ABOUT THIS PUBLICATION

FOR SERVICE ASSISTANCE

Customer Service
1.704.898.0770

North Carolina General Statues is published by The Muliti-Media Group of Greater Charlotte in Charlotte, North Carolina. Copyright 2015 by the Multi-Media Group of Greater Charlotte. This book or parts thereof may not be reproduced in any form, stored in a retrieval system, or transmitted in any form by any means—electronic, mechanical, photocopy, recording or otherwise—without prior written permission of the publisher, except as provided by United States of America copyright law.

The records required by U.S. Code 2257(a) through (c) and the pertinent regulations 28 C.F.R. Cli. 1, Part 75 with respect to this publication and all materials associated with such records are maintained by The Multi-Media Group of Greater Charlotte, Publisher and available for review by Attorney General.

www.visionbooks.org

Copyright © 2015 by MMGGC
All rights reserved!

TID: 5071796
ISBN (10) digit: 1502988240
ISBN (13) digit: 978-1502988249

123-4-56789-01239-Paperback
123-4-56789-01239-Hardback

First Edition

090520140547

Printed in the United States of America

2015 EDITION

North Carolina Criminal Law And Procedure-Pamphlet # 61

Printed In conjunction with the Administration of the Courts

North Carolina Criminal Law and Procedure
Pamphlet Reference Guide

Chapters	Pamphlet
Chapter 1 Civil Procedure	1
Chapter 1 Civil Procedure (Continue)	2
Chapter 1A Rules of Civil Procedure	2
Chapter 1B Contribution.	2
Chapter 1C Enforcement of Judgments.	2
Chapter 1D Punitive Damages.	2
Chapter 1E Eastern Band of Cherokee Indians.	2
Chapter 1F North Carolina Uniform Interstate Depositions and Discovery Act.	2
Chapter 2 - Clerk of Superior Court [Repealed and Transferred.]	3
Chapter 3 - Commissioners of Affidavits and Deeds [Repealed.]	3
Chapter 4 - Common Law	3
Chapter 5 - Contempt [Repealed.]	3
Chapter 5A - Contempt	3
Chapter 6 - Liability for Court Costs	3
Chapter 7 - Courts [Repealed and Transferred.]	3
Chapter 7A – Judicial Department	3
Chapter 7A – Continuation (Judicial Department)	4
Chapter 7A – Continuation (Judicial Department)	5
Chapter 7B - Juvenile Code	5
Chapter 8 - Evidence	6
Chapter 8A - Interpreters for Deaf Persons [Recodified.]	6
Chapter 8B - Interpreters for Deaf Persons	6
Chapter 8C - Evidence Code	6
Chapter 9 - Jurors	6
Chapter 10 - Notaries [Repealed.]	6
Chapter 10A - Notaries [Recodified.]	6
Chapter 10B - Notaries	6
Chapter 11 - Oaths	6
Chapter 12 - Statutory Construction	6
Chapter 13 - Citizenship Restored	6
Chapter 14 - Criminal Law	7
Chapter 14 –Criminal Law (Continuation)	8
Chapter 15 - Criminal Procedure	9
Chapter 15A - Criminal Procedure Act (Continuation)	10
Chapter 15A - Criminal Procedure Act (Continuation)	11
Chapter 15B - Victims Compensation	11
Chapter 15C - Address Confidentiality Program	11
Chapter 16 - Gaming Contracts and Futures	11
Chapter 17 - Habeas Corpus	11

Chapter 17A - Law-Enforcement Officers [Recodified.]	11
Chapter 17B - North Carolina Criminal Justice Education and Training System [Recodified.]	11
Chapter 17C - North Carolina Criminal Justice Education and Training Standards Commission	11
Chapter 17D - North Carolina Justice Academy	11
Chapter 17E - North Carolina Sheriffs' Education and Training Standards Commission	11
Chapter 18 - Regulation of Intoxicating Liquors [Repealed.]	12
Chapter 18A - Regulation of Intoxicating Liquors [Repealed.]	12
Chapter 18B - Regulation of Alcoholic Beverages	12
Chapter 18C - North Carolina State Lottery	12
Chapter 19 - Offenses against Public Morals	12
Chapter 19A - Protection of Animals	12
Chapter 20 - Motor Vehicles	13
Chapter 20 - Motor Vehicles (Continuation)	14
Chapter 20 - Motor Vehicles (Continuation)	15
Chapter 20 - Motor Vehicles (Continuation)	16
Chapter 21 - Bills of Lading	17
Chapter 22 - Contracts Requiring Writing	17
Chapter 22A - Signatures	17
Chapter 22B - Contracts Against Public Policy	17
Chapter 22C - Payments to Subcontractors	17
Chapter 23 - Debtor and Creditor	17
Chapter 24 – Interest	17
Chapter 25 – Uniform Commercial Code	18
Chapter 25 – Uniform Commercial Code (Continuation)	19
Chapter 25A – Retail Installment Sales Act	20
Chapter 25B - Credit	20
Chapter 25C - Sales of Artwork	20
Chapter 26 - Suretyship	20
Chapter 27 - Warehouse Receipts [Repealed.]	20
Chapter 28 - Administration [Repealed.]	20
Chapter 28A - Administration of Decedents' Estates	20
Chapter 28B - Estates of Absentees in Military Service	20
Chapter 28C - Estates of Missing Persons	20
Chapter 29 - Intestate Succession	21
Chapter 30 - Surviving Spouses	21
Chapter 31 - Wills	21
Chapter 31A - Acts Barring Property Rights	21
Chapter 31B - Renunciation of Property and Renunciation of Fiduciary Powers Act	21
Chapter 31C - Uniform Disposition of Community Property Rights at Death Act	21
Chapter 32 - Fiduciaries	21
Chapter 32A - Powers of Attorney	21
Chapter 33 - Guardian and Ward [Repealed and Recodified.]	21

Chapter 33A - North Carolina Uniform Transfers to Minors Act	21
Chapter 33B - North Carolina Uniform Custodial Trust Act	21
Chapter 34 - Veterans' Guardianship Act	22
Chapter 35 - Sterilization Procedures	22
Chapter 35A - Incompetency and Guardianship	22
Chapter 36 - Trusts and Trustees [Repealed.]	22
Chapter 36A - Trusts and Trustees	22
Chapter 36B - Uniform Management of Institutional Funds Act [Repealed.]	22
Chapter 36C - North Carolina Uniform Trust Code	22
Chapter 36D - North Carolina Community Third Party Trusts, Pooled Trusts	23
Chapter 36E - Uniform Prudent Management of Institutional Funds Act	23
Chapter 37 - Allocation of Principal and Income [Repealed.]	23
Chapter 37A - Uniform Principal and Income Act	23
Chapter 38 - Boundaries	23
Chapter 38A - Landowner Liability	23
Chapter 39 - Conveyances	23
Chapter 39A - Transfer Fee Covenants Prohibited	23
Chapter 40 - Eminent Domain [Repealed.]	23
Chapter 40A - Eminent Domain	23
Chapter 41 - Estates	23
Chapter 41A - State Fair Housing Act	23
Chapter 42 - Landlord and Tenant	23
Chapter 42A - Vacation Rental Act	23
Chapter 43 - Land Registration	23
Chapter 44 - Liens	24
Chapter 44A - Statutory Liens and Charges	24
Chapter 45 - Mortgages and Deeds of Trust	24
Chapter 45A - Good Funds Settlement Act	24
Chapter 46 - Partition	24
Chapter 47 - Probate and Registration	25
Chapter 47A - Unit Ownership	25
Chapter 47B - Real Property Marketable Title Act	25
Chapter 47C - North Carolina Condominium Act	25
Chapter 47D - Notice of Settlement Act [Expired.]	25
Chapter 47E - Residential Property Disclosure Act	25
Chapter 47F - North Carolina Planned Community Act	25
Chapter 47G - Option to Purchase Contracts	25
Chapter 47H - Contracts for Deed	25
Chapter 48 - Adoptions +	26
Chapter 48A - Minors	26
Chapter 49 - Bastardy	26
Chapter 49A - Rights of Children	26
Chapter 50 - Divorce and Alimony	26
Chapter 50A - Uniform Child-Custody Jurisdiction and	

Enforcement Act	26
Chapter 50B - Domestic Violence	26
Chapter 50C - Civil No-Contact Orders	26
Chapter 51 - Marriage	26
Chapter 52 - Powers and Liabilities of Married Persons	27
Chapter 52A - Uniform Reciprocal Enforcement of Support Act [Repealed.]	27
Chapter 52B - Uniform Premarital Agreement Act	27
Chapter 52C - Uniform Interstate Family Support Act	27
Chapter 53 - Banks	27
Chapter 53A - Business Development Corporations and North Carolina Capital Resource Corporations	28
Chapter 53B - Financial Privacy Act	28
Chapter 54 - Cooperative Organizations	28
Chapter 54A - Capital Stock Savings and Loan Associations [Repealed.]	28
Chapter 54B - Savings and Loan Associations	29
Chapter 54C - Savings Banks	29
Chapter 55 - North Carolina Business Corporation Act	30
Chapter 55A - North Carolina Nonprofit Corporation Act	31
Chapter 55B - Professional Corporation Act	31
Chapter 55C - Foreign Trade Zones	31
Chapter 55D - Filings, Names, and Registered Agents for Corporations, Nonprofit Corporations, and Partnerships	31
Chapter 56 - Electric, Telegraph and Power Companies [Repealed.]	31
Chapter 57 - Hospital, Medical and Dental Service Corporations [Recodified.]	31
Chapter 57A - Health Maintenance Organization Act [Recodified.]	31
Chapter 57B - Health Maintenance Organization Act [Recodified.]	31
Chapter 57C - North Carolina Limited Liability Company Act.	31
Chapter 58 - Insurance.	32
Chapter 58 - Insurance (Continuation)	33
Chapter 58 - Insurance (Continuation)	34
Chapter 58 - Insurance (Continuation)	35
Chapter 58 - Insurance (Continuation)	36
Chapter 58 - Insurance (Continuation)	37
Chapter 58 - Insurance (Continuation)	38
Chapter 58A - North Carolina Health Insurance Trust Commission [Recodified.]	38
Chapter 59 - Partnership.	39
Chapter 59B - Uniform Unincorporated Nonprofit Association Act.	39
Chapter 60 - Railroads and Other Carriers [Repealed and Transferred.]	39
Chapter 61 - Religious Societies	39
Chapter 62 - Public Utilities	39

Chapter 62 - Public Utilities (Continuation)	40
Chapter 62A - Public Safety Telephone Service And Wireless Telephone Service	40
Chapter 63 - Aeronautics	40
Chapter 63A - North Carolina Global TransPark Authority	40
Chapter 64 - Aliens	40
Chapter 65 – Cemeteries	40
Chapter 66 - Commerce and Business	41
Chapter 67 - Dogs	41
Chapter 68 - Fences and Stock Law	41
Chapter 69 - Fire Protection	41
Chapter 70 - Indian Antiquities, Archaeological Resources and Unmarked Human Skeletal Remains Protection	42
Chapter 71 - Indians [Repealed.]	42
Chapter 71A - Indians	42
Chapter 72 - Inns, Hotels and Restaurants	42
Chapter 73 - Mills	42
Chapter 74 - Mines and Quarries	42
Chapter 74A - Company Police [Repealed.]	42
Chapter 74B - Private Protective Services Act [Repealed.]	42
Chapter 74C - Private Protective Services	42
Chapter 74D - Alarm Systems	42
Chapter 74E - Company Police Act	42
Chapter 74F - Locksmith Licensing Act	42
Chapter 74G - Campus Police Act	42
Chapter 75 - Monopolies, Trusts and Consumer Protection	42
Chapter 75A - Boating and Water Safety	43
Chapter 75B - Discrimination in Business	43
Chapter 75C - Motion Picture Fair Competition Act	43
Chapter 75D - Racketeer Influenced and Corrupt Organizations	43
Chapter 75E - Unlawful Activities in Connection With Certain Corporate Transactions	43
Chapter 76 - Navigation	43
Chapter 76A - Navigation and Pilotage Commissions	43
Chapter 77 - Rivers, Creeks, and Coastal Waters	43
Chapter 78 - Securities Law [Repealed.]	43
Chapter 78A - North Carolina Securities Act	43
Chapter 78B - Tender Offer Disclosure Act [Repealed.]	43
Chapter 78C - Investment Advisers	43
Chapter 78D - Commodities Act	43
Chapter 79 - Strays [Repealed.]	43
Chapter 80 - Trademarks, Brands, etc.	44
Chapter 81 - Weights and Measures [Recodified.]	44
Chapter 81A - Weights and Measures Act of 1975.	44
Chapter 82 - Wrecks [Repealed.]	44
Chapter 83 - Architects [Recodified.]	44

Chapter 83A - Architects	44
Chapter 84 - Attorneys-at-Law	44
Chapter 84A - Foreign Legal Consultants	44
Chapter 85 - Auctions and Auctioneers [Repealed.]	44
Chapter 85A - Bail Bondsmen and Runners [Recodified.]	44
Chapter 85B - Auctions and Auctioneers	44
Chapter 85C - Bail Bondsmen and Runners [Recodified.]	44
Chapter 86 - Barbers [Recodified.]	44
Chapter 86A - Barbers	44
Chapter 87 - Contractors	44
Chapter 88 - Cosmetic Art [Repealed.]	44
Chapter 88A - Electrolysis Practice Act	44
Chapter 88B - Cosmetic Art	45
Chapter 89 - Engineering and Land Surveying [Recodified.]	45
Chapter 89A - Landscape Architects	45
Chapter 89B - Foresters	45
Chapter 89C - Engineering and Land Surveying	45
Chapter 89D - Landscape Contractors	45
Chapter 89E - Geologists Licensing Act	45
Chapter 89F - North Carolina Soil Scientist Licensing Act	45
Chapter 89G - Irrigation Contractors	45
Chapter 90 - Medicine and Allied Occupations	45
Chapter 90 - Medicine and Allied Occupations (Continuation)	46
Chapter 90 - Medicine and Allied Occupations (Continuation)	47
Chapter 90 - Medicine and Allied Occupations (Continuation)	48
Chapter 90A - Sanitarians and Water and Wastewater Treatment Facility Operators	48
Chapter 90B - Social Worker Certification and Licensure Act	48
Chapter 90C - North Carolina Recreational Therapy Licensure Act	48
Chapter 90D - Interpreters and Transliterators	48
Chapter 91 - Pawnbrokers [Repealed.]	48
Chapter 91A - Pawnbrokers Modernization Act of 1989	48
Chapter 92 - Photographers [Deleted.]	48
Chapter 93 - Certified Public Accountants	48
Chapter 93A - Real Estate License Law	49
Chapter 93B - Occupational Licensing Boards	49
Chapter 93C - Watchmakers [Repealed.]	49
Chapter 93D - North Carolina State Hearing Aid Dealers and Fitters Board.	49
Chapter 93E - North Carolina Appraisers Act	49
Chapter 94 - Apprenticeship	49
Chapter 95 - Department of Labor and Labor Regulations	49
Chapter 95 - Department of Labor and Labor Regulations (Continuation)	50
Chapter 96 - Employment Security	50
Chapter 97 - Workers' Compensation Act	50
Chapter 97 - Workers' Compensation Act (Continuation)	51

Chapter 98 - Burnt and Lost Records	51
Chapter 99 - Libel and Slander	51
Chapter 99A - Civil Remedies for Criminal Actions	51
Chapter 99B - Products Liability	51
Chapter 99C - Actions Relating to Winter Sports Safety and Accidents	51
Chapter 99D - Civil Rights	51
Chapter 99E - Special Liability Provisions	51
Chapter 100 - Monuments, Memorials and Parks	51
Chapter 101 - Names of Persons	51
Chapter 102 - Official Survey Base	51
Chapter 103 - Sundays, Holidays and Special Days	51
Chapter 104 - United States Lands	51
Chapter 104A - Degrees of Kinship	51
Chapter 104B - Hurricanes or Other Acts of Nature	51
Chapter 104C - Atomic Energy, Radioactivity and Ionizing Radiation [Repealed and Recodified.]	51
Chapter 104D - Southern States Energy Compact	51
Chapter 104E - North Carolina Radiation Protection Act	51
Chapter 104F - Southeast Interstate Low-Level Radioactive Waste Management Compact [Repealed]	51
Chapter 104G - North Carolina Low-Level Radioactive Waste Management Authority Act of 1987 [Repealed]	51
Chapter 105 - Taxation	51
Chapter 105 - Taxation (Continuation)	52
Chapter 105 - Taxation (Continuation)	53
Chapter 105 - Taxation (Continuation)	54
Chapter 105A - Setoff Debt Collection Act	55
Chapter 105B - Defaulted Student Loan Recovery Act	55
Chapter 106 - Agriculture	55
Chapter 106 - Agriculture (Continue)	56
Chapter 106 - Agriculture (Continue)	57
Chapter 107 - Agricultural Development Districts [Repealed.]	57
Chapter 108 - Social Services [Repealed and Recodified.]	57
Chapter 108A - Social Services	57
Chapter 108B - Community Action Programs	58
Chapter 108C Medicaid and Health Choice Provider Requirements.	58
Chapter 108D Medicaid Managed Care for Behavioral Health Services.	58
Chapter 109 - Bonds [Recodified.]	58
Chapter 110 - Child Welfare	58
Chapter 111 - Aid to the Blind	58
Chapter 112 - Confederate Homes and Pensions [Repealed.]	58
Chapter 113 - Conservation and Development	58
Chapter 113 - Conservation and Development (Continuation)	59

Chapter 113A - Pollution Control and Environment	59
Chapter 113A - Pollution Control and Environment (Continuation)	60
Chapter 113B - North Carolina Energy Policy Act of 1975	60
Chapter 114 - Department of Justice	60
Chapter 115 - Elementary and Secondary Education [Repealed.]	60
Chapter 115A - Community Colleges, Technical Institutes, and Industrial Education Centers [Repealed.]	60
Chapter 115B - Tuition and Fee Waivers	60
Chapter 115C - Elementary and Secondary Education	60
Chapter 115C - Elementary and Secondary Education (Continuation)	61
Chapter 115C - Elementary and Secondary Education (Continuation)	62
Chapter 115C - Elementary and Secondary Education (Continuation)	63
Chapter 115D - Community Colleges	63
Chapter 115E - Private Educational Facilities Finance Act [Recodified]	63
Chapter 116 - Higher Education	63
Chapter 116 - Higher Education (Continuation)	63
Chapter 116A - Escheats and Abandoned Property [Repealed.]	64
Chapter 116B - Escheats and Abandoned Property	64
Chapter 116C - Continuum of Education Programs	64
Chapter 116D - Higher Education Bonds	64
Chapter 117 - Electrification	64
Chapter 118 - Firemen's and Rescue Squad Workers' Relief and Pension Funds [Recodified.]	64
Chapter 118A - Firemen's Death Benefit Act [Repealed.]	64
Chapter 118B - Members of a Rescue Squad Death Benefit Act [Repealed.]	64
Chapter 119 - Gasoline and Oil Inspection and Regulation	64
Chapter 120 - General Assembly	65
Chapter 120 - General Assembly (Continuation)	66
Chapter 120 - General Assembly (Continuation)	67
Chapter 120C - Lobbying	67
Chapter 121 - Archives and History	67
Chapter 122 - Hospitals for the Mentally Disordered [Repealed.]	67
Chapter 122A - North Carolina Housing Finance Agency	67
Chapter 122B - North Carolina Agricultural Facilities Finance Act [Repealed.]	67
Chapter 122C - Mental Health, Developmental Disabilities, and Substance Abuse Act of 1985	67
Chapter 122C - Mental Health, Developmental Disabilities, and Substance Abuse Act of 1985 (Continuation)	68
Chapter 122D - North Carolina Agricultural Finance Act	68

Chapter 122E - North Carolina Housing Trust and Oil Overcharge Act	68
Chapter 123 - Impeachment	69
Chapter 123A - Industrial Development [Repealed.]	69
Chapter 124 - Internal Improvements	69
Chapter 125 - Libraries	69
Chapter 126 - State Personnel System	69
Chapter 127 - Militia [Repealed.]	69
Chapter 127A - Militia	69
Chapter 127B - Military Affairs	69
Chapter 127C - Advisory Commission on Military Affairs	69
Chapter 128 - Offices and Public Officers	69
Chapter 128 - Offices and Public Officers (Continuation)	70
Chapter 129 - Public Buildings and Grounds	70
Chapter 130 - Public Health [Repealed.]	70
Chapter 130A - Public Health	70
Chapter 130A - Public Health (Continuation)	71
Chapter 130A - Public Health (Continuation)	72
Chapter 130B - Hazardous Waste Management Commission [Repealed.]	72
Chapter 131 - Public Hospitals [Repealed.]	72
Chapter 131A - Health Care Facilities Finance Act	72
Chapter 131B - Licensing of Ambulatory Surgical Facilities [Repealed.]	72
Chapter 131C - Charitable Solicitation Licensure Act [Repealed.]	72
Chapter 131D - Inspection and Licensing of Facilities	72
Chapter 131E - Health Care Facilities and Services	72
Chapter 131E - Health Care Facilities and Services (Continuation)	73
Chapter 131F - Solicitation of Contributions	73
Chapter 132 - Public Records	73
Chapter 133 - Public Works	74
Chapter 134 - Youth Development [Recodified.]	74
Chapter 134A - Youth Services [Repealed.]	74
Chapter 135 - Retirement System for Teachers and State Employees; Social Security; Health Insurance Program for Children	74
Chapter 135 - Retirement System for Teachers and State Employees; Social Security; Health Insurance Program for Children	75
Chapter 136 - Transportation	75
Chapter 136 - Transportation (Continuation)	76
Chapter 137 - Rural Rehabilitation [Repealed.]	76
Chapter 138 - Salaries, Fees and Allowances	76
Chapter 138A - State Government Ethics Act	76
Chapter 139 - Soil and Water Conservation Districts	76

Chapter 140 - State Art Museum; Symphony and Art Societies	76
Chapter 140A - State Awards System	76
Chapter 141 - State Boundaries	76
Chapter 142 - State Debt	76
Chapter 143 - State Departments, Institutions, and Commissions	77
Chapter 143 - State Departments, Institutions, and Commissions (Continuation)	78
Chapter 143 - State Departments, Institutions, and Commissions (Continuation)	79
Chapter 143 - State Departments, Institutions, and Commissions (Continuation)	80
Chapter 143A - State Government Reorganization	80
Chapter 143B - Executive Organization Act of 1973	80
Chapter 143B - Executive Organization Act of 1973 (Continuation)	81
Chapter 143B - Executive Organization Act of 1973 (Continuation)	82
Chapter 143C - State Budget Act	83
Chapter 143D - The State Governmental Accountability and Internal Control Act	83
Chapter 144 - State Flag, Official Governmental Flags, Motto, and Colors	83
Chapter 145 - State Symbols and Other Official Adoptions.	83
Chapter 146 - State Lands	83
Chapter 147 - State Officers	83
Chapter 148 - State Prison System	84
Chapter 149 - State Song and Toast	84
Chapter 150 - Uniform Revocation of Licenses [Repealed.]	84
Chapter 150A - Administrative Procedure Act [Recodified.]	84
Chapter 150B - Administrative Procedure Act	84
Chapter 151 - Constables [Repealed.]	84
Chapter 152 - Coroners	84
Chapter 152A - County Medical Examiner [Repealed.]	84
Chapter 152A - County Medical Examiner [Repealed.] (Continuation)	85
Chapter 153 - Counties and County Commissioners [Repealed.]	85
Chapter 153A - Counties	85
Chapter 153B - Mountain Resources Planning Act	85
Chapter 153C - Uwharrie Regional Resources Act	85
Chapter 154 - County Surveyor [Repealed.]	85
Chapter 155 - County Treasurer [Repealed.]	85
Chapter 156 - Drainage	85
Chapter 156 – Drainage (Continuation)	86

Chapter 157 - Housing Authorities and Projects	86
Chapter 157A - Historic Properties Commissions [Transferred.]	86
Chapter 158 - Local Development	86
Chapter 159 - Local Government Finance	86
Chapter 159 - Local Government Finance (Continuation)	87
Chapter 159A - Pollution Abatement and Industrial Facilities Financing Act [Unconstitutional.]	87
Chapter 159B - Joint Municipal Electric Power and Energy Act	87
Chapter 159C - Industrial and Pollution Control Facilities Financing Act	87
Chapter 159D - The North Carolina Capital Facilities Financing Act	87
Chapter 159E - Registered Public Obligations Act	87
Chapter 159F - North Carolina Energy Development Authority [Repealed.]	87
Chapter 159G - Water Infrastructure	87
Chapter 159H - [Reserved.]	87
Chapter 159I - Solid Waste Management Loan Program and Local Government Special Obligation Bonds	87
Chapter 160 - Municipal Corporations [Repealed And Transferred.]	87
Chapter 160A - Cities and Towns	88
Chapter 160A - Cities and Towns (Continuation)	89
Chapter 160B - Consolidated City-County Act	89
Chapter 160C - Baseball Park Districts [Repealed.]	90
Chapter 161 - Register of Deeds	90
Chapter 162 - Sheriff	90
Chapter 162A - Water and Sewer Systems	90
Chapter 162B Continuity of Local Government in Emergency.	90
Chapter 163 Elections and Election Laws.	90
Chapter 163 Elections and Election Laws. (Continuation)	91
Chapter 164 Concerning the General Statutes of North Carolina.	92
Chapter 165 Veterans.	92
Chapter 166 Civil Preparedness Agencies [Repealed.]	92
Chapter 166A North Carolina Emergency Management Act.	92
Chapter 167 State Civil Air Patrol [Repealed.]	92
Chapter 168 Persons with Disabilities.	92
Chapter 168A Persons With Disabilities Protection Act.	92

§ 115C-51. Public comment period during regular meetings.

The local board of education shall provide at least one period for public comment per month at a regular meeting of the board. The board may adopt reasonable rules governing the conduct of the public comment period, including, but not limited to, rules (i) fixing the maximum time allotted to each speaker, (ii) providing for the designation of spokesmen for groups of persons supporting or opposing the same positions, (iii) providing for the selection of delegates from groups of persons supporting or opposing the same positions when the number of persons wishing to attend the hearing exceeds the capacity of the hall, and (iv) providing for the maintenance of order and decorum in the conduct of the hearing. The board is not required to provide a public comment period under this section if no regular meeting is held during the month. (2005-170, s. 1.)

§ 115C-52. Reserved for future codification purposes.

§ 115C-53. Reserved for future codification purposes.

Article 6.

Advisory Councils.

§ 115C-54: Repealed by Session Laws 1985 (Regular Session, 1986), c. 975, s. 1.

§ 115C-55. Advisory councils.

A board of education may appoint an advisory council for any school or schools within the local school administrative unit. The purpose and function of an advisory council shall be to serve in an advisory capacity to the board on matters affecting the school or schools for which it is appointed. The organization, terms, composition and regulations for the operation of such advisory council shall be determined by the board. (1955, c. 1372, art. 7, s. 2;

1957, c. 686, s. 2; 1965, c. 584, s. 8; 1981, c. 423, s. 1; 1985 (Reg. Sess., 1986), c. 975, s. 1.)

§§ 115C-56 through 115C-59: Repealed by Session Laws 1985 (Regular Session, 1986), c. 975, s. 1.

§§ 115C-60 through 115C-64. Reserved for future codification purposes.

Article 6A.

State Assistance and Intervention in Low Performing School Units.

§§ 115C-64.1 through 115C-64.5: Repealed by Session Laws 1995 (Regular Session, 1996), c. 716, s. 4.

Article 6B.

Dropout Prevention Grants.

§ 115C-64.6. Committee on Dropout Prevention.

(a) There is established the Committee on Dropout Prevention. The Committee shall be located administratively in the Department of Public Instruction but shall exercise its powers and duties independently of the Department of Public Instruction. The Department of Public Instruction shall provide for the administrative costs of the Committee and shall provide staff to the Committee.

(b) The Committee shall determine which local school administrative units, schools, agencies, and nonprofits shall receive dropout prevention grants under G.S. 115C-64.7, the amount of each grant, and eligible uses of the grant funding. The Committee shall consist of the following 15 members:

(1) The Governor shall appoint five members, of whom one is a superintendent of schools, one is a representative of a nonprofit, and one is a school social worker;

(2) The General Assembly upon the recommendation of the President Pro Tempore of the Senate shall appoint five members, of whom one is a principal, one is a representative of a school of education, and one is a school counselor; and

(3) The General Assembly upon the recommendation of the Speaker of the House of Representatives shall appoint five members, of whom one is a teacher, one is a member of the business community, and one is a representative of the juvenile justice system.

(c) The terms of the initial appointees expire December 1, 2010. Subsequent appointees shall serve for four-year terms.

The President Pro Tempore of the Senate and the Speaker of the House of Representatives shall each designate a cochair of the Committee. The members of the Committee shall assure they are in compliance with laws and rules governing conflicts of interest. (2007-323, s. 7.32(c), (e); 2008-107, ss. 7.14(a), 7.14A; 2010-31, s. 7.19(e), (g).)

§ 115C-64.7. Criteria for dropout prevention grants.

The following criteria apply to all types of dropout prevention grants approved by the Committee:

(1) Grants shall be issued in varying amounts up to a maximum of one hundred seventy-five thousand dollars ($175,000).

(2) These grants shall be provided to innovative programs and initiatives that target students at risk of dropping out of school and that demonstrate the potential to (i) be developed into effective, sustainable, and coordinated dropout prevention and reentry programs in middle schools and high schools and (ii) serve as effective models for other programs.

(3) Grants shall be distributed geographically throughout the State and throughout the eight educational districts as defined in G.S. 115C-65. No more than three grants shall be awarded in any one county under this section in a single fiscal year.

(4) Grants may be made to local school administrative units, schools, local agencies, or nonprofit organizations. Applications from nonprofits shall be subject to the additional fiscal accountability controls described in G.S. 115C-64.8.

(5) Grants shall be to programs and initiatives that hold all students to high academic and personal standards.

(6) Grant applications shall state (i) how grant funds will be used, (ii) what, if any, other resources will be used in conjunction with the grant funds, (iii) how the program or initiative will be coordinated to enhance the effectiveness of existing programs, initiatives, or services in the community, and (iv) a process for evaluating the success of the program or initiative.

(7) Programs and initiatives that receive grants under this section shall be based on best practices for helping at-risk students achieve successful academic progress, preventing students from dropping out of school, or for increasing the high school completion rate for those students who already have dropped out of school.

(8) Priority for grants shall be given to proposals that (i) demonstrate input from the local community and coordination with other available programs or resources and (ii) provide clear plans for sustaining the program in future years when State funding will no longer be provided.

(9) Grantees shall assure their compliance with applicable laws and rules regulating conflicts of interest.

(10) Priority for grants shall be given to programs that would serve students in local schools that have a four-year cohort graduation rate of less than sixty-five percent (65%). The Committee shall establish a grant rating cutoff score at such a level as to allow for consideration of all viable grants in this priority category. The Committee may require grantees to provide supplemental information in response to any prior reviewer comments.

(11) Priority for grants shall be given to proposals demonstrating the potential for success.

(12) The demonstrated need for a grant, level of collaboration, ability to increase attendance, persistence, academic success, ability to increase

parental involvement, and graduation shall be given more weight than the quality of the written grant.

(13) Grants shall be made no later than November 1, 2009.

The Committee shall report to the Joint Legislative Education Oversight Committee on the grants awarded under this section by March 1, 2010. (2009-451, s. 7.13(b); 2010-31, s. 7.19(c); 2011-266, s. 3.1; 2012-142, s. 7.13(e).)

§ 115C-64.8. Additional requirements for nonprofit organizations receiving dropout prevention grants.

As a condition for release of grant funds to a grantee, the Committee shall require each grantee to enter into a contract that requires the grantee to be (i) subject to monitoring by the Committee, (ii) fidelity bonded unless the grant is for less than one hundred thousand dollars ($100,000), (iii) subject to audit oversight by the State Auditor, and (iv) subject to the requirements of Article 6, Part 3 of Chapter 143C of the General Statutes. (2009-451, s. 7.13(e).)

§ 115C-64.9. Evaluation.

The Committee shall evaluate the impact of the dropout prevention grants awarded under this Article. In evaluating the impact of the grants, the Committee shall consider:

(1) How grant funds were used, including the services provided for teen pregnancy prevention and for pregnant and parenting teens;

(2) The success of the program or initiative, as indicated by the evaluation process stated in its grant application;

(3) The extent to which the program or initiative has improved students' attendance, test scores, persistence, and graduation rates;

(4) How the program or initiative was coordinated to enhance the effectiveness of existing programs, initiatives, or services in the community;

(5) What, if any, other resources were used in conjunction with the grant funds;

(6) The sustainability of the program;

(7) The number, gender, ethnicity, and grade level of students being served as well as whether the students left school due to pregnancy or parenting responsibilities;

(8) The potential for the program to serve as a model for achieving successful academic progress for at-risk students; and

(9) Other indicators of the impact of the grant on dropout prevention.

The recipients of the dropout prevention grants awarded under this section shall report to the Committee on Dropout Prevention by January 31, 2011, and annually thereafter. The reports shall provide information to assist the Committee in conducting its evaluation. The reports shall include a statement that the recipients used grant funds for the purposes appropriated by the General Assembly and complied with applicable laws, regulations, and terms and conditions of the grant documents. The Committee shall make an interim report of the results of its evaluation of the grants awarded under this section by March 31, 2011, to the Joint Legislative Education Oversight Committee. The Committee shall make a final report of the results of its evaluation of the grants awarded under subsection (c) of this section by November 15, 2011, to the Joint Legislative Education Oversight Committee. (2009-451, s. 7.13(c); 2010-31, s. 7.19(d); 2011-266, s. 3.2.)

Article 6C.

Education and Workforce Innovation Program.

§ 115C-64.15. North Carolina Education and Workforce Innovation Commission.

(a) There is created the North Carolina Education and Workforce Innovation Commission (Commission). The Commission shall be located administratively in the Office of the Governor but shall exercise all its prescribed powers independently of the Office of the Governor. Of the funds appropriated for the Education and Workforce Innovation Program established under G.S. 115C-64.16, up to two hundred thousand dollars ($200,000) each fiscal year may be used by the Office of the Governor to provide technical assistance and administrative assistance, including staff, to the Commission and reimbursements and expenses for the Commission.

(b) The Commission shall consist of the following 11 members:

(1) The Secretary of Commerce.

(2) The State Superintendent of Public Instruction.

(3) The Chair of the State Board of Education.

(4) The President of The University of North Carolina.

(5) The President of the North Carolina Community College System.

(6) Two members appointed by the Governor who have experience in education.

(7) Two members appointed by the General Assembly upon recommendation of the Speaker of the House of Representatives, as provided in G.S. 120-121, who have experience in businesses operating in North Carolina.

(8) Two members appointed by the General Assembly upon the recommendation of the President Pro Tempore of the Senate, as provided in G.S. 120-121, who have experience in businesses operating in North Carolina.

(c) The Commission members shall elect a chair from the membership of the Commission. The Commission shall meet at least three times annually on the call of the Chair or as additionally provided by the Commission. A quorum is six members of the Commission. Members may not send designees to Commission meetings nor may they vote by proxy.

(d) The Commission shall develop and administer the Education and Workforce Innovation Program, as established under G.S. 115C-64.16, and make awards of grants under the Program. The Commission shall work closely with the North Carolina New Schools in administering the program.

(e)   The Commission shall publish a report on the Education and Workforce Innovation Program on or before April 30 of each year. The report shall be submitted to the Joint Legislative Education Oversight Committee, the State Board of Education, the State Board of Community Colleges, and the Board of Governors of The University of North Carolina. The report shall include at least all of the following information:

(1)   An accounting of how funds and personnel resources were utilized and their impact on student achievement, retention, and employability.

(2)   Recommended statutory and policy changes.

(3)   Recommendations for improvement of the program. (2013-360, s. 8.34(a); 2013-363, s. 3.10(a).)

§ 115C-64.16. The Education and Workforce Innovation Program.

(a)   Program Establishment. - There is established the Education and Workforce Innovation Program (Program) to foster innovation in education that will lead to more students graduating career and college ready. Funds appropriated to the Program shall be used to award competitive grants to an individual school, a local school administrative unit, or a regional partnership of more than one local school administrative unit to advance comprehensive, high-quality education that equips teachers with the knowledge and skill required to succeed with all students. Before receiving a grant, applicants must meet all of the following conditions:

(1)   Form a partnership, for the purposes of the grant, with either a public or private university or a community college.

(2)   Form a partnership, for the purposes of the grant, with regional businesses and business leaders.

(3)   Demonstrate the ability to sustain innovation once grant funding ends.

(b)   Applicant Categories and Specific Requirements. -

(1) Individual schools. - Individual public schools must demonstrate all of the following in their applications:

a. Partnerships with business and industry to determine the skills and competencies needed for students' transition into growth sectors of the regional economy.

b. Aligned pathways to employment, including students' acquisition of college credit or industry recognized credentials.

c. Development of systems, infrastructure, capacity, and culture to enable teachers and school leaders to continuously focus on improving individual student achievement.

(2) Local school administrative units. - Local school administrative units must demonstrate all of the following in their applications:

a. Implementation of comprehensive reform and innovation.

b. Appointment of a senior leader to manage and sustain the change process with a specific focus on providing parents with a portfolio of meaningful options among schools.

(3) Regional partnerships of two or more local school administrative units. - Partnerships of two or more local school administrative units must demonstrate all of the following in their applications:

a. Implementation of resources of partnered local school administrative units in creating a tailored workforce development system for the regional economy and fostering innovation in each of the partnered local school administrative units.

b. Promotion of the development of knowledge and skills in career clusters of critical importance to the region.

c. Benefits of the shared strengths of local businesses and higher education.

d. Usage of technology to deliver instruction over large geographic regions and build networks with industry.

e. Implementation of comprehensive reform and innovation that can be replicated in other local school administrative units.

(c) Consideration of Factors in Awarding of Grants. - All applications must include information on at least the following in order to be considered for a grant:

(1) Describe the aligned pathways from school to high-growth careers in regional economies.

(2) Leverage technology to efficiently and effectively drive teacher and principal development, connect students and teachers to online courses and resources, and foster virtual learning communities among faculty, higher education partners, and business partners.

(3) Establish a comprehensive approach to enhancing the knowledge and skills of teachers and administrators to successfully implement the proposed innovative program and to graduate all students ready for work and college.

(4) Link to a proven provider of professional development services for teachers and administrators capable of providing evidence-based training and tools aligned with the goals of the proposed innovative program.

(5) Form explicit partnerships with businesses and industry, which may include business advisory councils, internship programs, and other customized projects aligned with relevant workforce skills.

(6) Partner with community colleges or public or private universities to enable communities to challenge every student to graduate with workplace credentials or college credit.

(7) Align K-12 and postsecondary instruction and performance expectations to reduce the need for college remediation courses.

(8) Secure input from parents to foster broad ownership for school choice options and to foster greater understanding of the need for continued education beyond high school.

(9) Provide a description of the funds that will be used and a proposed budget for five years.

(10) Describe the source of matching funds required in subsection (d) of this section.

(11) Establish a strategy to achieve meaningful analysis of program outcomes due to the receipt of grant funds under this section.

(d) Matching Private and Local Funds. - All funds appropriated by the State must be matched by a combination of private and local funds. All grant applicants must fund twenty-five percent (25%) of program costs through local funds. An additional twenty-five percent (25%) of program costs must be raised by private funds.

(e) Grants. - Any grants awarded by the Commission may be spent over a five-year period from the initial award.

(f) Reporting Requirements. - No later than March 1 of each year, a grant recipient shall submit to the Commission an annual report for the preceding grant year that describes the academic progress made by the students and the implementation of program initiatives. (2013-360, s. 8.34(a).)

SUBCHAPTER III. SCHOOL DISTRICTS AND UNITS.

Article 7.

Organization of Schools.

§ 115C-65. State divided into districts.

The State of North Carolina shall be divided into eight educational districts embracing the counties herein set forth:

First District

Beaufort, Bertie, Camden, Chowan, Currituck, Dare, Gates, Hertford, Hyde, Martin, Pasquotank, Perquimans, Pitt, Tyrrell, Washington.

Second District

Brunswick, Carteret, Craven, Duplin, Greene, Jones, Lenoir, New Hanover, Onslow, Pamlico, Pender, Sampson, Wayne.

Third District

Durham, Edgecombe, Franklin, Granville, Halifax, Johnston, Nash, Northampton, Vance, Wake, Warren, Wilson.

Fourth District

Bladen, Columbus, Cumberland, Harnett, Hoke, Lee, Montgomery, Moore, Richmond, Robeson, Scotland.

Fifth District

Alamance, Caswell, Chatham, Davidson, Forsyth, Guilford, Orange, Person, Randolph, Rockingham, Stokes.

Sixth District

Anson, Cabarrus, Cleveland, Gaston, Lincoln, Mecklenburg, Stanly, Union.

Seventh District

Alexander, Alleghany, Ashe, Avery, Burke, Caldwell, Catawba, Davie, Iredell, Rowan, Surry, Watauga, Wilkes, Yadkin.

Eighth District

Buncombe, Cherokee, Clay, Graham, Haywood, Henderson, Jackson, Macon, Madison, McDowell, Mitchell, Polk, Rutherford, Swain, Transylvania, Yancey. (1955, c. 1372, art. 1, s. 3; 1981, c. 423, s. 1.)

§ 115C-66. Administrative units classified.

Each county of the State shall be classified as a county school administrative unit, the schools of which, except in city administrative units, shall be under the general supervision and control of a county board of education with a county superintendent as the administrative officer.

A city school administrative unit shall be classified as an area within a county or adjacent parts of two or more contiguous counties which has been or may be approved by the State Board of Education as such a unit for purposes of school administration. The general administration and supervision of a city administrative unit shall be under the control of a board of education with a city superintendent as the administrative officer.

All local school administrative units, whether city or county, shall be dealt with by the State school authorities in all matters of school administration in the same way.

For purposes of eligibility for federal grant funds, the Department of Health and Human Services is hereby classified as a public authority, which is the school administrative agency for the schools that it operates, and shall be considered as such by the State school authorities in the administration and distribution of federal grant funds. (1955, c. 1372, art. 1, s. 4; 1981, c. 423, s. 1; 2005-276, s. 7.54(b).)

§ 115C-67. Merger of units in same county.

City school administrative units may be consolidated and merged with contiguous city school administrative units and with county school administrative units upon approval by the State Board of Education of a plan for consolidation and merger submitted by the boards of education involved and bearing the approval of the board of county commissioners.

County and city boards of education desiring to consolidate and merge their school administrative units may do so by entering into a written plan which shall set forth the conditions of merger. The provisions of the plan shall be consistent with the General Statutes and shall contain, but not be limited to, the following:

(1) The name by which the merged school administrative unit shall be identified and known.

(2) The effective date of the merger.

(3) The establishment and maintenance of a board of education which shall administer all the public schools of the newly created unit, including:

a. The termination of any terms of office proposed in the reorganization of the board.

b. The method of constituting and continuing the board of education; the manner of selection of board members, including (i) the number of members of the board, (ii) the method of their election or appointment, (iii) whether members shall be nominated, elected, or appointed from districts or at large, (iv) the manner of determining the nominee, and (v) whether the election shall be partisan or nonpartisan; the length of the members' terms of office; the dates of induction into office; the organization of the board; the procedure for filling vacancies; and the compensation to be paid members of the board for expenses incurred in performance of their duties. To the extent that the method conflicts with G.S. 115C-35, G.S. 115C-37, or with any local act concerning any of the units being merged and consolidated, the plan of merger and consolidation shall prevail.

(4)   The authority, powers, and duties of the board of education with respect to the employment of personnel, the preparation of budgets, and any other related matters which may be particularly applicable to the merged unit not inconsistent with the General Statutes.

(5)   The transfer of all facilities, properties, structures, funds, contracts, deeds, titles, and other obligations, assets and liabilities to the board of education of the merged unit.

(6)   Whether or not there shall be continued in force any supplemental school tax which may be in effect in either or all local school administrative units involved.

(7)   A public hearing, which shall have been announced at least 10 days prior to the hearing, on the proposed plan of merger.

(8)   A statement as to whether the question of merger, in accordance with the projected plan, is to be contingent upon approval of the voters in the affected area.

(9)   Any other condition or prerequisite to merger, together with any other appropriate subject or function that may be necessary for the orderly consolidation and merger of the local school administrative units involved.

The plan referred to above shall be mutually agreed upon by the city and county boards of education involved and shall be accompanied by a certification that the plan was approved by the board of education on a given day and that the action has been duly recorded in the minutes of said board, together with a certification to the effect that the public hearing required above was announced and held. The plan, together with the required certifications, shall then be submitted to the board of county commissioners for its concurrence and approval. After such approval has been received, the plan shall be submitted to the State Board of Education for the approval of said State Board and the plan shall not become effective until such approval is granted. Upon approval by the State Board of Education, the plan of consolidation and merger shall become final and shall be deemed to have been made by authority of law and shall not be changed or amended except by an act of the General Assembly. The written plan of agreement shall be placed in the custody of the board of education operating and administering the public schools in the merged unit and a copy filed with the Secretary of State.

The plan may be, but it is not required that it be, submitted for the approval of the voters of the geographic area affected in a referendum or election called for such purpose, and such elections or referendums if held shall be held under the provisions governing elections or referendums as set forth in G.S. 115C-507, with authority of the board of county commissioners to have such election or referendum conducted by the board of elections of the county.

Upon approval of the plan of consolidation or merger by the State Board of Education, or upon approval of the plan of consolidation or merger by the voters in a referendum or election called for such purpose, and as soon as a provisional or interim board of education of the merged unit, or a permanent board of education of the merged unit, enters in and upon the duties of the administration of the public schools of the consolidated or merged unit, then the former boards of education and all public officers of the former boards of education of the separate units thus merged shall stand abolished, and said separate boards of education or administrative units thus merged shall stand dissolved and shall cease to exist for any and all purposes. All consolidations and mergers of county and city boards of education and of county and city school administrative units heretofore agreed to and finally approved, and all consolidation or merger proceedings entered into prior to June 9, 1969, are hereby declared to be effective, legal and according to law notwithstanding any defect in the merger or consolidation proceedings and notwithstanding any dissolution of the separate boards of education and public officers of the former, separate school units. (1967, c. 643, s. 3; 1969, c. 742; 1981, c. 423, s. 1; 1991 (Reg. Sess., 1992), c. 767, s. 3.)

§ 115C-68. Merger of units in adjoining counties.

(a) Boards of education of contiguous counties or boards of education in a group of counties in which each county is contiguous with at least one other county in the group, and any city school administrative unit located in counties to be merged, may merge school administrative units upon approval by the State Board of Education of a written plan for merger submitted by the boards of education involved and bearing the approval of the tax-levying body for the school units. The plan shall be consistent with the General Statutes, shall contain provisions covering those items listed in G.S. 115C-67 (providing for the merger of units in the same county), and shall contain any other provision deemed necessary or appropriate by the State Board of Education or the local boards of education for the merger of school units in two or more counties.

(b)   The plan of merger, including any arrangements for financing or taxing for the schools in the new local school administrative unit, may be, but is not required to be, submitted for the approval of the voters of the geographic area affected in a referendum or election called for the purpose of approving these matters. Such elections or referendums, if held, shall be held under the provisions governing elections or referendums as set forth in G.S. 115C-507. Each board of county commissioners shall have authority to have such elections or referendums conducted by the board of elections of its county under the provisions set forth in G.S. 115C-507.

(c)   If twenty percent (20%) of the qualified voters of a county to be merged petition the board of county commissioners of their county for an election as to whether their county shall be included in the proposed merger, the board of county commissioners shall call an election on this question for its county under the provisions of G.S. 115C-507. The petition must be submitted to the board of county commissioners within 10 days following the public hearing required by G.S. 115C-67 on the proposed plan of merger. The board of county commissioners shall have authority to have such an election conducted by the board of election of its county under the provisions set forth in G.S. 115C-507.

(d)   Boards of education considering a merger of two or more counties may spend money necessary for studying and preparing for such a merger. (1969, c. 828; 1981, c. 423, s. 1.)

§ 115C-68.1. Merger of units by the board of commissioners.

(a)   The board of commissioners of a county in which two or more local school administrative units are located, but all are located wholly within the county, may adopt a plan for the consolidation and merger of the units into a single countywide unit.

The plan adopted under this subsection shall require that the county adopting the plan provide local funding per average daily membership to the resulting local school administrative unit for subsequent years of at least the highest level of any local school administrative unit in the county during the preceding five fiscal years before the merger.

The board of commissioners shall forward a copy of the plan it adopts to the boards of education of all local school administrative units located within the county, immediately upon adoption.

(b)   The boards of commissioners of two counties in which one local school administrative unit is located in both counties may jointly adopt plans for each of their counties, including a plan of consolidation and merger for such unit that is located in more than one county. The results of such consolidation and merger shall be that there is only one countywide local school administrative unit in each county, or that the entirety of the unit located within two counties is merged and consolidated with the county unit of one of the two counties. Such plans shall also merge and consolidate any other city school administrative unit located wholly within one of the two counties. Within the two-county area, all the plans shall take effect on the same day.

The plans jointly adopted under this subsection shall require that the counties jointly adopting the plans provide local funding per average daily membership to the resulting local school administrative units for subsequent fiscal years of at least the highest level of any local school administrative unit being merged during the preceding five fiscal years before the merger.

The boards of commissioners of each of the two counties shall forward copies of the plans they adopt to the boards of education of all local school administrative units located within the county, immediately upon adoption.

(c)   The plans under this section shall be prepared and approved in accordance with G.S. 115C-67 as provided by general law, or G.S. 115C-68 as provided by general law, as applicable, except that the county and city boards of education shall not participate by preparing, entering into, submitting, or agreeing to a plan, and the plan shall not be contingent upon approval of the voters.

(d) For the purpose of this section, local funding per average daily membership means the budgeted local expense per average daily membership. The State Board of Education shall establish guidelines for the computation of this amount and the amount shall be set out in the plan for consolidation and merger.

(e) If the State Board of Education fails to approve a plan submitted to it under this section, such failure to approve does not preclude the approval of the plan by the General Assembly by local act. (1991, c. 689, s. 37(b).)

§ 115C-68.2. Merger of units by the local boards of education.

If a city board of education notifies the State Board of Education that it is dissolving itself, the State Board of Education shall adopt a plan of consolidation and merger of that city school administrative unit with the county school administrative unit in the county in which the city unit is located; provided, however, if a city school administrative unit located in more than one county notifies the State Board of Education that it is dissolving itself, the State Board shall adopt a plan that divides the city unit along the county line and consolidates and merges the part of the city unit in each county with the county unit in that county and the plans shall take effect on the same day. The plans shall be prepared and approved in accordance with G.S. 115C-67 as provided by general law, and G.S. 115C-68 as provided by general law, as applicable, except that the county and city boards of education and the boards of commissioners shall not participate by preparing, entering into, submitting, or agreeing to a plan, and the plan shall not be contingent upon approval by the voters. (1991, c. 689, s. 37(c).)

§ 115C-68.3. Validation of plans of consolidation and merger.

All plans for consolidation and merger of school administrative units entered into between June 9, 1969, and May 26, 1992, under G.S. 115C-67, 115C-68.1, 115C-68.2, former G.S. 115-74.1, or under any local act authorizing such mergers, are ratified and considered to have been adopted by act of the General Assembly. This Article prevails over G.S. 153A-76(4). (1991 (Reg. Sess., 1992), c. 767, s. 2; c. 1030, s. 51.2.)

§ 115C-69. Types of districts defined.

The term "district" here used is defined to mean any convenient territorial division or subdivision of a county, created for the purpose of maintaining within its boundaries one or more public schools. It may include one or more incorporated towns or cities, or parts thereof, or one or more townships, or parts thereof, all of which territory is included in a common boundary. There shall be three different kinds of districts:

(1) The "nontax district" is a territorial division of a local school administrative unit under the control of the local board of education, having no special local tax fund voted by the people for supplementing State and county funds.

(2) The "local tax district" is a territorial division of a local school administrative unit under the control of the local board of education, having in addition to State and county funds, a special local tax fund voted by the people for supplementing State and county funds.

(3) The "administrative district" is a territorial division of a county school administrative unit under the control of a county board of education which is established for administrative purposes and which consists of any combination of one or more local tax districts, nontax areas or bond districts of the county school administrative unit. (1955, c. 1372, art. 1, s. 7; 1965, c. 584, s. 1; 1981, c. 423, s. 1; 1985 (Reg. Sess., 1986), c. 975, s. 12.)

§ 115C-70. Repealed by Session Laws 1985 (Regular Session, 1986), c. 975, s. 24.

§ 115C-71. Districts formed from portions of contiguous counties.

School districts may be formed out of contiguous counties by agreement of the county boards of education of the respective counties subject to the approval of the State Board of Education. Rules for the organization, support and operation of districts so formed are subject to the agreement of the boards of education concerned, and as a guide to the working out of such agreements the formulas contained in G.S. 115C-510 should be followed as far as applicable. (1955, c. 1372, art. 8, s. 2; 1981, c. 423, s. 1.)

§ 115C-72. Consolidation of districts and discontinuance of schools.

(a) Local boards of education shall have the power and authority to close or consolidate schools located in the same district, and with the approval of the State Board of Education, to consolidate school districts or other school areas over which the board has full control, whenever and wherever in its judgment the closing or consolidation will better serve the educational interest of the local school administrative unit or any part of it.

In determining whether two or more public schools shall be consolidated, or in determining whether or not a school shall be closed and the pupils transferred therefrom, local boards of education of the several counties shall observe and be bound by the following rules:

(1) In any question involving the closing or consolidation of any public school, the local board of education of the school administrative unit in which such school is located shall cause a thorough study of such school to be made, having in mind primarily the welfare of the students to be affected by a proposed closing or consolidation and including in such study, among other factors, geographic conditions, anticipated increase or decrease in school enrollment, the inconvenience or hardship that might result to the pupils to be affected by such closing or consolidation, the cost of providing additional school facilities in the event of such closing or consolidation, and such other factors as the board shall consider germane. Before the entry of any order of closing or consolidation, the local board of education shall provide for a public hearing in regard to such proposed closing or consolidation, at which hearing the public shall be afforded an opportunity to express their views. Upon the basis of the study so made and after such hearing, said board may, in the exercise of its discretion, approve the closing or consolidation proposed.

(2) The provisions of this section shall not deprive any local board of education of the authority to assign or enroll any and all pupils in schools in accordance with the provisions of G.S. 115C-366(b) and 115C-367 to 115C-370.

(b) This section does not govern merger of a city school administrative unit with another school administrative unit. Such merger is governed by G.S. 115C-67. (1955, c. 1372, art. 8, s. 3; 1981, c. 423, s. 1; 1983, c. 308; c. 752; 2009-570, s. 27.)

§ 115C-73. Enlarging tax districts and city units by permanently attaching contiguous property.

The county boards of education with the approval of the State Board of Education may transfer from nontax territory and attach permanently to local tax districts or to city school administrative units, real property contiguous to said local tax districts or city school administrative units, upon the written petition of the owners thereof and the taxpayers of the families living on such real property, and there shall be levied upon the property of each individual in the area so attached, including landowners and tenants, the same tax as is levied upon other property in said district or unit: Provided, that such transfer shall be subject to the approval of the board of education of such city unit: Provided, the petition must be signed by a majority of the persons who are the owners thereof and a majority of the taxpayers of the families living on such real property on the date the petition is filed with the county board of education: Provided, further, that a person or corporation owning only an easement in real property shall not be considered an owner of said property within contemplation of this section: Provided, further that no right of action or defense founded upon the invalidity of such transfer shall be asserted, nor shall the validity of such transfer be open to question in any court upon any ground whatever, except in an action or proceeding commenced within 60 days after the approval of such transfer is given by the State Board of Education.

Any qualified voter residing in the area attached shall be permitted to vote in any election for members of the board of education having jurisdiction over the attached area. (1955, c. 1372, art. 8, s. 4; 1959, c. 573, s. 4; 1971, c. 672; 1973, c. 1155; 1981, c. 423, s. 1; 1985 (Reg. Sess., 1986), c. 975, s. 13.)

§ 115C-74. School system defined.

The school system of each local school administrative unit shall consist of 12 years of study or grades, and shall be graded on the basis of a school year of not less than nine months. Schools within the system may be organized in the discretion of the local board of education. (1955, c. 1372, art. 1, s. 5; 1959, c. 573, s. 1; 1981, c. 423, s. 1; 2001-97, s. 1.)

§ 115C-75. Recommended school classification.

(a) The different types of public schools are classified and defined as follows:

(1) An "elementary school" is a school that includes all or part of the first through eighth grade and that may have a kindergarten or other early childhood program.

(2) A "high school" is a school that includes all or part of grades nine through 12 and that offers at least the minimum high school course of study prescribed by the State Board of Education.

(3) Repealed by Session Laws 2001-97, s. 2.

(4) A "junior high school" is a school that includes all or part of grades seven through nine.

(4a) A "middle school" is a school that includes all or part of grades six through nine.

(5) A "senior high school" is a school that includes the tenth, eleventh and twelfth grades.

(6) A "union school" is a school that includes elementary, middle, and high school grades.

(b) The school classifications in subsection (a) of this section are recommendations only and do not prohibit local boards of education from classifying schools in other ways. (1955, c. 1372, art. 1, s. 6; 1959, c. 915, s. 1; 1963, c. 448, s. 24; 1969, c. 1213, s. 2; 1981, c. 423, s. 1; 2001-97, s. 2.)

§§ 115C-76 through 115C-80. Reserved for future codification purposes.

SUBCHAPTER IV. EDUCATION PROGRAM.

Article 8.

General Education.

Part 1. Courses of Study.

§ 115C-81. Basic Education Program.

(a) The General Assembly believes that all children can learn. It is the intent of the General Assembly that the mission of the public school community is to challenge with high expectations each child to learn, to achieve, and to fulfill his or her potential. With that mission as its guide, the State Board of Education shall adopt a Basic Education Program for the public schools of the State. Before it adopts or revises the Basic Education Program, the State Board shall consult with an Advisory Committee, including at least eight members of local boards of education, that the State Board appoints from a list of nominees submitted by the North Carolina School Boards Association.

The State Board shall implement the Basic Education Program within funds appropriated for that purpose by the General Assembly and by units of local government. It is the intent of the General Assembly that until the Basic Education Program is fully funded, the implementation of the Basic Education Program shall be the focus of State educational funding. It is the goal of the General Assembly that the Basic Education Program be fully funded and completely operational in each local school administrative unit by July 1, 1995.

It is further a goal of the General Assembly to provide supplemental funds to low-wealth counties to allow those counties to enhance the instructional program and student achievement.

(a1) The Basic Education Program shall describe the education program to be offered to every child in the public schools. It shall provide every student in the State equal access to a Basic Education Program. Instruction shall be offered in the areas of arts, communication skills, physical education and personal health and safety, mathematics, media and computer skills, science, second languages, social studies, and vocational and technical education.

Instruction in vocational and technical education under the Basic Education Program shall be based on factors including:

(1) The integration of academic and vocational and technical education;

(2) A sequential course of study leading to both academic and occupational competencies;

(3) Increased student work skill attainment and job placement;

(4) Increased linkages, where geographically feasible, between public schools and community colleges, so the public schools can emphasize academic preparation and the community colleges can emphasize specific job training; and

(5) Instruction and experience, to the extent practicable, in all aspects of the industry the students are prepared to enter.

(a2) Repealed by Session Laws 1995, c. 534, s. 1.

(a3) Alcohol and Drug Education Program to Be Recommended and Implemented:

(1) A comprehensive education program that includes alcohol and drug use prevention education must be available to every child in North Carolina schools in kindergarten through high school.

(2) The State Board of Education shall develop and maintain a recommended list of alcohol and drug use prevention education materials that include components for teacher training and ongoing assessment and evaluation to verify success and ensure the use of up-to-date information and strategies.

(3) The Department of Public Instruction will work to strengthen instructional offerings in the content and skill areas of the Basic Education Program in which alcohol and drug use prevention education is addressed. Curricular materials and resources will be developed that meet, extend, and supplement drug and alcohol education as outlined in the North Carolina Standard Course of Study and the Teacher Handbook for the competency-based curriculum.

(4) The Department of Public Instruction shall recommend to the State Board of Education any drug use prevention education support materials that should be removed or added to the recommended list of curricular resources developed and maintained by the State Board of Education.

(5) Local boards of education may select supplemental alcohol and drug use prevention education materials from the list maintained by the State Board of Education, or develop their own supplemental materials to be approved by the State Board of Education.

(6) Local boards of education shall implement alcohol and drug use prevention education as a primary part of their comprehensive health education program.

(7) Local boards of education will provide for ongoing evaluation of drug use prevention education resources, to include participation in on-going evaluations with the Department of Public Instruction.

(8) Local boards of education must implement an approved drug and alcohol education prevention program for kindergarten through sixth grade by the 1990-91 school year, and for seventh grade through twelfth grade by the 1991-92 school year.

(9) Repealed by Session Laws 2005-155, s. 2, effective July 5, 2005.

(10) The Department of Public Instruction, in conjunction with local school districts, will provide for staff development to train educators and support personnel to implement a comprehensive alcohol and drug use prevention education program.

(11) Sequential, age-appropriate instruction will be provided that has the following features:

a. Reaches all students in all grades;

b. Presents a clear and consistent message that the use of alcohol and illicit drugs and the misuse of other drugs is unhealthy and harmful;

c. Reflects current research and theory;

d. Includes all abusable substances;

e. Utilizes information that is current and accurate;

f. Involves students in active "hands-on" learning experiences;

g. Integrates substance abuse education with other health and social issues and other subject and skill areas of the North Carolina Basic Education Program and Standard Course of Study;

h. Promotes understanding and respect for the law and values of society;

i. Encourages health, safe, and responsible attitudes and behaviors;

j. Includes strategies to involve parents, family members, and the community;

k. Includes information on intervention and treatment services;

l. Is continually open to revision, expansion and improvement.

(a4) Conflict Resolution and Mediation Models: The State Board of Education shall develop a list of recommended conflict resolution and mediation materials, models, and curricula that address responsible decision making, the causes and effects of school violence and harassment, cultural diversity, and nonviolent methods for resolving conflict, including peer mediation and shall make the list available to local school administrative units and school buildings by the beginning of the 1994-95 school year. In developing this list, the Board shall emphasize materials, models, and curricula that currently are being used in North Carolina and that the Board determines to be effective. The Board shall include at least one model that includes instruction and guidance for the voluntary implementation of peer mediation programs and one model that provides instruction and guidance for teachers concerning the integration of conflict resolution and mediation lessons into the existing classroom curriculum.

(b) The Basic Education Program shall include course requirements and descriptions similar in format to materials previously contained in the standard course of study and it shall provide:

(1) A core curriculum for all students that takes into account the special needs of children;

(2) A set of competencies, by grade level, for each curriculum area;

(3) A list of textbooks for use in providing the curriculum;

(4) Standards for student performance and promotion based on the mastery of competencies, including standards for graduation, that take into account children with disabilities and, in particular, include appropriate modifications;

(5) A program of remedial education;

(6) Required support programs;

(7) A definition of the instructional day;

(8) Class size recommendations and requirements;

(9) Prescribed staffing allotment ratios;

(10) Material and equipment allotment ratios;

(11) Facilities guidelines that reflect educational program appropriateness, long-term cost efficiency, and safety considerations; and

(12) Any other information the Board considers appropriate and necessary.

The State Board shall not adopt or enforce any rule that requires Algebra I as a graduation standard or as a requirement for a high school diploma for any student whose individualized education program (i) identifies the student as learning disabled in the area of mathematics and (ii) states that this learning disability will prevent the student from mastering Algebra I.

The State Board shall not require any student to prepare a high school graduation project as a condition of graduation from high school; local boards of education may, however, require their students to complete a high school graduation project.

(b1) Both the standard course of study and the Basic Education Program shall include the requirement that the public schools provide to all students one yearlong course of instruction on North Carolina history and geography in elementary school and one yearlong course of instruction in middle school on North Carolina history with United States history integrated into this instruction. The course of instruction shall include contributions to the history and geography of the State and the nation by the racial and ethnic groups that have contributed to the development and diversity of the State and nation. Each course of instruction may include up to two weeks of instruction relating to the local area in which the students reside.

(c)   (For final effective date, see notes) Local boards of education shall provide for the efficient teaching at appropriate grade levels of all materials set forth in the standard course of study, including integrated instruction in the areas of citizenship in the United States of America, government of the State of North Carolina, government of the United States, fire prevention, the free enterprise system, and the dangers of harmful or illegal drugs, including alcohol.

Except when a board authorizes teaching in a foreign language in order to comply with federal law, local boards of education shall require all teachers and principals to conduct classes except foreign language classes in English. Any teacher or principal who refuses to do so may be dismissed.

(c)   (For future effective date, see notes) Local boards of education shall provide for the efficient teaching at appropriate grade levels of all materials set forth in the Basic Education Program, including integrated instruction in the areas of citizenship in the United States of America, government of the State of North Carolina, government of the United States, fire prevention, the free enterprise system, and the dangers of harmful or illegal drugs, including alcohol.

Except when a board authorizes teaching in a foreign language in order to comply with federal law, local boards of education shall require all teachers and principals to conduct classes except foreign language classes in English. Any teacher or principal who refuses to do so may be dismissed.

(d)   The standard course of study as it exists on January 1, 1985, and as subsequently revised by the State Board, shall remain in effect until its components have been fully incorporated and implemented as a part of the Basic Education Program.

(e)   Repealed by Session Laws 1995, c. 534, s. 2.

(e1)   School Health Education Program to Be Developed and Administered.

(1)   A comprehensive school health education program shall be developed and taught to pupils of the public schools of this State from kindergarten through ninth grade. This program includes age-appropriate instruction in the following subject areas, regardless of whether this instruction is described as, or incorporated into a description of, "family life education", "family health

education", "health education", "family living", "health", "healthful living curriculum", or "self-esteem":

a. Mental and emotional health.

b. Drug and alcohol abuse prevention.

c. Nutrition.

d. Dental health.

e. Environmental health.

f. Family living.

g. Consumer health.

h. Disease control.

i. Growth and development.

j. First aid and emergency care, including the teaching of cardiopulmonary resuscitation (CPR) and the Heimlich maneuver by using hands-on training with mannequins so that students pass a test approved by the American Heart Association, or American Red Cross. Schools shall use for this purpose an instructional program developed by the American Heart Association, the American Red Cross, or other nationally recognized programs that is based on the most current national evidence-based emergency cardiovascular care guidelines for CPR. Schools shall maintain documentation in an electronic database that students have successfully completed CPR instruction to meet Healthful Living Essential Standards. Successful completion of instruction in CPR shall be a requirement for high school graduation by the 2014-2015 school year.

k. Preventing sexually transmitted diseases, including HIV/AIDS, and other communicable diseases.

l. Reproductive health and safety education.

m. Bicycle safety.

As used in this subsection, "HIV/AIDS" means Human Immunodeficiency Virus/Acquired Immune Deficiency Syndrome.

(2) The State Board of Education shall supervise the development and operation of a statewide comprehensive school health education program including curriculum development, in-service training provision and promotion of collegiate training, learning material review, and assessment and evaluation of local programs in the same manner as for other programs. The State Board of Education shall adopt objectives for the instruction of the subject areas listed in subdivision (1) of this subsection that are appropriate for each grade level. In addition, the State Board shall approve textbooks and other materials incorporating these objectives that local school administrative units may purchase with State funds. The State Board of Education, through the Department of Public Instruction, shall, on a regular basis, review materials related to these objectives, and distribute these reviews to local school administrative units for their information.

(3) Repealed by Session Laws 2009-213, s. 3, effective June 30, 2009, and applicable beginning with the 2010-2011 school year.

(4) Each local school administrative unit shall provide a reproductive health and safety education program commencing in the seventh grade that includes the following instruction:

a. Teaches that abstinence from sexual activity outside of marriage is the expected standard for all school-age children.

b. Presents techniques and strategies to deal with peer pressure and offering positive reinforcement.

c. Presents reasons, skills, and strategies for remaining or becoming abstinent from sexual activity.

d. Teaches that abstinence from sexual activity is the only certain means of avoiding out-of-wedlock pregnancy, sexually transmitted diseases when transmitted through sexual contact, including HIV/AIDS, and other associated health and emotional problems.

e. Teaches that a mutually faithful monogamous heterosexual relationship in the context of marriage is the best lifelong means of avoiding sexually transmitted diseases, including HIV/AIDS.

f. Teaches the positive benefits of abstinence until marriage and the risks of premarital sexual activity.

g. Provides opportunities that allow for interaction between the parent or legal guardian and the student.

h. Provides factually accurate biological or pathological information that is related to the human reproductive system.

i. Teaches about the preventable risks for preterm birth in subsequent pregnancies, including induced abortion, smoking, alcohol consumption, the use of illicit drugs, and inadequate prenatal care.

Materials used in this instruction shall be age appropriate for use with students. Information conveyed during the instruction shall be objective and based upon scientific research that is peer reviewed and accepted by professionals and credentialed experts in the field of sexual health education.

(4a) Each local school administrative unit shall also include as part of the instruction required under subdivision (4) of this subsection the following instruction:

a. Teaches about sexually transmitted diseases. Instruction shall include how sexually transmitted diseases are and are not transmitted, the effectiveness and safety of all federal Food and Drug Administration (FDA)-approved methods of reducing the risk of contracting sexually transmitted diseases, and information on local resources for testing and medical care for sexually transmitted diseases. Instruction shall include the rates of infection among pre-teen and teens of each known sexually transmitted disease and the effects of contracting each sexually transmitted disease. In particular, the instruction shall include information about the effects of contracting the Human Papilloma Virus, including sterility and cervical cancer.

b. Teaches about the effectiveness and safety of all FDA-approved contraceptive methods in preventing pregnancy.

c. Teaches awareness of sexual assault, sexual abuse, and risk reduction. The instruction and materials shall:

1. Focus on healthy relationships.

2. Teach students what constitutes sexual assault and sexual abuse, the causes of those behaviors, and risk reduction.

3. Inform students about resources and reporting procedures if they experience sexual assault or sexual abuse.

4. Examine common misconceptions and stereotypes about sexual assault and sexual abuse.

Materials used in this instruction shall be age appropriate for use with students. Information conveyed during the instruction shall be objective and based upon scientific research that is peer reviewed and accepted by professionals and credentialed experts in the field of sexual health education. Each local board of education shall adopt a policy and provide a mechanism to allow a parent or a guardian to withdraw his or her child from instruction required under this subdivision.

(5) The State Board of Education shall make available to all local school administrative units for review by the parents and legal guardians of students enrolled at that unit any State-developed objectives for instruction, any approved textbooks, the list of reviewed materials, and any other State-developed or approved materials that pertain to or are intended to impart information or promote discussion or understanding in regard to the prevention of sexually transmitted diseases, including HIV/AIDS, to the avoidance of out-of-wedlock pregnancy, or to the reproductive health and safety education curriculum. The review period shall extend for at least 60 days before use.

(6) Repealed by Session Laws 2009-213, s. 7, effective June 30, 2009, and applicable beginning with the 2010-2011 school year.

(7) Each school year, before students may participate in any portion of (i) a program that pertains to or is intended to impart information or promote discussion or understanding in regard to the prevention of sexually transmitted diseases, including HIV/AIDS, or to the avoidance of out-of-wedlock pregnancy, or (ii) a reproductive health and safety education program, whether developed by the State or by the local board of education, the parents and legal guardians of those students shall be given an opportunity to review the objectives and materials. Local boards of education shall adopt policies to provide opportunities either for parents and legal guardians to consent or for parents and legal guardians to withhold their consent to the students' participation in any or all of these programs.

(8) Students may receive information about where to obtain contraceptives and abortion referral services only in accordance with a local board's policy regarding parental consent. Any instruction concerning the use of contraceptives or prophylactics shall provide accurate statistical information on their effectiveness and failure rates for preventing pregnancy and sexually transmitted diseases, including HIV/AIDS, in actual use among adolescent populations and shall explain clearly the difference between risk reduction and risk elimination through abstinence. The Department of Health and Human Services shall provide the most current available information at the beginning of each school year.

(9) Contraceptives, including condoms and other devices, shall not be made available or distributed on school property.

(10) School health coordinators may be employed to assist in the instruction of any portion of the comprehensive school health education program. Where feasible, a school health coordinator should serve more than one local school administrative unit. Each person initially employed as a State-funded school health coordinator after June 30, 1987, shall have a degree in health education.

(11) Each local school administrative unit shall provide a comprehensive school health education program that meets all the requirements of this subsection and all the objectives established by the State Board. Each local board of education may expand on the subject areas to be included in the program and on the instructional objectives to be met.

(e2) Honors-Level Courses in Healthful Living Education to be Developed and Administered. - The State Board of Education shall develop or identify academically rigorous honors-level courses in healthful living education that can be offered at the high school level. These honors-level courses shall be more rigorous than standard-level courses, include advanced content, provide multiple opportunities for students to take greater responsibility for their learning, and require higher quality work from the students than standard courses.

(f) Establishment and Maintenance of Kindergartens. -

(1) Local boards of education shall provide for their respective local school administrative unit kindergartens as a part of the public school system for all children living in the local school administrative unit who are eligible for admission pursuant to subdivision (2) of this subsection provided that funds are

available from State, local, federal or other sources to operate a kindergarten program as provided in this subsection.

All kindergarten programs so established shall be subject to the supervision of the Department of Public Instruction and shall be operated in accordance with the standards adopted by the State Board of Education, upon recommendation of the Superintendent of Public Instruction.

Among the standards to be adopted by the State Board of Education shall be a provision that the Board will allocate funds for the purpose of operating and administering kindergartens to each school administrative unit in the State based on the average daily membership for the best continuous three out of the first four school months of pupils in the kindergarten program during the last school year in that respective school administrative unit. Such allocations are to be made from funds appropriated to the State Board of Education for the kindergarten program.

(2) Any child who meets the requirements of G.S. 115C-364 shall be eligible for enrollment in kindergarten. Any child who is enrolled in kindergarten and not withdrawn by the child's parent or guardian shall attend kindergarten.

(3) Notwithstanding any other provision of law to the contrary, subject to the approval of the State Board of Education, any local board of education may elect not to establish and maintain a kindergarten program. Any funds allocated to a local board of education which does not operate a kindergarten program may be reallocated by the State Board of Education, within the discretion of the Board, to a county or city board of education which will operate such a program.

(g) Civic Literacy. -

(1) Local boards of education shall require during the high school years the teaching of a semester course "American History I - The Founding Principles," to include at least the following:

a. The Creator-endowed inalienable rights of the people.

b. Structure of government, separation of powers with checks and balances.

c. Frequent and free elections in a representative government.

d. Rule of law.

e. Equal justice under the law.

f. Private property rights.

g. Federalism.

h. Due process.

i. Individual rights as set forth in the Bill of Rights.

j. Individual responsibility.

A passing grade in the course shall be required for graduation from high school.

(2), (3) Repealed by Session Laws 2011-273, s. 2, effective June 23, 2011, and applicable beginning with the 2014-2015 school year.

(3a) Local boards of education shall allow and may encourage any public school teacher or administrator to read or post in a public school building, classroom, or event, excerpts or portions of writings, documents, and records that reflect the history of the United States, including, but not limited to, (i) the preamble to the North Carolina Constitution, (ii) the Declaration of Independence, (iii) the United States Constitution, (iv) the Mayflower Compact, (v) the national motto, (vi) the National Anthem, (vii) the Pledge of Allegiance, (viii) the writings, speeches, documents, and proclamations of the founding fathers and Presidents of the United States, (ix) decisions of the Supreme Court of the United States, and (x) acts of the Congress of the United States, including the published text of the Congressional Record. Local boards, superintendents, principals, and supervisors shall not allow content-based censorship of American history in the public schools of this State, including religious references in these writings, documents, and records. Local boards and professional school personnel may develop curricula and use materials that are limited to specified topics provided the curricula and materials are aligned with the standard course of study or are grade level appropriate.

(3b) A local school administrative unit may display on real property controlled by that local school administrative unit documents and objects of historical significance that have formed and influenced the United States legal or governmental system and that exemplify the development of the rule of law, such as the Magna Carta, the Mecklenburg Declaration, the Ten Commandments, the Justinian Code, and documents set out in subdivision (3a) of this subsection. This display may include, but shall not be limited to, documents that contain words associated with a religion; provided however, no display shall seek to establish or promote religion or to persuade any person to embrace a particular religion, denomination of a religion, or other philosophy. The display of a document containing words associated with a religion shall be in the same manner and appearance generally as other documents and objects displayed and shall not be presented or displayed in any fashion that results in calling attention to it apart from the other displayed documents and objects. The display also shall be accompanied by a prominent sign quoting the First Amendment of the United States Constitution as follows: "Congress shall make no law respecting an establishment of religion, or prohibiting the free exercise thereof; or abridging the freedom of speech, or of the press; or the right of the people peaceably to assemble, and to petition the government for a redress of grievances."

(4) The State Board of Education shall require that any high school level curriculum-based tests developed and administered statewide beginning with the 2014-2015 academic year include questions related to the philosophical foundations of our form of government and the principles underlying the Declaration of Independence, the United States Constitution and its amendments, and the most important of the Federalist Papers.

(5) The Department of Public Instruction and the local boards of education, as appropriate, shall provide or cause to be provided curriculum content for the semester course required in subdivision (1) of this subsection and teacher training to ensure that the intent and provisions of this subsection are carried out. The curriculum content established shall include a review of the contributions made by Americans of all races.

(6) The Department of Public Instruction shall submit a biennial report by October 15 of each odd-numbered year to the Joint Legislative Education Oversight Committee covering the implementation of this subsection.

(g1) Modifications to the social studies curriculum to instruct students on participation in the democratic process and to give them hands-on experience in participating in the democratic process:

(1) The State Board of Education shall modify the high school social studies curriculum to include instruction in civic and citizenship education. The State

Board of Education is strongly encouraged to include, at a minimum, the following components in the high school civic and citizenship education curriculum:

a. That students write to a local, State, or federal elected official about an issue that is important to them;

b. Instruction on the importance of voting and otherwise participating in the democratic process, including instruction on voter registration;

c. Information about current events and governmental structure; and

d. Information about the democratic process and how laws are made.

(2) The State Board of Education shall modify the middle school social studies curriculum to include instruction in civic and citizenship education. The State Board of Education is strongly encouraged to include, at a minimum, the following components in the middle school civic and citizenship education curriculum:

a. A tour of representative local government facilities such as the local jail, the courthouse, or a town hall, to help students understand the way their community is governed;

b. That students choose and analyze a community problem and offer public policy recommendations on the problem to local officials; and

c. Information about getting involved in community groups.

(g2) Student Councils. - All high schools and middle schools shall be encouraged to have elected student councils through which students have input into policies and decisions that affect them. All other schools are encouraged to have student councils.

The purpose of these student councils is to build civic skills and attitudes such as participation in elections, discussion and debate of issues, and collaborative decision making. Schools shall encourage active, broad-based participation in these student councils.

(g3) Current Events. - Schools should encourage discussions of current events in a wide range of classes, especially social studies and language arts classes. All high schools and middle schools are encouraged to have at least two classes per grade level to offer interactive current events discussions at least every four weeks.

(h) Character Education. - Each local board of education shall develop and implement character education instruction with input from the local community. The instruction shall be incorporated into the standard curriculum and should address the following traits:

(1) Courage. - Having the determination to do the right thing even when others don't and the strength to follow your conscience rather than the crowd; and attempting difficult things that are worthwhile.

(2) Good judgment. - Choosing worthy goals and setting proper priorities; thinking through the consequences of your actions; and basing decisions on practical wisdom and good sense.

(3) Integrity. - Having the inner strength to be truthful, trustworthy, and honest in all things; acting justly and honorably.

(4) Kindness. - Being considerate, courteous, helpful, and understanding of others; showing care, compassion, friendship, and generosity; and treating others as you would like to be treated.

(5) Perseverance. - Being persistent in the pursuit of worthy objectives in spite of difficulty, opposition, or discouragement; and exhibiting patience and having the fortitude to try again when confronted with delays, mistakes, or failures.

(6) Respect. - Showing high regard for authority, for other people, for self, for property, and for country; and understanding that all people have value as human beings.

(7) Responsibility. - Being dependable in carrying out obligations and duties; showing reliability and consistency in words and conduct; being accountable for your own actions; and being committed to active involvement in your community.

(8) Self-Discipline. - Demonstrating hard work and commitment to purpose; regulating yourself for improvement and restraining from inappropriate behaviors; being in proper control of your words, actions, impulses, and desires;

choosing abstinence from premarital sex, drugs, alcohol, and other harmful substances and behaviors; and doing your best in all situations.

(h1) In addition to the instruction under subsection (h) of this section, local boards of education are encouraged to include instruction on the following responsibilities:

(1) Respect for school personnel. - In the school environment, respect includes holding teachers, school administrators, and all school personnel in high esteem and demonstrating in words and deeds that all school personnel deserve to be treated with courtesy and proper deference.

(2) Responsibility for school safety. - Helping to create a harmonious school atmosphere that is free from threats, weapons, and violent or disruptive behavior; cultivate an orderly learning environment in which students and school personnel feel safe and secure; and encourage the resolution of conflicts and disagreements through peaceful means including peer mediation. Instruction in this responsibility should include a consistent and age-appropriate antiviolence message and a conflict resolution component for students in kindergarten through twelfth grade. These messages should include media-awareness education to help children recognize stereotypes and messages portraying violence.

(3) Service to others. - Engaging in meaningful service to their schools and their communities. Schools may teach service-learning by (i) incorporating it into their standard curriculum, or (ii) involving a classroom of students or some other group of students in one or more hands-on community-service projects. All schools are encouraged to provide opportunities for student involvement in community service or service-learning projects.

(4) Good citizenship. - Obeying the laws of the nation and this State; abiding by school rules; and understanding the rights and responsibilities of a member of a republic.

(i) Both the standard course of study and the Basic Education Program shall include the requirement that the public schools provide instruction in personal financial literacy for all students. Each student shall receive personal financial literacy instruction that shall include (i) the true cost of credit, (ii) choosing and managing a credit card, (iii) borrowing money for an automobile or other large purchase, (iv) home mortgages, (v) credit scoring and credit reports, and (vi) other relevant financial literacy issues.

The State Board of Education shall determine the other components of personal financial literacy that will be covered in the curriculum. The State Board shall also review the high school standard course of study to determine into which courses and grade levels the personal financial literacy curriculum shall be integrated.

(j) Disability History and Awareness. - Each local board of education shall provide instruction on disability, people with disabilities, and the disability rights movement in conjunction with Disability History and Awareness Month, established pursuant to G.S. 103-11. This instruction shall be incorporated into the standard curriculum through measures that include: (i) supplementing existing lesson plans, (ii) holding school assemblies, (iii) hosting disability-focused film festivals, or (iv) organizing other school activities. Local boards of education are encouraged to incorporate individuals with disabilities or knowledgeable guest speakers from the disability community into the delivery of this instruction.

(k) Cursive Writing. - The standard course of study shall include the requirement that the public schools provide instruction in cursive writing so that students create readable documents through legible cursive handwriting by the end of fifth grade.

(l) Multiplication Tables. - The standard course of study shall include the requirement that students enrolled in public schools memorize multiplication tables to demonstrate competency in efficiently multiplying numbers. (1955, c. 1372, art. 5, s. 20; art. 23, ss. 1, 5, 6; 1957, cc. 845, 1101; 1969, c. 487, ss. 1, 2; 1971, c. 356; 1973, c. 476, s. 128; 1975, c. 65, ss. 1, 2; 1977, 2nd Sess., c. 1256, s. 1; 1981, c. 423, s. 1; 1983, c. 656, s. 2; 1983 (Reg. Sess., 1984), c. 1034, s. 81; c. 1103, s. 2; 1985, c. 479, ss. 55(c)(1), 55(c)(2); 1987, c. 630; c. 738, ss. 186(a), 186(b), 187(a); 1989, c. 370; c. 801; 1989 (Reg. Sess., 1990), c. 1066, s. 100; 1991, c. 636, s. 9; c. 689, ss. 196(a), 198; c. 739, s. 11; 1991 (Reg. Sess., 1992), c. 769, s. 1; c. 900, s. 75.1(h); 1993, c. 180, s. 1; c. 321, s. 139(d); c. 359, s. 1; 1993 (Reg. Sess., 1994), c. 769, s. 19.5(a); 1995, c. 371, s. 1; c. 450, ss. 5, 6, 7; c. 507, s. 17.14; c. 509, ss. 61, 62; c. 534, ss. 1, 2, 3; 1995 (Reg. Sess., 1996), c. 716, s. 8.6; 1996, 2nd Ex. Sess., c. 18, ss. 18.17(a), 18.24(a); 1997-18, s. 15(f); 1997-204, s. 2; 1997-273, ss. 1, 2; 1997-422, s. 1; 2001-363, ss. 1, 2(b), 2(d); 2003-284, s. 7.40(a), (b); 2005-155, s. 2; 2005-276, s. 7.59(a); 2006-69, s. 3(a); 2006-264, s. 54(a)-(c); 2007-274, s. 2; 2009-60, s. 1; 2009-213, ss. 2-9; 2009-236, s. 1; 2009-504, s. 1; 2009-541, s. 28(a); 2010-33, s. 1; 2010-35, s. 1; 2011-273, s. 2; 2012-197, s. 1; 2013-71, s. 1; 2013-307, s. 1; 2013-381, s. 12.1(g).)

§ 115C-81.1. Basic Education Program Funds not to supplant Local funds for schools.

It is the intent of the General Assembly that budget funds appropriated by the General Assembly for vocational and technical education programs and clerical personnel to implement the Basic Education Program be used to supplement and not supplant existing State and local funding for the public schools. Therefore, to the extent that local school administrative units receive additional State funds for vocational and technical education programs and clerical personnel positions that were previously funded in whole or in part with nonstate funds, the local governments shall continue to spend for public school operating or capital purposes in the local school administrative units the amount of money they would have spent to provide the vocational and technical education programs and the school clerical personnel previously funded with nonstate funds.

Priority shall be given to funding capital needs, particularly those resulting from implementation of the Basic Education Program. (1987, c. 830, s. 88; 1993, c. 180, s. 2.)

§ 115C-81.2: Repealed by Session Laws 2012-142, s. 7A.1(a), effective July 2, 2012.

§ 115C-81.3. Instruction in American Sign Language.

(a) The State Board of Education shall encourage schools to offer American Sign Language classes in high schools as a modern foreign language.

(b) The State Board of Education shall adopt and implement standards for the certification of teachers of American Sign Language and shall set standards for teacher preparation programs that prepare students for certification as American Sign Language teachers. (2007-154, s. 1(a).)

§ 115C-81.4. Science safety requirements.

(a) Prior to July 1, 2010, and annually thereafter, each local board of education shall certify to the State Board of Education that its high school and middle school science laboratories are equipped with appropriate personal protective equipment for students and teachers.

(b) Each local board of education shall ensure that its high schools and middle schools comply with all State Board of Education policies related to science laboratory safety. (2009-59, s. 1.)

§ 115C-82: Repealed by Session Laws 1987 (Reg. Sess., 1988), c. 1086, s. 89(d).

§ 115C-83: Repealed by Session Laws 1997-18, s. 4.

Part 1A. North Carolina Read to Achieve Program.

§ 115C-83.1. State goal.

The goal of the State is to ensure that every student read at or above grade level by the end of third grade and continue to progress in reading proficiency so that he or she can read, comprehend, integrate, and apply complex texts needed for secondary education and career success. (2012-142, s. 7A.1(b).)

§ 115C-83.2. Purposes.

(a) The purposes of this Part are to ensure that (i) difficulty with reading development is identified as early as possible; (ii) students receive appropriate instructional and support services to address difficulty with reading development and to remediate reading deficiencies; and (iii) each student and his or her parent or guardian be continuously informed of the student's academic needs and progress.

(b) In addition to the purposes listed in subsection (a) of this section, the purpose of this Part is to determine that progression from one grade to another be based, in part, upon proficiency in reading. (2012-142, s. 7A.1(b).)

§ 115C-83.3. Definitions.

The following definitions apply in this Part:

(1) "Accelerated reading class" means a class where focused instructional supports and services are provided to increase a student's reading level at least two grades in one school year.

(2) "Alternative assessment" means a valid and reliable standardized assessment of reading comprehension, approved by the State Board of Education, that is not the same test as the State-approved standardized test of reading comprehension administered to third grade students.

(3) "Difficulty with reading development" means not demonstrating appropriate developmental abilities in any of the major reading areas, including, but not limited to, oral language, phonological or phonemic awareness, vocabulary, fluency, or comprehension, according to observation-based, diagnostic, or formative assessments.

(4) "Instructional supports and services" mean intentional strategies used with a majority of students to facilitate reading development and remediate emerging difficulty with reading development. Instructional supports and services include, but are not limited to, small group instruction, reduced teacher-student ratios, frequent progress monitoring, and extended learning time.

(5) "Reading deficiency" means not reading at the third grade level by the end of the student's third grade year, demonstrated by the results of the State-approved standardized test of reading comprehension administered to third grade students.

(6) "Reading interventions" mean evidence-based strategies frequently used to remediate reading deficiencies and include, but are not limited to, individual instruction, tutoring, or mentoring that target specific reading skills and abilities.

(7) "Reading proficiency" means reading at or above the third grade level by the end of a student's third grade year, demonstrated by the results of the State-approved standardized test of reading comprehension administered to third grade students.

(8) "Student reading portfolio" means a compilation of independently produced student work selected by the student's teacher, and signed by the teacher and principal, as an accurate picture of the student's reading ability. The student reading portfolio shall include an organized collection of evidence of the student's mastery of the State's reading standards that are assessed by the State-approved standardized test of reading comprehension administered to third grade students. For each benchmark, there shall be three examples of student work demonstrating mastery by a grade of seventy percent (70%) or above.

(9) "Summer reading camp" means an additional educational program outside of the instructional calendar provided by the local school administrative unit to any student who does not demonstrate reading proficiency. Parents or guardians of the student not demonstrating reading proficiency shall make the final decision regarding the student's summer camp attendance. Summer camps shall (i) be six to eight weeks long, four or five days per week; (ii) include at least three hours of instructional time per day; (iii) be taught by compensated, licensed teachers selected based on demonstrated student outcomes in reading proficiency; and (iv) allow volunteer mentors to read with students.

(10) "Transitional third and fourth class combination" means a classroom specifically designed to produce learning gains sufficient to meet fourth grade performance standards while continuing to remediate areas of reading deficiency. (2012-142, s. 7A.1(b).)

§ 115C-83.4. Comprehensive plan for reading achievement.

(a) The State Board of Education shall develop, implement, and continuously evaluate a comprehensive plan to improve reading achievement in the public schools. The plan shall be based on reading instructional practices with strong evidence of effectiveness in current empirical research in reading development. The plan shall be developed with the active involvement of teachers, college and university educators, parents and guardians of students, and other interested parties. The plan shall, when appropriate to reflect research, include revision of the standard course of study or other curricular standards, revision of teacher licensure and renewal standards, and revision of teacher education program standards.

(b) The State Board of Education shall report biennially to the Joint Legislative Education Oversight Committee by October 1 of each even-numbered year on the implementation, evaluation, and revisions to the comprehensive plan for reading achievement and shall include recommendations for legislative changes to enable implementation of current empirical research in reading development. (2012-142, s. 7A.1(b).)

§ 115C-83.4A. Advanced courses.

(a) It is the intent of the State to enhance accessibility and encourage students to enroll in and successfully complete more rigorous advanced courses to enable success in postsecondary education for all students. For the purposes of this section, an advanced course is an Advanced Placement or International Baccalaureate Diploma Programme course. To attain this goal, to the extent funds are made available for this purpose, students enrolled in public schools shall be exempt from paying any fees for administration of examinations for advanced courses and registration fees for advanced courses in which the student is enrolled regardless of the score the student achieves on an examination.

(b) Eligible secondary students shall be encouraged to enroll in advanced courses to expose them to more rigorous coursework while still in secondary school. Successfully completing advanced courses will increase the quality and level of students' preparation for postsecondary career paths and their pursuit of higher education.

(c) The results of student diagnostic tests administered pursuant to G.S. 115C-174.18 and G.S. 115C-174.22, such as the Preliminary SAT/National Merit Scholarship Qualifying Test (PSAT/NMSQT) and ACT, shall be used to identify students who are prepared or who need additional work to be prepared to enroll and be successful in advanced courses. Students may also be identified for potential enrollment in advanced courses based on other criteria established by schools to increase access to those courses for their students.

(d) Local boards of education shall provide information to students and parents on available opportunities and the enrollment process for students to take advanced courses. The information shall explain the value of advanced courses in preparing students for postsecondary level coursework, enabling students to gain access to postsecondary opportunities, and qualifying for scholarships and other financial aid opportunities.

(e)   Local boards of education shall ensure that all high school students have access to advanced courses in language arts, mathematics, science, and social studies. Such access may be provided through enrollment in courses offered through or approved by the North Carolina Virtual Public School.

(f)   The State Board of Education shall seek a partner, such as the College Board, to form the North Carolina Advanced Placement Partnership, hereinafter referred to as Partnership, to assist in improving college readiness of secondary students and to assist secondary schools to ensure that students have access to high-quality, rigorous academics with a focus on access to Advanced Placement courses.

In order to implement its responsibilities under this section, the partner selected by the State Board of Education shall provide staff to do the following:

(1)   Provide professional development in the form of support and training to enable teachers of Advanced Placement courses to have the necessary content knowledge, instructional skills, and materials to prepare students for success in Advanced Placement courses and examinations and mastery of postsecondary course content.

(2)   Provide administrators, including principals and counselors, with professional development that will enable them to create strong and effective Advanced Placement courses in their schools.

(3)   Provide teachers of students in grades seven through 12 with preadvanced course professional development and materials that prepare students for success in Advanced Placement courses.

(4)   Provide consulting expertise and technical assistance to support implementation.

(5)   Prioritize assistance to schools designated as low-performing by the State Board of Education and provide for frequent visits to the schools targeted by the Partnership.

(g)   The Partnership shall report annually to the Department of Public Instruction on the Partnership's implementation of its responsibilities under subsection (f) of this section.

(h)   Beginning October 1, 2014, the State Board of Education shall report annually to the Joint Legislative Education Oversight Committee on advanced courses in North Carolina. The report shall include, at a minimum, the following information:

(1)   The North Carolina Advanced Placement Partnership's report to the Department of Public Instruction as required by subsection (g) of this section and the State Board's assessment of that report.

(2)   Number of students enrolled in advanced courses and participating in advanced course examinations, including demographic information by gender, race, and free and reduced-price lunch status.

(3)   Student performance on advanced course examinations, including information by course, local school administrative unit, and school.

(4)   Number of students participating in 10th grade PSAT/NMSQT testing.

(5)   Number of teachers attending summer institutes offered by the North Carolina Advanced Placement Partnership.

(6)   Distribution of funding appropriated for advanced course testing fees and professional development by local school administrative unit and school.

(7)   Status and efforts of the North Carolina Advanced Placement Partnership.

(8)   Other trends in advanced courses and examinations. (2013-360, s. 8.27(b).)

§ 115C-83.5. Developmental screening and kindergarten entry assessment.

(a)   The State Board of Education shall ensure that every student entering kindergarten shall be administered a developmental screening of early language, literacy, and math skills within 30 days of enrollment.

(b)   The State Board of Education shall ensure that every student entering kindergarten shall complete a kindergarten entry assessment within 60 days of enrollment.

(c)   The developmental screening instrument may be composed of subsections of the kindergarten entry assessment.

(d)   The kindergarten entry assessment shall address the five essential domains of school readiness: language and literacy development, cognition and general knowledge, approaches toward learning, physical well-being and motor development, and social and emotional development.

(e)   The kindergarten entry assessment shall be (i) administered at the classroom level in all local school administrative units; (ii) aligned to North Carolina's early learning and development standards and to the standard course of study; and (iii) reliable, valid, and appropriate for use with all children, including those with disabilities and those who are English language learners.

(f)   The results of the developmental screening and the kindergarten entry assessment shall be used to inform the following:

(1)   The status of children's learning at kindergarten entry.

(2)   Instruction of each child.

(3)   Efforts to reduce the achievement gap at kindergarten entry.

(4)   Continuous improvement of the early childhood system. (2012-142, s. 7A.1(b).)

§ 115C-83.6. Facilitating early grade reading proficiency.

(a)   Kindergarten, first, second, and third grade students shall be assessed with valid, reliable, formative, and diagnostic reading assessments made available to local school administrative units by the State Board of Education pursuant to G.S. 115C-174.11(a). Difficulty with reading development identified through administration of formative and diagnostic assessments shall be addressed with instructional supports and services. To the greatest extent possible, kindergarten through third grade reading assessments shall yield data that can be used with the Education Value-Added Assessment System (EVAAS), or a compatible and comparable system approved by the State Board of Education, to analyze student data to identify root causes for difficulty with reading development and to determine actions to address them.

(b) Formative and diagnostic assessments and resultant instructional supports and services shall address oral language, phonological and phonemic awareness, phonics, vocabulary, fluency, and comprehension using developmentally appropriate practices.

(c) Local school administrative units are encouraged to partner with community organizations, businesses, and other groups to provide volunteers, mentors, or tutors to assist with the provision of instructional supports and services that enhance reading development and proficiency. (2012-142, s. 7A.1(b).)

§ 115C-83.7. Elimination of social promotion.

(a) The State Board of Education shall require that a student be retained in the third grade if the student fails to demonstrate reading proficiency appropriate for a third grade student, as demonstrated on a State-approved standardized test of reading comprehension administered to third grade students. The test may be readministered once prior to the end of the school year.

(b) Students may be exempt from mandatory retention in third grade for good cause but shall continue to receive instructional supports and services and reading interventions appropriate for their age and reading level. Good cause exemptions shall be limited to the following:

(1) Limited English Proficient students with less than two years of instruction in an English as a Second Language program.

(2) Students with disabilities, as defined in G.S. 115C-106.3(1), whose individualized education program indicates the use of alternative assessments and reading interventions.

(3) Students who demonstrate reading proficiency appropriate for third grade students on an alternative assessment approved by the State Board of Education. Teachers may administer the alternative assessment following the

administration of the State-approved standardized test of reading comprehension typically given to third grade students at the end of the school year, or after a student's participation in the local school administrative unit's summer reading camp.

(4) Students who demonstrate, through a student reading portfolio, reading proficiency appropriate for third grade students. Teachers may submit the student reading portfolio at the end of the school year or after a student's participation in the local school administrative unit's summer reading camp. The student reading portfolio and review process shall be established by the State Board of Education.

(5) Students who have (i) received reading intervention and (ii) previously been retained more than once in kindergarten, first, second, or third grades.

(c) The superintendent shall determine whether a student may be exempt from mandatory retention on the basis of a good cause exemption. The following steps shall be taken in making the determination:

(1) The teacher of a student eligible for a good cause exemption shall submit documentation of the relevant exemption and evidence that promotion of the student is appropriate based on the student's academic record to the principal. Such evidence shall be limited to the student's personal education plan, individual education program, if applicable, alternative assessment, or student reading portfolio.

(2) The principal shall review the documentation and make an initial determination whether the student should be promoted. If the principal determines the student should be promoted, the principal shall make a written recommendation of promotion to the superintendent for final determination. The superintendent's acceptance or rejection of the recommendation shall be in writing. (2012-142, s. 7A.1(b).)

§ 115C-83.8. Successful reading development for retained students.

(a) Students not demonstrating reading proficiency shall be enrolled in a summer reading camp provided by the local school administrative unit prior to being retained. Students who demonstrate reading proficiency on an alternative assessment of reading comprehension or student reading portfolio after completing a summer reading camp shall be promoted to the fourth grade. Students who do not demonstrate reading proficiency on these measures after completing a summer reading camp shall be retained under G.S. 115C-83.7(a) and provided with the instruction listed in subsection (b) of this section during the retained year.

(b)   Students retained under G.S. 115C-83.7(a) shall be provided with a teacher selected based on demonstrated student outcomes in reading proficiency and placed in an accelerated reading class or a transitional third and fourth grade class combination, as appropriate. Classroom instruction shall include at least 90 minutes of daily, uninterrupted, evidence-based reading instruction, not to include independent reading time, and other appropriate instructional supports and services and reading interventions.

(c)   The State Board of Education shall establish a midyear promotion policy for any student retained under G.S. 115C-83.7(a) who, by November 1, demonstrates reading proficiency through administration of the alternative assessment of reading comprehension or student reading portfolio review.

(d)   Repealed by Session Laws 2013-360, s. 8.30, effective July 1, 2013.

(e)   Parents or guardians of students who have been retained twice under the provisions of G.S. 115C-83.7(a) shall be offered supplemental tutoring for the retained student in evidence-based reading services outside the instructional day. (2012-142, s. 7A.1(b); 2013-360, s. 8.30.)

§ 115C-83.9. Notification requirements to parents and guardians.

(a)   Parents or guardians shall be notified in writing, and in a timely manner, that the student shall be retained, unless he or she is exempt from mandatory retention for good cause, if the student is not demonstrating reading proficiency by the end of third grade. Parents or guardians shall receive this notice when a kindergarten, first, second, or third grade student (i) is demonstrating difficulty with reading development; (ii) is not reading at grade level; or (iii) has a personal education plan under G.S. 115C-105.41.

(b)   Parents or guardians of any student who is to be retained under the provisions of G.S. 115C-83.7(a) shall be notified in writing of the reason the student is not eligible for a good cause exemption as provided in G.S. 115C-

83.7(b). Written notification shall also include a description of proposed reading interventions that will be provided to the student to remediate identified areas of reading deficiency.

(c)   Parents or guardians of students retained under G.S. 115C-83.7(a) shall receive at least monthly written reports on student progress toward reading proficiency. The evaluation of the student's progress shall be based upon the student's classroom work, observations, tests, assessments, and other relevant information.

(d)   Teachers and principals shall provide opportunities to discuss with parents and guardians the notifications listed in this section. (2012-142, s. 7A.1(b).)

§ 115C-83.10. Accountability measures.

(a)   Each local board of education shall publish annually on a Web site maintained by that local school administrative unit and report in writing to the State Board of Education by September 1 of each year the following information on the prior school year:

(1)   The number and percentage of third grade students demonstrating and not demonstrating reading proficiency on the State-approved standardized test of reading comprehension administered to third grade students.

(2)   The number and percentage of third grade students who take and pass the alternative assessment of reading comprehension.

(3)   The number and percentage of third grade students retained for not demonstrating reading proficiency.

(4)   The number and percentage of third grade students exempt from mandatory third grade retention by category of exemption as listed in G.S. 115C-83.7(b).

(b)   Each local board of education shall report annually in writing to the State Board of Education by September 1 of each year a description of all reading interventions provided to students who have been retained under G.S. 115C-83.7(a).

(c) The State Board of Education shall establish a uniform format for local boards of education to report the required information listed in subsections (a) and (b) of this section and shall provide the format to local boards of education no later than 90 days prior to the annual due date. The State Board of Education shall compile annually this information and submit a State-level summary to the Governor, the President Pro Tempore of the Senate, the Speaker of the House of Representatives, and the Joint Legislative Education Oversight Committee by October 1 of each year, beginning with the 2014-2015 school year.

(d) The State Board of Education and the Department of Public Instruction shall provide technical assistance as needed to aid local school administrative units to implement all provisions of this Part. (2012-142, s. 7A.1(b).)

§ 115C-83.11: Reserved for future codification purposes.

§ 115C-83.12: Reserved for future codification purposes.

§ 115C-83.13: Reserved for future codification purposes.

§ 115C-83.14: Reserved for future codification purposes.

Part 1B. School Performance.

§ 115C-83.15. School achievement, growth, performance scores, and grades.

(a) School Scores and Grades. - The State Board of Education shall award school achievement, growth, and performance scores and an associated performance grade as required by G.S. 115C-12(9)c1., and calculated as provided in this section. The State Board of Education shall enter all necessary data into the Education Value-Added Assessment System (EVAAS) in order to calculate school performance scores and grades.

(b) Calculation of the School Achievement Score. - In calculating the overall school achievement score earned by schools, the State Board of Education shall total the sum of points earned by a school on all of the following indicators that are measured for that school:

(1) One point for each percent of students who score at or above proficient on annual assessments for mathematics in grades three through eight.

(2) One point for each percent of students who score at or above proficient on annual assessments for reading in grades three through eight.

(3) One point for each percent of students who score at or above proficient on annual assessments for science in grades five and eight.

(4) One point for each percent of students who score at or above proficient on the Algebra I or Integrated Math I end-of-course test.

(5) One point for each percent of students who score at or above proficient on the English II end-of-course test.

(6) One point for each percent of students who score at or above proficient on the Biology end-of-course test.

(7) One point for each percent of students who complete Algebra II or Integrated Math III with a passing grade.

(8) One point for each percent of students who achieve the minimum score required for admission into a constituent institution of The University of North Carolina on a nationally normed test of college readiness.

(9) One point for each percent of students enrolled in Career and Technical Education courses who meet the standard when scoring at Silver, Gold, or Platinum levels on a nationally normed test of workplace readiness.

(10) One point for each percent of students who graduate within four years of entering high school.

Each school achievement indicator shall be of equal value when used to determine the overall school achievement score. The overall school achievement score shall be translated to a 100-point scale and used for school reporting purposes as provided in G.S. 115C-12(9)c1., 115C-238.29F, and 115C-238.66.

(c) Calculation of the School Growth Score. - Using EVAAS, the State Board shall calculate the overall growth score earned by schools. In calculating the total growth score earned by schools, the State Board of Education shall weight student growth on the achievement indicators as provided in subsection (b) of this section that have available growth values. The numerical values used to determine whether a school has met, exceeded, or has not met expected growth shall be translated to a 100-point scale and used for school reporting purposes as provided in G.S. 115C-12(9)c1., 115C-238.29F, and 115C-238.66.

(d) Calculation of the School Performance Scores and Grades. - For schools exceeding or not meeting expected school growth, the State Board of Education shall use EVAAS to calculate the school performance score by adding the school achievement score, as provided in subsection (b) of this section, and the school growth score, as provided in subsection (c) of this section, earned by a school. The school achievement score shall account for eighty percent (80%), and the school growth score shall account for (20%) of the total sum. For schools meeting expected growth, and with a school achievement score of eighty percent (80%) or higher, the school performance score shall solely reflect the achievement score. For schools meeting expected growth, and with a school achievement score below eighty percent (80%), the school achievement score shall account for eighty percent (80%), and the school growth score shall account for twenty percent (20%) of the total sum. For all schools, the total school performance score shall be converted to a 100-point scale and used to determine a school performance grade based on the following scale:

(1) A school performance score of at least 90 is equivalent to an overall school performance grade of A.

(2) A school performance score of at least 80 is equivalent to an overall school performance grade of B.

(3) A school performance score of at least 70 is equivalent to an overall school performance grade of C.

(4) A school performance score of at least 60 is equivalent to an overall school performance grade of D.

(5) A school performance score of less than 60 points is equivalent to an overall school performance grade of F.

(e) Elementary and Middle School Reading and Math Achievement Scores. - For schools serving students in kindergarten through eighth grade, the school achievement scores in reading and mathematics, respectively, shall be reported separately on the annual school report card provided under G.S. 115C-12(9)c1., 115C-238.29F, and 115C-238.66.

(f) Indication of Growth. - In addition to awarding the overall school scores for achievement, growth, and performance and the performance grade, using EVAAS, the State Board shall designate that a school has met, exceeded, or has not met expected growth. The designation of student growth shall be clearly displayed in the annual school report card provided under G.S. 115C-12(9)c1., 115C-238.29F, and 115C-238.66. (2013-360, s. 9.4(b); 2013-363, s. 3.6.)

Part 2. Calendar.

§ 115C-84: Repealed by Session Laws 1997-443, s. 8.38(a).

§ 115C-84.1: Repealed by Session Laws 1997-443, s. 1.

§ 115C-84.2. School calendar.

(a) School Calendar. - Each local board of education shall adopt a school calendar consisting of 215 days all of which shall fall within the fiscal year. A school calendar shall include the following:

(1) A minimum of 185 days or 1,025 hours of instruction covering at least nine calendar months. The local board shall designate when the instructional days shall occur. The number of instructional hours in an instructional day may vary according to local board policy and does not have to be uniform among the schools in the administrative unit. Local boards may approve school improvement plans that include days with varying amounts of instructional time. If school is closed early due to inclement weather, the day and the scheduled amount of instructional hours may count towards the required minimum to the extent allowed by State Board policy. The school calendar shall include a plan for making up days and instructional hours missed when schools are not opened due to inclement weather.

(1a) Repealed by Session Laws 2004-180, s. 1, effective August 9, 2004.

(2) A minimum of 10 annual vacation leave days.

(3) The same or an equivalent number of legal holidays occurring within the school calendar as those designated by the State Human Resources Commission for State employees.

(4) Repealed by Session Laws 2011-145, s. 7.29(a), effective July 1, 2011.

(5) The remaining days scheduled by the local board in consultation with each school's principal for use as teacher workdays, additional instructional days, or other lawful purposes. Before consulting with the local board, each principal shall work with the school improvement team to determine the days to be scheduled and the purposes for which they should be scheduled. Days may be scheduled and planned for different purposes for different personnel and there is no requirement to schedule the same dates for all personnel. In order to make up days for school closing because of inclement weather, the local board may designate any of the days in this subdivision as additional make-up days to be scheduled after the last day of student attendance.

Local boards and individual schools are encouraged to use the calendar flexibility in order to meet the annual performance standards set by the State Board. Local boards of education shall consult with parents and the employed public school personnel in the development of the school calendar.

Local boards shall designate at least two days scheduled under subdivision (5) of this subsection as days on which teachers may take accumulated vacation leave. Local boards may designate the remaining days scheduled in subdivision (5) of this subsection as days on which teachers may take accumulated vacation leave, but local boards shall give teachers at least 14 calendar days' notice before requiring a teacher to work instead of taking vacation leave on any of these days. A teacher may elect to waive this notice requirement for one or more of these days.

(b) Limitations. - The following limitations apply when developing the school calendar:

(1) The total number of teacher workdays for teachers employed for a 10 month term shall not exceed 195 days.

(2) The calendar shall include at least 42 consecutive days when teacher attendance is not required unless: (i) the school is a year-round school; or (ii) the teacher is employed for a term in excess of 10 months. At the request of the local board of education or of the principal of a school, a teacher may elect to work on one of the 42 days when teacher attendance is not required in lieu of another scheduled workday.

(3) School shall not be held on Sundays.

(4) Veterans Day shall be a holiday for all public school personnel and for all students enrolled in the public schools.

(c) Emergency Conditions. - During any period of emergency in any section of the State where emergency conditions make it necessary, the State Board of Education may order general, and if necessary, extended recesses or adjournment of the public schools.

(d) Opening and Closing Dates. - Local boards of education shall determine the dates of opening and closing the public schools under subdivision (a)(1) of this section. Except for year-round schools, the opening date for students shall be no earlier than the Monday closest to August 26, and the closing date for students shall be no later than the Friday closest to June 11. On a showing of good cause, the State Board of Education may waive the requirement that the opening date for students be no earlier than the Monday closest to August 26 and may allow the local board of education to set an opening date no earlier than the Monday closest to August 19, to the extent that school calendars are able to provide sufficient days to accommodate anticipated makeup days due to school closings. A local board may revise the scheduled closing date if necessary in order to comply with the minimum requirements for instructional days or instructional time. For purposes of this subsection, the term "good cause" means that schools in any local school administrative unit in a county have been closed eight days per year during any four of the last 10 years because of severe weather conditions, energy shortages, power failures, or other emergency situations.

The required opening and closing dates under this subsection shall not apply to any school that a local board designated as having a modified calendar for the 2003-2004 school year or to any school that was part of a planned program in the 2003-2004 school year for a system of modified calendar schools, so long as the school operates under a modified calendar.

(e) Nothing in this section prohibits a local board of education from offering supplemental or additional educational programs or activities outside the calendar adopted under this section. (1997-443, s. 8.38(c); 1998-212, s. 9.18(b); 1999-373, s. 1; 1999-463, Ex. Sess., s. 7A; 2003-8, s. 1; 2003-131, s. 1; 2004-180, s. 1; 2004-203, s. 44; 2006-264, s. 25; 2010-10, s. 1(a); 2010-114, s. 1; 2011-93, s. 1; 2011-145, ss. 7.13(c), (d), 7.29(a); 2011-391, s. 14(b); 2012-142, s. 7A.11(a); 2012-145, s. 2.5; 2013-382, s. 9.1(c).)

Part 3. Textbooks.

§ 115C-85. Textbook needs are determined by course of study.

When the State Board of Education has adopted, upon the recommendation of the Superintendent of Public Instruction, a standard course of study at each instructional level in the elementary school and the secondary school, setting forth what subjects shall be taught at each level, it shall proceed to select and adopt textbooks.

As used in this part, "textbook" means systematically organized material comprehensive enough to cover the primary objectives outlined in the standard course of study for a grade or course. Formats for textbooks may be print or nonprint, including hardbound books, softbound books, activity-oriented programs, classroom kits, and technology-based programs that require the use of electronic equipment in order to be used in the learning process.

Textbooks adopted in accordance with the provisions of this Part shall be used by the public schools of the State except as provided in G.S. 115C-98(b1). (1955, c. 1372, art. 24, s. 1; 1959, c. 693, s. 1; 1969, c. 519, s. 1; 1981, c. 423, s. 1; 1993 (Reg. Sess., 1994), c. 677, s. 20; 1995 (Reg. Sess., 1996), c. 716, s. 18.)

§ 115C-86. State Board of Education to select and adopt textbooks.

The Board shall select and adopt for a period determined to be most advantageous to the State public school system for the exclusive use in the public schools of North Carolina the basic textbooks or series of books needed for instructional purposes at each instructional level on all subject matter required by law to be taught in elementary and secondary schools of North Carolina. (1955, c. 1372, art. 24, s. 2; 1959, c. 693, s. 2; 1965, c. 584, s. 18; 1969, c. 519, s. 1; 1981, c. 423, s. 1.)

§ 115C-87. Appointment of Textbook Commission.

Shortly after assuming office, the Governor shall appoint a Textbook Commission of 23 members who shall hold office for four years, or until their successors are appointed and qualified. The members of the Commission shall be appointed by the Governor upon recommendation of the Superintendent. Five of these members shall be teachers or principals in grades K-5; five shall be teachers or principals in grades 6-8; four shall be superintendents, teachers, or principals in grades 9-12; one shall be a superintendent of a local school administrative unit, three shall be parents of students in grades K-5 at the time of appointment; three shall be parents of students in grades 6-8 at the time of appointment; and two shall be parents of students in grades 9-12 at the time of appointment. The Governor shall fill all vacancies by appointment for the unexpired term. The Commission shall elect a chairman, subject to the approval of the Superintendent. The Commission shall meet four times a year or at the call of the chair. The members shall be entitled to compensation for each day spent on the work of the Commission as approved by the Board and to reimbursement for travel and subsistence expense incurred in the performance of their duties at the rates specified in G.S. 138-5(a). Compensation shall be paid from funds available to the State Board of Education. (1955, c. 1372, art. 24, s. 3; 1969, c. 519, s. 1; 1977, c. 1113; 1981, c. 423, s. 1; 1999-237, s. 8.30(a).)

§ 115C-88. Commission to evaluate textbooks offered for adoption.

(a) The Commission shall evaluate all textbooks offered for adoption.

Each proposed textbook shall be read by at least one expert certified in the discipline for which the textbook would be used. The Commission may use external experts if no Commission member or advisory committee member qualifies as an expert certified in a particular discipline.

The Commission may consider any review of a proposed textbook by other experts certified in the discipline who are not involved in the textbook adoption process. However, these reviews may not substitute for the direct examination of the proposed textbook by a Commission member, an advisory committee member, or any other expert retained by the Commission.

(b) Each member shall examine carefully and file a written evaluation of each proposed textbook for which the member is responsible.

The evaluation report shall give special consideration to the suitability of the textbook to the instructional level for which it is offered, the content or subject matter, whether the textbook is aligned with the Standard Course of Study, and other criteria prescribed by the Board.

Each evaluation report shall be signed by the member making the report and filed with the Board not later than a day fixed by the Board when the call for adoption is made. (1955, c. 1372, art. 24, s. 4; 1969, c. 519, s. 1; 1981, c. 423, s. 1; 1993 (Reg. Sess., 1994), c. 777, s. 3(a); 1999-237, s. 8.30(b).)

§ 115C-89. Selection of textbooks by Board.

At the next meeting of the Board after the reports have been filed, the Textbook Commission and the Board shall jointly examine the reports. From the books evaluated the Board shall select those that it thinks will meet the teaching requirements of the State public schools in the instructional levels for which they are offered. The Board shall request sealed bids from the publishers on all the books being considered.

The Board shall make all necessary rules and regulations concerning requests for bids, notification to publishers of calls for adoption, execution and delivery of contracts, requirement of performance bonds, cancellation clauses, and such other material matters as may affect the validity of the contracts. (1955, c. 1372, art. 24, s. 5; 1969, c. 519, s. 1; 1981, c. 423, s. 1; 1989, c. 798, s. 1.)

§ 115C-90. Adoption of textbooks and contracts with publishers.

The publishers' sealed bids shall be opened in the presence of two persons designated by the State Board of Education and one person designated by the Superintendent of Public Instruction. The Board may then adopt the books required by the courses of study and enter into contracts with the publisher of adopted books. It may refuse to adopt any of the books offered at the prices bid and call for new bids. When bids are accepted and a contract entered into, the contract may require, in the Board's discretion, that the total sales of each book in the State of North Carolina be reported annually to the Board.

All textbook contracts shall include a clause granting to the State Board of Education the license to produce Braille, large print, and audio-cassette tape copies of the textbooks for use in the State public schools. Also, the General

Assembly urges the State Board of Education to request such a license from textbook publishers with whom a contract was entered into prior to August 1, 1987. (1955, c. 1372, art. 24, s. 6; 1969, c. 519, s. 1; 1981, c. 423, s. 1; 1983, c. 549, s. 1; 1987, c. 738, s. 190; 1987 (Reg. Sess., 1988), c. 1025, s. 10.)

§ 115C-91. Continuance and discontinuance of contracts with publishers.

When an existing or future contract expires, the Board may, with the publisher's approval, continue the contract for any particular book or books for a period not less than one or more than five years. If a publisher desires to terminate a contract that has been extended beyond the original contract period, he shall give notice to the Board 90 days prior to May 1. The Board may then proceed to a new adoption. (1955, c. 1372, art. 24, s. 7; 1969, c. 519, s. 1; 1981, c. 423, s. 1.)

§ 115C-92. Procedure for change of textbook.

The Superintendent may at any time communicate to the Board that a particular book is unsatisfactory for the schools, whereupon the Board may call for a new selection and adoption. If the Board votes to change a textbook, it shall give the publisher 90 days' notice prior to May 1, after which it may adopt a new book or books on the subject for which a book is sought. (1955, c. 1372, art. 24, s. 7; 1969, c. 519, s. 1; 1981, c. 423, s. 1.)

§ 115C-93. Advice from and suits by Attorney General.

The form and legality of contracts between the Board and publishers of textbooks shall be subject to the approval of the Attorney General.

When requested by the Board, the Attorney General shall bring suit against any publisher who fails to keep his contract as to prices, distribution, adequate supply of books in the edition adopted, or in any other way violates the terms of his contract. The suit shall be brought for an amount sufficient to enforce the contract or to compensate the State for any loss sustained by the publisher's failure to keep his contract. (1955, c. 1372, art. 24, s. 8; 1969, c. 519, s. 1; 1981, c. 423, s. 1.)

§ 115C-94. Publishers to register.

Any publisher who submits books for adoption shall register in the office of the Superintendent of Public Instruction the names of all agents or other employees authorized to represent that company in the State, and this registration list shall be open to the public for inspection. (1955, c. 1372, art. 24, s. 9; 1969, c. 519, s. 1; 1981, c. 423, s. 1.)

§ 115C-95. Sale of books at lower price reduces price to State.

Every contract made by the Board with the publisher of any school textbook on the State-adopted list shall be deemed to have written therein a condition providing that if that publisher, during the life of his contract with this State, contracts with any other governmental unit or places that textbook on sale anywhere in the United States for a price less than that stipulated in his contract with the State of North Carolina, the publisher shall immediately furnish that textbook to this State at a price not greater than that for which the book is furnished, sold, or placed on sale anywhere else in the nation. (1955, c. 1372, art. 24, s. 10; 1969, c. 519, s. 1; 1981, c. 423, s. 1.)

§ 115C-96. Powers and duties of the State Board of Education in regard to textbooks.

The children of the public elementary and secondary schools of the State shall be provided with free basic textbooks within the appropriation of the General Assembly for that purpose. To implement this directive, the State Board of Education shall evaluate annually the amount of money necessary to provide textbooks based on the actual cost and availability of textbooks and shall request sufficient appropriations from the General Assembly.

The State Board of Education shall administer a fund and establish rules and regulations necessary to:

(1) Acquire by contract such basic textbooks as are or may be on the adopted list of the State of North Carolina which the Board finds necessary to meet the needs of the State public school system and to carry out the provisions of this Part.

(2) Provide a system of distribution of these textbooks and distribute the books that are provided without using any depository or warehouse facilities other than those operated by the State Board of Education.

(3) Provide for the free use, with proper care and return, of elementary and secondary basic textbooks. The title of said books shall be vested in the State. (1955, c. 1372, art. 25, s. 1; 1965, c. 584, s. 19; 1969, c. 519, s. 1; 1981, c. 423, s. 1; 1991 (Reg. Sess., 1992), c. 900, s. 81(a).)

§ 115C-97. State Board of Education authorized to discontinue handling supplementary and library books.

The State Board of Education may discontinue the adoption of supplementary textbooks and, at the expiration of existing contracts, may discontinue the purchase, warehousing, and distribution of supplementary textbooks. The Board may also discontinue the purchase and resale of library books. Funds appropriated to the State Board of Education for supplementary textbooks shall be transferred to the State Public School Fund for allotment to each local school administrative unit, based on its average daily membership, for the purchase of supplementary textbooks, library books, periodicals, and other instructional materials. (1969, c. 519, s. 1; 1981, c. 423, s. 1.)

§ 115C-98. Local boards of education to provide for local operation of the textbook program, the selection and procurement of other instructional materials, and the use of nonadopted textbooks.

(a) Local boards of education shall adopt rules not inconsistent with the policies of the State Board of Education concerning the local operation of the textbook program.

(b) Local boards of education shall adopt written policies concerning the procedures to be followed in their local school administrative units for the selection and procurement of supplementary textbooks, library books, periodicals, audiovisual materials, and other supplementary instructional materials needed for instructional purposes in the public schools of their units.

Local boards of education shall have sole authority to select and procure supplementary instructional materials, whether or not the materials contain commercial advertising, to determine if the materials are related to and within the limits of the prescribed curriculum, and to determine when the materials may be presented to students during the school day. Supplementary materials and contracts for supplementary materials are not subject to approval by the State Board of Education.

Supplementary books and other instructional materials shall neither displace nor be used to the exclusion of basic textbooks.

(b1)   A local board of education may establish a community media advisory committee to investigate and evaluate challenges from parents, teachers, and members of the public to textbooks and supplementary instructional materials on the grounds that they are educationally unsuitable, pervasively vulgar, or inappropriate to the age, maturity, or grade level of the students. The State Board of Education shall review its rules and policies concerning these challenges and shall establish guidelines to be followed by community media advisory committees.

The local board, at all times, has sole authority and discretion to determine whether a challenge has merit and whether challenged material should be retained or removed.

(b2)   Local boards of education may:

(1)   Select, procure, and use textbooks that have not been adopted by the State Board of Education for use throughout the local school administrative unit for selected grade levels and courses; and

(2)   Approve school improvement plans developed under G.S. 115C-105.27 that include provisions for using textbooks that have not been adopted by the State Board of Education for selected grade levels and courses.

All textbook contracts made under this subsection shall include a clause granting to the local board of education the license to produce braille, large print, and audiocassette tape copies of the textbooks for use in the local school administrative unit.

(c)   Funds allocated by the State Board of Education or appropriated in the current expense or capital outlay budgets of the local school administrative units, may be used for the above-stated purposes. (1969, c. 519, s. 1; 1981, c. 423, s. 1; 1989 (Reg. Sess., 1990), c. 1074, s. 23(a); 1995 (Reg. Sess., 1996), c. 716, ss. 8.7, 19; 2011-145, s. 7.13(e); 2011-391, s. 14(b).)

§ 115C-99. Legal custodians of textbooks furnished by State.

Local boards of education are the custodians of all textbooks purchased by the local boards with State funds. They shall provide adequate and safe storage facilities for the proper care of these textbooks and emphasize to all students the necessity for proper care of textbooks. (1955, c. 1372, art. 25, s. 3; 1969, c. 519, s. 1; 1981, c. 423, s. 1; 1993 (Reg. Sess., 1994), c. 777, s. 3(b).)

§ 115C-100. Rental fees for textbooks prohibited; damage fees authorized.

No local board of education may charge any pupil a rental fee for the use of textbooks. A pupil's parents or legal guardians may be charged damage fees for abuse or loss of textbooks under rules adopted by the State Board of Education. All money collected from the sale of textbooks purchased with State funds under the provisions of this Part shall be paid annually as collected to the State Board of Education. (1969, c. 519, s. 1; 1981, c. 423, s. 1; 1983, c. 549, s. 2; 1985, c. 581, s. 1; 1993 (Reg. Sess., 1994), c. 777, s. 3(c).)

§ 115C-101. Duties and authority of superintendents of local school administrative units.

The superintendent of each local school administrative unit, as an official agent of the State Board of Education, shall administer the provisions of this Part and the rules and regulations of the Board insofar as they apply to his unit. The superintendent of each local school administrative unit shall have authority to require the cooperation of principals and teachers so that the children may receive the best possible service, and so that all the books and moneys may be accounted for properly. If any principal or teacher fails to comply with the provisions of this section, his superintendent shall withhold his salary vouchers until the duties imposed by this section have been performed.

If any superintendent fails to comply with the provisions of this section, the State Superintendent, as secretary to the State Board of Education, shall notify the State Board of Education and the State Treasurer. The State Board and the State Superintendent shall withhold the superintendent's salary vouchers, and the State Treasurer shall make no payment until the State Superintendent notifies him that the provisions of this section have been complied with. (1955, c. 1372, art. 25, s. 8; 1969, c. 519, s. 1; 1981, c. 423, s. 1.)

§ 115C-102. Right to purchase; disposal of textbooks and materials.

(a)   Any parent, guardian, or person in loco parentis may purchase any instructional material needed for any child in the public schools of the State from the board of education of the local school administrative unit in which the child is enrolled or, in the case of basic textbooks, from the State Board of Education.

(b)   Notwithstanding Article 3A of Chapter 143 of the General Statutes, G.S. 143-49(4), or any other provision of law, the State Board of Education may adopt rules authorizing local boards of education to dispose of discontinued instructional material, including State-adopted textbooks. (1955, c. 1372, art. 25, s. 2; 1969, c. 519, s. 1; 1981, c. 423, s. 1; 1991, c. 328.)

§§ 115C-102.1 through 115C-102.4. Reserved for future codification purposes.

Part 3A. School Technology.

§ 115C-102.5. Commission on School Technology created; membership.

(a)   There is created the Commission on School Technology. The Commission shall be located administratively in the Department of Public Instruction.

The purpose of the Commission shall be to advise the State Board of Education on the development of a State School Technology Plan that (i) ensures the effective use of technology is built into the North Carolina Public School System for the purpose of preparing a globally competitive workforce and citizenry for the 21st century and (ii) ensures equity and access to school technology for all segments of the public school population in North Carolina.

The Commission shall meet at least twice each fiscal year and shall provide input and feedback on the State School Technology Plan prior to approval.

(b) The Commission shall consist of the following members:

(1) The State Superintendent of Public Instruction or a designee;

(2) One representative of The University of North Carolina, appointed by the President of The University of North Carolina;

(3) One representative of the North Carolina Community College System, appointed by the President of the North Carolina Community College System;

(4) Repealed by Session Laws 2009-451, s. 7.31, effective July 1, 2009.

(5) Two members appointed by the Governor;

(6) Two members appointed by the President Pro Tempore of the Senate;

(7) Two members appointed by the Speaker of the House of Representatives; and

(8) Repealed by Session Laws 2009-451, s. 7.31, effective July 1, 2009.

(9) The State Chief Information Officer, or a designee.

In appointing members pursuant to subdivisions (5), (6), and (7) of this subsection, the appointing persons shall select individuals with technical or applied knowledge or experience in learning and instructional management technologies or individuals with expertise in curriculum or instruction who have successfully used learning and instructional management technologies.

No producers, vendors, or consultants to producers or vendors of learning or instructional management technologies shall serve on the Commission.

Members shall serve for two-year terms. Vacancies in terms of members shall be filled by the appointing officer. Persons appointed to fill vacancies shall qualify in the same manner as persons appointed for full terms.

(c) Repealed by Session Laws 1997-443, s. 8.26(a).

(d) Members of the Commission who are also members of the General Assembly shall be paid subsistence and travel expenses at the rate set forth in G.S. 120-3.1. Members of the Commission who are officials or employees of the State shall receive travel allowances at the rate set forth in G.S. 138-6. All other members of the Commission shall be paid the per diem and allowances set forth in G.S. 138-5.

(d1) The Chair of the State Board of Education shall select the Commission member or members who shall serve as chair or cochairs of the Commission.

(e) The Department of Public Instruction shall provide requested professional and clerical staff to the Commission. (1993, c. 321, s. 135(a); c. 522, s. 20; 1993 (Reg. Sess., 1994), c. 591, s. 11(a); 1997-148, s. 7; 1997-443, s. 8.26(a); 1998-131, s. 7; 1998-220, s. 1; 2004-199, s. 4; 2009-451, s. 7.31.)

§ 115C-102.6. Duty to propose a State school technology plan.

The State Board of Education shall propose a State school technology plan that ensures the effective use of technology is built into the North Carolina Public School System for the purpose of preparing a globally competitive workforce and citizenry for the 21st century. The Commission on School Technology will advise the State Board of Education on the State School Technology Plan and its components. (1993, c. 321, s. 135(a); 1993 (Reg. Sess., 1994), c. 769, s. 19.26(a); 2009-451, s. 7.31.)

§ 115C-102.6A. Elements of the State school technology plan.

(a) The State school technology plan shall be a comprehensive State implementation plan for using funds from the State School Technology Fund and other sources to improve student performance in the public schools through the use of learning and instructional management technologies. The purpose of the plan shall be to provide a cost-effective foundation of flexible technology and infrastructure to promote substantial gains in student achievement.

(b) Repealed by Session Laws 2009-451, s. 7.31, effective July 1, 2009.

(c) Components of the State school technology plan shall include at least the following:

(1) Common technical standards and uniform practices and procedures that provide statewide economies of scale in procurements, training, support, planning, and operations.

(2) Conceptual technical architecture that includes:

a. Principles - Statements of direction, goals, and concepts to guide the development of technical architecture;

b. Standards for interoperability - Detailed specifications to ensure hardware, software, databases, and other products that may have been developed independently or purchased from different vendors or manufacturers will work together, to the extent that interoperability facilitates meeting instructional or administrative goals; and

c. Implementation strategies - Approaches or guidelines for developing and installing the components of the technical infrastructure.

(3) A quality assurance policy for all school technology projects, training programs, systems documentation, and maintenance plans.

(4) Policies and procedures for the fair and competitive procurement of school technology that provide local school administrative units with a vendor-neutral operating environment in which different school technology hardware, software, and networks operate together easily and reliably, to the extent feasible consistent with meeting instructional or administrative goals. The operating environment includes all hardware and software components and configurations necessary to accomplish the integrated functions for school technology such as (i) types and sizes of computer platforms, telecommunications equipment, and associated communications protocols; (ii) operating systems for the computer processors; (iii) applications and other operating and support software; and (iv) other equipment, items, and software,

such as printers, terminals, data and image storage devices, and other input, output, and storage devices.

(5)   A comprehensive policy for inventory control.

(6)   Parameters for continuous, ongoing training for all personnel involved in the use of school technology. Training shall focus on the integration of technology and instruction and on the use of particular applications.

(7)   Recommendations to the State Board of Education of requirements for preservice teacher training on the integration of teaching and school technology.

(8)   Proposals for leadership training on the use of school technology to improve instruction and as a management tool.

(9)   Development of expertise at the State and regional levels on school technology.

(10)   Flexibility to enable local school administrative units and individual schools to meet individual school unit and building needs.

(11)   Flexibility to meet the needs of all students, allow support to students with a wide range of abilities, and ensure access to challenging curricula and instruction for children at risk of school failure.

(12)   Use of technologies to support challenging State, federal, and local educational performance goals.

(13)   Effective and integrated use of technologies compatible with (i) the standard course of study, (ii) the State assessment program, and (iii) related student data management.

(14)   Use of technologies as a communication, instructional, and management tool and for problem-solving, exploration, and advanced skills.

(15)   Proposals for addressing equipment needs for State curricula areas.

(16)   Specifications for minimum components of local school system technology plans.

(17)   A baseline template for:

a. Technology and service application infrastructure, including broadband connectivity, personnel recommendations, and other resources needed to operate effectively from the classroom desktop to local, regional, and State networks, and

b. An evaluation component that provides for local school administrative unit accountability for maintaining quality upgradeable systems. (1993 (Reg. Sess., 1994), c. 769, s. 19.26(b); 2005-276, s. 7.43(a); 2009-451, s. 7.31.)

§ 115C-102.6B. Approval of State school technology plan.

(a) The State Board of Education shall review, revise as needed, and approve the State School Technology Plan at a minimum every two years in the odd-numbered year, beginning in 2011. The plan shall be updated more often, as required, as in cases where significant changes occur related to Board goals, curriculum standards, and available technology.

(b) The Board shall submit the plan to the State Chief Information Officer for approval of the technical components of the plan set out in G.S. 115C-102.6A(1) through (4). At least one-fourth of the members of any technical committee that reviews the plan for the State Chief Information Officer shall be people actively involved in primary or secondary education.

The Board shall report annually by February 1 of each year to the Joint Legislative Education Oversight Committee on the status of the State School Technology Plan.

(c) Repealed by Session Laws 2009-451, s. 7.31, effective July 1, 2009. (1993 (Reg. Sess., 1994), c. 769, s. 19.26(b); 1997-443, s. 8.26(b); 2004-129, s. 29; 2009-451, s. 7.31; 2009-570, s. 37; 2010-96, s. 13.)

§ 115C-102.6C: Repealed by Session Laws 2011-145, 7.13(aa), effective July 1, 2011.

§ 115C-102.6D. Establishment of the State School Technology Fund; allocation and use of funds.

(a) There is established under the control and direction of the State Board of Education the State School Technology Fund. This fund shall be a nonreverting special revenue fund consisting of any monies appropriated to it by the General Assembly and any monies credited to it under G.S. 20-81.12 from the sale of School Technology special license plates.

(b) Funds in the State School Technology Fund shall be allocated to local school administrative units as directed by the General Assembly. Funds allocated to each local school administrative unit shall be credited with interest by the State Treasurer pursuant to G.S. 147-69.2 and G.S. 147-69.3.

(c) Repealed by Session Laws 2009-451, s. 7.31, effective July 1, 2009.

(d) Repealed by Session Laws 2011-145, s. 7.13(bb), effective July 1, 2011. (1993 (Reg. Sess., 1994), c. 769, s. 19.26(b); 1997-484, s. 7; 2009-451, s. 7.31; 2011-145, s. 7.13(bb).)

§ 115C-102.7. Monitoring and evaluation of State and local school system technology plans; reports.

(a) The Department of Public Instruction shall monitor and evaluate the development and implementation of the State technology plan. The evaluation shall consider the effects of technology on student learning, the effects of technology on students' workforce readiness, the effects of technology on teacher productivity, and the cost-effectiveness of the technology.

(a1) Repealed by Session Laws 1997-18, s. 15(k).

(b) Repealed by Session Laws 2009-451, s. 7.31, effective July 1, 2009.

(c) Repealed by Session Laws 2011-145, s. 7.13(cc), effective July 1, 2011. (1993, c. 321, s. 135(a); 1993 (Reg. Sess., 1994), c. 769, s. 19.26(c); 1997-18, s. 15(k); 2004-129, s. 31; 2005-276, s. 7.43(c); 2009-451, s. 7.31; 2011-145, s. 7.13(cc).)

§ 115C-102.8: Repealed by Session Laws 1997-18, s. 5.

Part 3B. Technology Alliance.

§ 115C-102.15: Repealed by Session Laws 2009-451, s. 7.15(a), effective July 1, 2009.

Part 4. Fees.

§ 115C-103. Fees.

Fees, charges and costs may be collected from students, their parents or guardians, and school personnel in accordance with the provisions of G.S. 115C-47(6). (1981, c. 423, s. 1; 1985, c. 581, s. 2.)

Part 5. Interstate Compact on Education.

§ 115C-104. Enactment of Compact.

The Compact for Education is hereby entered into and enacted into law, with all jurisdictions legally joining therein. Pursuant to Article III(9) of the Compact, the commission shall file a copy of its bylaws and any amendment thereto with the Secretary of State of North Carolina. The form of the Compact is substantially as follows:

COMPACT FOR EDUCATION.

Article I. Policy and Purpose.

It is the purpose of this Compact to:

(1)   Establish and maintain close cooperation and understanding among executive, legislative, professional, educational and lay leadership on a nationwide basis at the state and local levels.

(2)   Provide a forum for the discussion, development, crystallization and recommendation of public policy alternatives in the field of education.

(3)   Provide a clearinghouse of information on matters relating to educational problems and how they are being met in different places throughout the nation, so that the executive and legislative branches of state government and of local communities may have ready access to the experience and record of the entire country, and so that both lay and professional groups in the field of education may have additional avenues for the sharing of experience and the interchange of ideas in the formation of public policy in education.

(4)   Facilitate the improvement of state and local educational systems so that all of them will be able to meet adequate and desirable goals in a society which requires continuous qualitative and quantitative advances in educational opportunities, methods and facilities.

(5)   It is the policy of this Compact to encourage and promote local and state initiative in the development, maintenance, improvement and administration of educational systems and institutions in a manner which will accord with the needs and advantages of diversity among localities and states.

(6)   The party states recognize that each of them has an interest in the quality and quantity of education furnished in each of the other states, as well as in the excellence of its own educational systems and institutions, because of the highly mobile character of individuals within the nation, and because of the products and services contributing to the health, welfare and economic advancement of each state which are supplied in significant part by persons educated in other states.

Article II. State Defined.

As used in this Compact, "state" means a state, territory or possession of the United States, the District of Columbia, or the Commonwealth of Puerto Rico.

Article III. The Commission.

(1)   The education commission of the states, hereinafter called "the commission," is hereby established. The commission shall consist of seven members representing each party state. One of such members shall be the governor; two shall be members of the state legislature selected by its respective houses and serving in such manner as the legislature may determine; and four shall be appointed by and serve at the pleasure of the governor, unless the laws of the state otherwise provide. If the laws of a state prevent legislators from serving on the commission, six members shall be appointed and serve at the pleasure of the governor, unless the laws of the state otherwise provide. In addition to any other principles or requirements which a state may establish for the appointment and service of its members of the commission, the guiding principle for the composition of the membership on the commission from each party state shall be that the members representing such state shall, by virtue of their training, experience, knowledge or affiliations be in a position collectively to reflect broadly the interests of the state government, higher education, the state education system, local education, lay and professional, public and nonpublic educational leadership. Of those appointees, one shall be the head of a state agency or institution, designated by the governor, having responsibility for one or more programs of public education. In addition to the members of the commission representing the party states, there may be not to exceed 10 nonvoting commissioners selected by the steering committee for terms of one year. Such commissioners shall represent leading national organizations of professional educators or persons concerned with educational administration.

(2)   The members of the commission shall be entitled to one vote each on the commission. No action of the commission shall be binding unless taken at a meeting at which a majority of the total number of votes on the commission are cast in favor thereof. Action of the commission shall be only at a meeting at which a majority of the commissioners are present. The commission shall meet at least once a year. In its bylaws, and subject to such directions and limitations as may be contained therein, the commission may delegate the exercise of any of its powers to the steering committee or the executive director, except for the power to approve budgets or requests for appropriations, the power to make policy recommendations pursuant to Article IV and adoption of the annual report pursuant to Article III(10).

(3) The commission shall have a seal.

(4) The commission shall elect annually, from among its members, a chairman, who shall be a governor, a vice-chairman and a treasurer. The commission shall provide for the appointment of an executive director. Such executive director shall serve at the pleasure of the commission, and together with the treasurer and such other personnel as the commission may deem appropriate shall be bonded in such amount as the commission shall determine. The executive director shall be secretary.

(5) Irrespective of the civil service, personnel or other merit system laws of any of the party states, the executive director subject to the approval of the steering committee shall appoint, remove or discharge such personnel as may be necessary for the performance of the functions of the commission, and shall fix the duties and compensation of such personnel. The commission in its bylaws shall provide for the personnel policies and programs of the commission.

(6) The commission may borrow, accept or contract for the services of personnel from any party jurisdiction, the United States, or any subdivision or agency of the aforementioned governments, or from any agency of two or more of the party jurisdictions or their subdivisions.

(7) The commission may accept for any of its purposes and functions under this Compact any and all donations, and grants of money, equipment, supplies, materials and services, conditional or otherwise, from any state, the United States, or any other governmental agency, or from any person, firm, association, foundation, or corporation, and may receive, utilize and dispose of the same. Any donation or grant accepted by the commission pursuant to this paragraph or services borrowed pursuant to paragraph (6) of this article shall be reported in the annual report of the commission. Such report shall include the nature, amount and conditions, if any, of the donation, grant, or services borrowed, and the identity of the donor or lender.

(8) The commission may establish and maintain such facilities as may be necessary for the transaction of its business. The commission may acquire, hold, and convey real and personal property and any interest therein.

(9) The commission shall adopt bylaws for the conduct of its business and shall have the power to amend and rescind these bylaws. The commission shall publish its bylaws in convenient form and shall file a copy thereof and a

copy of any amendment thereto, with the appropriate agency or officer in each of the party states.

(10) The commission annually shall make to the governor and legislature of each party state a report covering the activities of the commission for the preceding year. The commission may make such additional reports as it may deem desirable.

Article IV. Powers.

In addition to authority conferred on the commission by other provisions of the Compact, the commission shall have authority to:

(1) Collect, correlate, analyze and interpret information and data concerning educational needs and resources.

(2) Encourage and foster research in all aspects of education, but with special reference to the desirable scope of instruction, organization, administration, and instructional methods and standards employed or suitable for employment in public educational systems.

(3) Develop proposals for adequate financing of education as a whole and at each of its many levels.

(4) Conduct or participate in research of the types referred to in this article in any instance where the commission finds that such research is necessary for the advancement of the purposes and policies of this Compact, utilizing fully the resources of national associations, regional compact organizations for higher education, and other agencies and institutions, both public and private.

(5) Formulate suggested policies and plans for the improvement of public education as a whole, or for any segment thereof, and make recommendations with respect thereto available to the appropriate governmental units, agencies and public officials.

(6) Do such other things as may be necessary or incidental to the administration of any of its authority or functions pursuant to this Compact.

Article V. Cooperation with Federal Government.

(1)   If the laws of the United States specifically so provide, or if administrative provision is made therefor within the federal government, the United States may be represented on the commission by not to exceed 10 representatives. Any such representative or representatives of the United States shall be appointed and serve in such manner as may be provided by or pursuant to federal law, and may be drawn from any one or more branches of the federal government, but no such representatives shall have a vote on the commission.

(2)   The commission may provide information and make recommendations to any executive or legislative agency or officer of the federal government concerning the common educational policies of the states, and may advise with any such agencies or officers concerning any matter of mutual interest.

Article VI. Committees.

(1)   To assist in the expeditious conduct of its business when the full commission is not meeting, the commission shall elect a steering committee of 32 members which, subject to the provisions of this Compact and consistent with the policies of the commission, shall be constituted and function as provided in the bylaws of the commission. One fourth of the voting membership of the steering committee shall consist of governors, one fourth shall consist of legislators, and the remainder shall consist of other members of the commission. A federal representative on the commission may serve with the steering committee, but without vote. The voting members of the steering committee shall serve for terms of two years, except that members elected to the first steering committee of the commission shall be elected as follows: 16 for one year and 16 for two years. The chairman, vice-chairman, and treasurer of the commission shall be members of the steering committee and, anything in this paragraph to the contrary notwithstanding, shall serve during their continuance in these offices. Vacancies in the steering committee shall not affect its authority to act, but the commission at its next regularly ensuing meeting following the occurrence of any vacancy shall fill it for the unexpired

term. No person shall serve more than two terms as a member of the steering committee; provided that service for a partial term of one year or less shall not be counted toward the two-term limitation.

(2)   The commission may establish advisory and technical committees composed of state, local, and federal officials, and private persons to advise it with respect to any one or more of its functions. Any advisory or technical committee may, on request of the states concerned, be established to consider any matter of special concern to two or more of the party states.

(3)   The commission may establish such additional committees as its bylaws may provide.

Article VII.   Finance.

(1)   The commission shall advise the governor or designated officer or officers of each party state of its budget and estimated expenditures for such period as may be required by the laws of that party state. Each of the commission's budgets of estimated expenditures shall contain specific recommendations of the amount or amounts to be appropriated by each of the party states.

(2)   The total amount of appropriation requests under any budget shall be apportioned among the party states. In making such apportionment, the commission shall devise and employ a formula which takes equitable account of the populations and per capita income levels of the party states.

(3)   The commission shall not pledge the credit of any party states. The commission may meet any of its obligations in whole or in part with funds available to it pursuant to Article III(7) of this Compact, provided that the commission takes specific action setting aside such funds prior to incurring an obligation to be met in whole or in part in such manner. Except where the commission makes use of funds available to it pursuant to Article III(7) thereof, the commission shall not incur any obligation prior to the allotment of funds by the party states adequate to meet the same.

(4) The commission shall keep accurate accounts of all receipts and disbursements. The receipts and disbursements of the commission shall be subject to the audit and accounting procedures established by its bylaws. However, all receipts and disbursements of funds handled by the commission shall be audited yearly by a qualified public accountant, and the report of the audit shall be included in and become part of the annual reports of the commission.

(5) The accounts of the commission shall be open at any reasonable time for inspection by duly constituted officers of the party states and by any persons authorized by the commission.

(6) Nothing contained herein shall be construed to prevent commission compliance with laws relating to audit or inspection of accounts by or on behalf of any government contributing to the support of the commission.

Article VIII. Eligible Parties' Entry into and Withdrawal.

(1) This Compact shall have as eligible parties all states, territories, and possessions of the United States, the District of Columbia, and the Commonwealth of Puerto Rico. In respect of any such jurisdiction not having a governor, the term "governor," as used in this Compact, shall mean the closest equivalent official of such jurisdiction.

(2) Any state or other eligible jurisdiction may enter into this Compact and it shall become binding thereon when it has adopted the same: Provided that in order to enter into initial effect, adoption by at least 10 eligible party jurisdictions shall be required.

(3) Adoption of the Compact may be either by enactment thereof or by adherence thereto by the governor; provided that in the absence of enactment, adherence by the governor shall be sufficient to make his state a party only until December 31, 1967. During any period when a state is participating in this Compact through gubernatorial action, the governor shall appoint those persons who, in addition to himself, shall serve as the members of the commission from his state, and shall provide to the commission an equitable share of the financial support of the commission from any source available to him.

(4) Except for a withdrawal effective on December 31, 1967, in accordance with paragraph (3) of this article, any party state may withdraw from this Compact by enacting a statute repealing the same, but no such withdrawal shall take effect until one year after the governor of the withdrawing state has given notice in writing of the withdrawal to the governors of all other party states. No withdrawal shall affect any liability already incurred by or chargeable to a party state prior to the time of such withdrawal.

Article IX. Construction and Severability.

This Compact shall be liberally construed so as to effectuate the purposes thereof. The provisions of this Compact shall be severable and if any phrase, clause, sentence or provision of this Compact is declared to be contrary to the constitution of any state or of the United States, or the application thereof to any government, agency, person or circumstance is held invalid, the validity of the remainder of this Compact and the applicability thereof to any government, agency, person or circumstance shall not be affected thereby. If this Compact shall be held contrary to the constitution of any state participating therein, the Compact shall remain in full force and effect as to the state affected as to all severable matters. (1967, c. 1020; 1981, c. 423, s. 1; 1991, c. 369, s. 1.)

§ 115C-105: Repealed by Session Laws 1991, c. 369, s. 2.

Article 8A.

North Carolina Education Standards and Accountability Commission.

§§ 115C-105.1 through 115C-105.10: Repealed by Session Laws 1997-443, s. 8.27(c).

§§ 115C-105.11 through 115C-105.19. Reserved for future codification purposes.

Article 8B.

School-Based Management and Accountability Program.

Part 1. Implementation of Program.

§ 115C-105.20. School-Based Management and Accountability Program.

(a) The General Assembly believes that all children can learn. It is the intent of the General Assembly that the mission of the public school community is to challenge with high expectations each child to learn, to achieve, and to fulfill his or her potential. With that mission as its guide, the State Board of Education shall develop a School-Based Management and Accountability Program. The primary goal of the Program shall be to improve student performance.

(b) In order to support local boards of education and schools in the implementation of this Program, the State Board of Education shall adopt guidelines, including guidelines to:

(1) Assist local boards and schools in the development and implementation of school-based management under Part 2 of this Article.

(2) Recognize the schools that meet or exceed their goals.

(3) Identify low-performing schools under G.S. 115C-105.37, and create assistance teams that the Board may assign to schools identified as low-performing under G.S. 115C-105.37. The assistance teams should consist of currently practicing teachers and staff, representatives of institutions of higher education, school administrators, and others the State Board considers appropriate.

(4) Enable assistance teams to make appropriate recommendations under G.S. 115C-105.38.

(5) Establish a process to resolve disputes between local boards and schools in the development and implementation of school improvement plans

under G.S. 115C-105.27. This process shall provide for final resolution of the disputes. (1989, c. 778, s. 3; 1991 (Reg. Sess., 1992), c. 900, s. 75.1(a); 1993, c. 321, s. 144.2(a); 1995, c. 272, s. 1; 1995 (Reg. Sess., 1996), c. 716, ss. 2, 3; 2011-145, s. 7.13(f); 2011-391, s. 14(b).)

§ 115C-105.21. Local participation in the Program.

(a) Local school administrative units shall participate in the School-Based Management and Accountability Program.

(b) The School-Based Management and Accountability Program shall provide increased local control of schools with the goal of improving student performance. Local boards of education:

(1) Are allowed increased flexibility in the expenditure of State funds, in accordance with G.S. 115C-105.25; and

(2) May be granted waivers of certain State laws, regulations, and policies that inhibit their ability to reach local accountability goals, in accordance with G.S. 115C-105.26.

(c) The School-Based Management and Accountability Program shall be based upon an accountability, recognition, assistance, and intervention process in order to hold each school and the school's personnel accountable for improved student performance in the school. (1989, c. 778, s. 3; 1991, c. 331, s. 1; 1993, c. 263, s. 1; c. 522, s. 3; 1995, c. 272, s. 2; c. 450, s. 12; 1995 (Reg. Sess., 1996), c. 716, ss. 2, 3.)

§ 115C-105.22. Reserved for future codification purposes.

§ 115C-105.23. Reserved for future codification purposes.

§ 115C-105.24. Reserved for future codification purposes.

Part 2. School-Based Management.

§ 115C-105.25. Budget flexibility.

(a)   Consistent with improving student performance, a local board shall provide maximum flexibility to schools in the use of funds to enable the schools to accomplish their goals.

(b)   Subject to the following limitations, local boards of education may transfer and may approve transfers of funds between funding allotment categories:

(1)   Repealed by Session Laws 2013-360, s. 8.14, effective July 1, 2013.

(1a)   Funds for children with disabilities, career and technical education, and other purposes may be transferred only as permitted by federal law and the conditions of federal grants or as provided through any rules that the State Board of Education adopts to ensure compliance with federal regulations.

(2),   (2a) Repealed by Session Laws 2013-360, s. 8.14, effective July 1, 2013.

(3)   No funds shall be transferred into the central office administration allotment category.

(4),   (5) Repealed by Session Laws 2013-360, s. 8.14, effective July 1, 2013.

(5a)   Positions allocated for classroom teachers may be converted to dollar equivalents to contract for visiting international exchange teachers. These positions shall be converted at the statewide average salary for classroom teachers, including benefits. The converted funds shall be used only to cover the costs associated with bringing visiting international exchange teachers to the local school administrative unit through a State-approved visiting international exchange teacher program and supporting the visiting exchange teachers.

(5b)   Except as provided in subdivision (5a) of this subsection, positions allocated for classroom teachers and instructional support personnel may be converted to dollar equivalents for any purpose authorized by the policies of the State Board of Education. These positions shall be converted at the salary on the first step of the "A" Teachers Salary Schedule. Certified position allotments shall not be transferred to dollars to hire the same type of position.

(5c)   Funds allocated for school building administration may be converted for any purpose authorized by the policies of the State Board of Education. For funds related to principal positions, the salary transferred shall be based on the first step of the Principal III Salary Schedule. For funds related to assistant principal months of employment, the salary transferred shall be based on the first step of the Assistant Principal Salary Schedule. Certified position allotments shall not be transferred to dollars to hire the same type of position.

(6) through (9) Repealed by Session Laws 2013-360, s. 8.14, effective July 1, 2013.

(10) Funds to carry out the elements of the Excellent Public Schools Act that are contained in Section 7A.1 of S.L. 2012-142 shall not be transferred.

(c) To ensure that parents, educators, and the general public are informed on how State funds have been used to address local educational priorities, each local school administrative unit shall publish the following information on its Web site by October 15 of each year:

(1) A description of each program report code, written in plain English, and a summary of the prior fiscal year's expenditure of State funds within each program report code.

(2) A description of each object code within a program report code, written in plain English, and a summary of the prior fiscal year's expenditure of State funds for each object code.

(3) A description of each allotment transfer that increased or decreased the initial allotment amount by more than five percent (5%) and the educational priorities that necessitated the transfer. (1995 (Reg. Sess., 1996), c. 716, s. 3; 1996, 2nd Ex. Sess., c. 18, ss. 18.24(h)-(k); 1998-212, s. 9.20(b); 1999-237, s. 8.25(c); 2001-424, s. 28.22; 2005-276, s. 7.22(a); 2006-69, s. 3(b); 2011-145, s. 7.13(g); 2011-391, s. 14(b); 2013-360, s. 8.14.)

§ 115C-105.26. Waivers of State laws, rules, or policies.

(a) When included as part of a school improvement plan accepted under G.S. 115C-105.27, local boards of education shall submit requests for waivers of State laws, rules, or policies to the State Board of Education. A request for a waiver shall (i) identify the school making the request, (ii) identify the State laws, rules, or policies that inhibit the school's ability to improve student performance, (iii) set out with specificity the circumstances under which the waiver may be used, and (iv) explain how the requested waiver will permit the school to improve student performance. Except as provided in subsection (c) of this section, the State Board shall grant waivers only for the specific schools for which they are requested and shall be used only under the specific circumstances for which they are requested.

(b) When requested as part of a school improvement plan, the State Board of Education may grant waivers of:

(1) State laws pertaining to class size and teacher certification; and

(2) (Effective until July 1, 2014) State rules and policies, except those pertaining to public school State salary schedules and employee benefits for school employees, the instructional program that must be offered under the Basic Education Program, the system of employment for public school teachers and administrators set out in G.S. 115C-287.1 and G.S. 115C-325, health and safety codes, compulsory attendance, the minimum lengths of the school day and year, and the Uniform Education Reporting System.

(2) (Effective July 1, 2014) State rules and policies, except those pertaining to public school State salary schedules and employee benefits for school employees, the instructional program that must be offered under the Basic Education Program, the system of employment for public school teachers and administrators set out in G.S. 115C-287.1 and in Part 3 of Article 22 of this Chapter, health and safety codes, compulsory attendance, the minimum lengths of the school day and year, and the Uniform Education Reporting System.

(c) The State Board also may grant requests received from local boards for waivers of State laws, rules, or policies that affect the organization, duties, and assignment of central office staff only. However, none of the duties to be performed under G.S. 115C-436 may be waived.

(c1) The State Board also may grant requests received from local boards for waivers of State laws, rules, or policies that require that each local school administrative unit provide at least one alternative school or at least one alternative learning program.

(d) Notwithstanding subsections (b) and (c) of this section, the State Board shall not grant waivers of G.S. 115C-12(16)b. regarding the placement of State-allotted office support personnel, teacher assistants, and custodial personnel on the salary schedule adopted by the State Board.

(e) Notwithstanding subsection (b) of this section, the State Board may grant requests received from local boards for waivers of State laws, rules, or policies pertaining to the placement of principals on the State salary schedule for public school administrators in order to provide financial incentives to encourage principals to accept employment in a school that has been identified as low-performing under G.S. 115C-105.37. The State Board shall act on requests under this subsection at the first Board meeting following receipt of each request.

(f) Except as provided in subsection (e) of this section, the State Board shall act within 60 days of receipt of all requests for waivers under this section.

(g) The State Board shall, on a regular basis, review all waivers it has granted to determine whether any rules should be repealed or modified or whether the Board should recommend to the General Assembly the repeal or modification of any laws. (1995 (Reg. Sess., 1996), c. 716, s. 3; 1999-237, s. 8.25(b); 2006-153, s. 2; 2011-145, s. 7.13(h); 2011-391, s. 14(b); 2013-360, s. 9.7(a).)

§ 115C-105.27. Development and approval of school improvement plans.

(a) School Improvement Team. - The principal of each school, representatives of the assistant principals, instructional personnel, instructional support personnel, and teacher assistants assigned to the school building, and parents of children enrolled in the school shall constitute a school improvement team. The team shall develop a school improvement plan to improve student performance.

Representatives of the assistant principals, instructional personnel, instructional support personnel, and teacher assistants shall be elected by their respective groups by secret ballot.

Unless the local board of education has adopted an election policy, parents shall be elected by parents of children enrolled in the school in an election conducted by the parent and teacher organization of the school or, if none exists, by the largest organization of parents formed for this purpose. Parents serving on school improvement teams shall reflect the racial and socioeconomic composition of the students enrolled in that school and shall not be members of the building-level staff.

Parental involvement is a critical component of school success and positive student achievement; therefore, it is the intent of the General Assembly that parents, along with teachers, have a substantial role in developing school improvement plans. To this end, school improvement team meetings shall be held at a convenient time to assure substantial parent participation.

(a1)   Open Meetings. - School improvement team meetings are subject to the open meetings requirements of Article 33C of Chapter 143 of the General Statutes. Deliberations on the school safety components of the plan shall be in closed session in accordance with G.S. 143-318.11(a)(8). The principal shall ensure that these requirements are met.

(a2)   Public Records. - The school improvement plan, except for the school safety components of the plan, is a public record subject to Chapter 132 of the General Statutes and shall be posted on the school Web site. The names of the members of the school improvement team, their positions, and the date of their election to the school improvement team shall also be posted on the Web site.

The school safety components of the plan are not public records subject to Chapter 132 of the General Statutes.

(b)   School Improvement Plan. - In order to improve student performance, the school improvement team at each school shall develop a school improvement plan that takes into consideration the annual performance goal for that school that is set by the State Board under G.S. 115C-105.35 and the goals set out in the mission statement for the public schools adopted by the State Board of Education. All school improvement plans shall be, to the greatest extent possible, data-driven. School improvement teams shall use the Education Value-Added Assessment System (EVAAS) or a compatible and comparable system approved by the State Board of Education to (i) analyze student data and identify root causes for problems, (ii) determine actions to address them, and (iii) appropriately place students in courses such as Algebra I. School improvement plans shall contain clear, unambiguous targets, explicit indicators and actual measures, and expeditious time frames for meeting the measurement standards.

The strategies for improving student performance:

(1)   Shall include a plan for the use of staff development funds that may be made available to the school by the local board of education to implement the school improvement plan. The plan may provide that a portion of these funds is

used for mentor training and for release time and substitute teachers while mentors and teachers mentored are meeting;

(1a) Repealed by Session Laws 2012-142, s. 7A.1(c), effective July 2, 2012.

(2) Shall include a plan to address school safety and discipline concerns;

(3) May include a decision to use State funds in accordance with G.S. 115C-105.25;

(4) Shall include a plan that specifies the effective instructional practices and methods to be used to improve the academic performance of students identified as at risk of academic failure or at risk of dropping out of school;

(5) May include requests for waivers of State laws, rules, or policies for that school. A request for a waiver shall meet the requirements of G.S. 115C-105.26;

(6) Shall include a plan to provide a duty-free lunch period for every teacher on a daily basis or as otherwise approved by the school improvement team; and

(7) Shall include a plan to provide duty-free instructional planning time for every teacher under G.S. 115C-301.1, with the goal of providing an average of at least five hours of planning time per week; [and]

(8) Shall include a plan to identify and eliminate unnecessary and redundant reporting requirements for teachers and, to the extent practicable, streamline the school's reporting system and procedures, including requiring forms and reports to be in electronic form when possible and incorporating relevant documents into the student accessible components of the Instructional Improvement System.

(c) School Vote on the Plan. - Support among affected staff members is essential to successful implementation of a school improvement plan to address improved student performance at that school. The principal of the school shall present the proposed school improvement plan to all of the principals, assistant principals, instructional personnel, instructional support personnel, and teacher assistants assigned to the school building for their review and vote. The vote shall be by secret ballot. The principal shall submit the school improvement plan to the local board of education only if the proposed school improvement plan has the approval of a majority of the staff who voted on the plan.

(c1) Consideration of the School Safety Components of the Plan. - The superintendent shall review the school safety components of the school improvement plans and make written recommendations on them to the local board of education. Prior to a vote to accept a school's improvement plan in accordance with G.S. 115C-105.27(d), the local board of education shall review the school safety components of the plan for that school in closed session. The board shall make findings on the safety components of the plan. Neither the safety components of the plan nor the board's findings on the safety components of the plan shall be set out in the minutes of the board.

(d) Adoption of the Plan. - The local board of education shall accept or reject the school improvement plan. The local board shall not make any substantive changes in any school improvement plan that it accepts. If the local board rejects a school improvement plan, the local board shall state with specificity its reasons for rejecting the plan; the school improvement team may then prepare another plan, present it to the principals, assistant principals, instructional personnel, instructional support personnel, and teacher assistants assigned to the school building for a vote, and submit it to the local board to accept or reject. If no school improvement plan is accepted for a school within 60 days after its initial submission to the local board, the school or the local board may ask to use the process to resolve disagreements recommended in the guidelines developed by the State Board under G.S. 115C-105.20(b)(5). If this request is made, both the school and local board shall participate in the process to resolve disagreements. If there is no request to use that process, then the local board may develop a school improvement plan for the school. The General Assembly urges the local board to utilize the school's proposed school improvement plan to the maximum extent possible when developing such a plan.

(e) Effective Period of the Plan. - A school improvement plan shall remain in effect for no more than two years; however, the school improvement team may amend the plan as often as is necessary or appropriate. If, at any time, any part of a school improvement plan becomes unlawful or the local board finds that a school improvement plan is impeding student performance at a school, the local board may vacate the relevant portion of the plan and may direct the school to revise that portion. The procedures set out in this subsection shall apply to amendments and revisions to school improvement plans.

(f) Elimination of Other Unnecessary Plans. - If a local board of education finds that a school improvement plan adequately covers another plan that the local school administrative unit is otherwise required to prepare, the local school administrative unit shall not be required to prepare an additional plan on the matter.

(g) Compliance With Requirements. - Any employee, parent, or other interested individual or organization is encouraged to notify the principal of any concerns regarding compliance with this section. In addition, any employee, parent, or other interested individual or organization may submit in writing to the superintendent concerns regarding compliance with this section. The superintendent shall make a good-faith effort to investigate the concern. The superintendent shall upon request provide a written response to the concern. (1989, c. 778, s. 3; 1991 (Reg. Sess., 1992), c. 900, s. 75.1(b); 1993, c. 38, s. 1; c. 263, s. 2; c. 321, s. 144.2(b); 1995, c. 272, s. 3; c. 450, s. 13; 1995 (Reg. Sess., 1996), c. 716, ss. 2, 3; 1997-159, s. 1; 1997-443, s. 8.29(r)(2); 1999-271, s. 1; 1999-397, s. 1; 2000-67, s. 8.1; 2001-424, s. 28.30(c); 2006-153, s. 1; 2009-223, s. 2; 2010-110, s. 1; 2011-145, s. 7.13(i), (x); 2011-379, s. 6(b); 2011-391, s. 14(b); 2012-77, s. 2; 2012-142, s. 7A.1(c); 2013-226, s. 11(a); 2013-360, s. 8.41(a).)

§§ 115C-105.28, 115C-105.29: Repealed by Session Laws 1995 (Regular Session, 1996), c. 716, s. 3.

§ 115C-105.30. Distribution of staff development funds.

Any funds the local board of education makes available to an individual school building to implement the school improvement plan at that school shall be used in accordance with that plan.

Each local board shall distribute seventy-five percent (75%) of the funds in the staff development funding allotment to the schools to be used in accordance with that school's school improvement plan. By October 1 of each year, the principal shall disclose to all affected personnel the total allocation of all funds available to the school for staff development and the superintendent shall disclose to all affected personnel the total allocation of all funds available at the system level for staff development. At the end of the fiscal year, the principal shall make available to all affected personnel a report of all disbursements from the building-level staff development funds, and the superintendent shall make available to all affected personnel a report of all disbursements at the system level of staff development funds. (1993, c. 321, s. 144.2(c); 1995 (Reg. Sess., 1996), c. 716, ss. 2, 3; 2011-145, s. 7.13(j); 2011-391, s. 14(b).)

§ 115C-105.31: Repealed by Session Laws 2011-266, s. 1.18, effective July 1, 2011.

§ 115C-105.32. Parent involvement programs and conflict resolution programs as part of school improvement plans.

A school is encouraged to include a comprehensive parent involvement program as part of its school improvement plan under G.S. 115C-105.27. The State Board of Education shall develop a list of recommended strategies that it determines to be effective, which building level committees may use to establish parent involvement programs designed to meet the specific needs of their schools. The Board shall make the list available to local school administrative units and school buildings by the beginning of the 1994-95 school year.

A school is encouraged to review its need for a comprehensive conflict resolution program as part of the development of its school improvement plan under G.S. 115C-105.27. If a school determines that this program is needed, it may select from the list developed by the State Board of Education under G.S. 115C-81(a4) or may develop its own materials and curricula to be approved by the local board of education. (1993, c. 509, ss. 2, 3; 1995 (Reg. Sess., 1996), c. 716, ss. 2, 3; 2011-145, s. 7.13(l); 2011-391, s. 14(b).)

§ 115C-105.33. Safe and orderly schools.

A school improvement team or a parent organization at a school may ask the local board of education to provide assistance in promoting or restoring safety and an orderly learning environment at a school. The school improvement team or parent organization shall file a copy of this request with the State Board. If the local board fails to provide adequate assistance to the school, then the school improvement team or parent organization may ask the State Board to provide an assistance team to the school.

The State Board may provide an assistance team, established under G.S. 115C-105.38, to a school in order to promote or restore safety and an orderly learning environment at that school if one of the following applies:

(1)   The local board of education or superintendent requests that the State Board provide an assistance team to a school and the State Board determines that the school needs assistance.

(2)   The State Board determines within 10 days after its receipt of the request for assistance from a school improvement team or parent organization of a school that the school needs assistance and that the local board has failed to provide adequate assistance to that school.

If an assistance team is assigned to a school under this section, the team shall spend a sufficient amount of time at the school to assess the problems at the school, assist school personnel with resolving those problems, and work with school personnel and others to develop a long-term plan for restoring and maintaining safety and an orderly learning environment at the school. The assistance team also shall make recommendations to the local board of education and the superintendent on actions the board and the superintendent should consider taking to resolve problems at the school. These recommendations shall be in writing and are public records. If an assistance team is assigned to a school under this section, the powers given to the State Board and the assistance team under G.S. 115C-105.38 and G.S. 115C-105.39 shall apply as if the school had been identified as low-performing under this Article. (1997-443, s. 8.29(a)(2); 2011-145, s. 7.13(m); 2011-391, s. 14(b).)

§ 115C-105.34. Reserved for future codification purposes.

Part 3. School-Based Accountability.

§ 115C-105.35. Annual performance goals.

(a)   The School-Based Management and Accountability Program shall (i) focus on student performance in the basics of reading, mathematics, and communications skills in elementary and middle schools, (ii) focus on student performance in courses required for graduation and on other measures required by the State Board in the high schools, and (iii) hold schools accountable for the educational growth of their students. To those ends, the State Board shall design and implement an accountability system that sets annual performance standards for each school in the State in order to measure the growth in performance of the students in each individual school. During the 2004-2005 school year and at least every five years thereafter, the State Board shall evaluate the accountability system and, if necessary, modify the testing standards to assure the testing standards continue to reasonably reflect the level of performance necessary to be successful at the next grade level or for more advanced study in the content area.

As part of this evaluation, the Board shall, where available, review the historical trend data on student academic performance on State tests. To the extent that the historical trend data suggest that the current standards for student performance may not be appropriate, the State Board shall adjust the standards to assure that they continue to reflect the State's high expectations for student performance.

(b) For purposes of this Article, the State Board shall include a "closing the achievement gap" component in its measurement of educational growth in student performance for each school. The "closing the achievement gap" component shall measure and compare the performance of each subgroup in a school's population to ensure that all subgroups as identified by the State Board are meeting State standards.

(c) The State Board shall consider incorporating into the School-Based Management and Accountability Program a character and civic education component which may include a requirement for student councils. (1995 (Reg. Sess., 1996), c. 716, s. 3; 2001-424, s. 28.30(a); 2003-284, s. 7.40(c); 2004-124, s. 7.12(a).)

§ 115C-105.36. Performance recognition.

(a) The personnel in schools that achieve a level of expected growth greater than one hundred percent (100%) at a level to be determined by the State Board of Education are eligible for financial awards in amounts set by the State Board. Schools and personnel shall not be required to apply for these awards. For the purpose of this section, "personnel" includes the principal, assistant principal, instructional personnel, instructional support personnel, and teacher assistants (i) serving students in one or more of the grades kindergarten through 12 or (ii) assigned to a public school prekindergarten program that is located within a public elementary school and is designed to prepare students for kindergarten at that school.

(b) The State Board shall establish a procedure to allocate the funds for these awards to the local school administrative units in which the eligible schools are located. Funds shall become available for expenditure July 1 of each fiscal year. Funds shall remain available until November 30 of the subsequent fiscal year for expenditure for awards to the personnel. Each local school administrative unit is encouraged to make these awards to each eligible person no later than the first regular teacher payroll following the local unit's receipt of the funds, and shall make these awards to each eligible person no later than the second regular teacher payroll following the local unit's receipt of the funds. (1995 (Reg. Sess., 1996), c. 716, s. 3; 1997-443, s. 8.14; 1998-220, s. 2.)

§ 115C-105.37. Identification of low-performing schools.

(a) The State Board of Education shall design and implement a procedure to identify low-performing schools on an annual basis. Low-performing schools are those in which there is a failure to meet the minimum growth standards, as defined by the State Board, and a majority of students are performing below grade level.

(a1) By July 10 of each year, each local school administrative unit shall do a preliminary analysis of test results to determine which of its schools the State Board may identify as low-performing under this section. The superintendent then shall proceed under G.S. 115C-105.39. In addition, within 30 days of the initial identification of a school as low-performing by the local school administrative unit or the State Board, whichever occurs first, the superintendent shall submit to the local board a preliminary plan for addressing the needs of that school, including how the superintendent and other central office administrators will work with the school and monitor the school's progress. Within 30 days of its receipt of this plan, the local board shall vote to approve, modify, or reject this plan. Before the board makes this vote, it shall make the plan available to the public, including the personnel assigned to that school and the parents and guardians of the students who are assigned to the school, and shall allow for written comments. The board shall submit the plan to the State

Board within five days of the board's vote. The State Board shall review the plan expeditiously and, if appropriate, may offer recommendations to modify the plan. The local board shall consider any recommendations made by the State Board.

(b)   Each school that the State Board identifies as low-performing shall provide written notification to the parents of students attending that school. The written notification shall include a statement that the State Board of Education has found that the school has "failed to meet the minimum growth standards, as defined by the State Board, and a majority of students in the school are performing below grade level." This notification also shall include information about the plan developed under subsection (a1) of this section and a description of any additional steps the school is taking to improve student performance. (1995 (Reg. Sess., 1996), c. 716, s. 3; 1997-221, s. 20(b); 1997-443, s. 8.45; 1998-59, s. 1; 2001-424, s. 29.4(a).)

§ 115C-105.37A. Continually low-performing schools; definition; assistance and intervention; reassignment of students.

(a)   Definition of Continually Low-Performing Schools. - A continually low-performing school is a school that has received State-mandated assistance and has been designated by the State Board as low performing for at least two of three consecutive years. If the State Board identifies a school as continually low performing:

(1)   The school improvement team at that school shall review its school improvement plan to ensure consistency with the plan adopted pursuant to G.S. 115C-105.38(b)(3), and

(2)   The plan must be reviewed and approved by the State Board of Education.

(b)   Assistance to Schools That Are Low Performing for Two Years. - If a school that has received State-mandated assistance is designated by the State Board as low performing for two consecutive years or for two of three consecutive years, the State Board shall provide a series of progressive assistance and intervention strategies to that school. These strategies shall be designed to improve student achievement and to maintain student achievement at appropriate levels and may include, to the extent that funds are available for this purpose, assistance such as reductions in class size, extension of teacher and assistant principal contracts, extension of the instructional year, and grant-based assistance.

(c) Intervention in Schools That Are Low Performing for Three or More Years. - The State Board of Education shall develop and implement a series of actions for providing assistance and intervention to schools that have previously received State-mandated assistance and have been designated by the State Board as low performing for three or more consecutive years or for at least three out of four years. These actions shall be the least intrusive actions that are consistent with the need to improve student achievement at each such school and shall be adapted to the unique characteristics of each such school and the effectiveness of other actions developed or implemented to improve student achievement at each such school. (2001-424, s. 29.3; 2009-223, s. 3; 2011-145, s. 7.13(n); 2011-391, s. 14(b).)

§ 115C-105.37B. Reform of continually low-performing schools.

(a) Notwithstanding any other provision of this Article, the State Board of Education is authorized to approve a local board of education's request to reform any school in its administrative unit which the State Board of Education has identified as one of the continually low-performing schools in North Carolina.

If the State Board of Education approves a local board of education's request to reform a school, the State Board of Education may authorize the local board of education to adopt one of the following models in accordance with State Board of Education requirements:

(1) Transformation model, which would address the following four specific areas critical to transforming a continually low-performing school:

a. Developing and increasing teacher and school leader effectiveness.

b. Comprehensive instructional reform strategies.

c. Increasing learning time and creating community-oriented schools.

d. Providing operational flexibility and sustained support.

(2) (Effective until July 1, 2014) Restart model, in which the State Board of Education would authorize the local board of education to operate the school with the same exemptions from statutes and rules as a charter school authorized under Part 6A of Article 16 of this Chapter, or under the management of an educational management organization that has been selected through a rigorous review process. A school operated under this subdivision remains under the control of the local board of education, and employees assigned to the school are employees of the local school administrative unit with the protections provided by G.S. 115C-325.

(2) (Effective July 1, 2014) Restart model, in which the State Board of Education would authorize the local board of education to operate the school with the same exemptions from statutes and rules as a charter school authorized under Part 6A of Article 16 of this Chapter, or under the management of an educational management organization that has been selected through a rigorous review process. A school operated under this subdivision remains under the control of the local board of education, and employees assigned to the school are employees of the local school administrative unit with the protections provided by Part 3 of Article 22 of this Chapter.

(3) Turnaround model, which would involve, among other actions, replacing the principal, if the principal has been in that position for at least three years, and rehiring no more than fifty percent (50%) of the school's staff, adopting a new governance structure at the school consistent with this Article, and implementing an instructional program aligned with the Standard Course of Study.

(4) School closure model, in which a local school administrative unit would close the school consistent with G.S. 115C-72 and enroll the students who attended the school in other, higher-achieving schools in the local school administrative unit consistent with Article 25 of this Chapter.

(b) The State Board of Education shall adopt rules to develop requirements for the models for school reform established in subsection (a) of this section.

(c) The State Board shall establish a procedure to implement this section. This procedure shall include annual reporting requirements from local boards that are authorized to use one of the models under this section and shall include a procedure for removing or continuing the authorization.

(d) Nothing in this section shall be construed to limit the authority of a local board of education as otherwise provided in this Chapter. (2010-1, s. 1; 2011-164, s. 2(b); 2013-360, s. 9.7(b).)

§ 115C-105.38. Assistance teams; review by State Board.

(a) The State Board of Education may assign an assistance team to any school identified as low-performing under this Article or to any other school that requests an assistance team and that the State Board determines would benefit from an assistance team. The State Board shall give priority to low-performing schools in which the educational performance of the students is declining. The Department of Public Instruction shall, with the approval of the State Board, provide staff as needed and requested by an assistance team.

(b) When assigned to an identified low-performing school, an assistance team shall:

(1) Review and investigate all facets of school operations and assist in developing recommendations for improving student performance at that school.

(2) Evaluate at least semiannually the personnel assigned to the school and make findings and recommendations concerning their performance.

(3) Collaborate with school staff, central offices, and local boards of education in the design, implementation, and monitoring of a plan that, if fully implemented, can reasonably be expected to alleviate problems and improve student performance at that school.

(4) Make recommendations as the school develops and implements this plan.

(5) Review the school's progress.

(6) Report, as appropriate, to the local board of education, the community, and the State Board on the school's progress. If an assistance team determines that an accepted school improvement plan developed under G.S. 115C-105.27 is impeding student performance at a school, the team may recommend to the local board that it vacate the relevant portions of that plan and direct the school to revise those portions.

(b1) Report to the State Board of Education if a school and its local board of education are not responsive to the team's recommendations. A copy of that report shall be made available to the local board, and the local board shall have an opportunity to respond. Notwithstanding G.S. 115C-36 and other provisions of this Chapter, if the State Board confirms that the school and local board have failed to take appropriate steps to improve student performance at that school, the State Board shall assume all powers and duties previously conferred upon that local board and that school and shall have general control and supervision of all matters pertaining to that school until student performance at the school meets or exceeds the standards set for the school. The State Board may, as it considers appropriate, delegate any powers and duties to that local board or school before the school meets or exceeds those standards.

(c) If a school fails to improve student performance after assistance is provided under this section, the assistance team may recommend that the assistance continues or that the State Board take further action under G.S. 115C-105.39.

(d) The State Board shall annually review the progress made in identified low-performing schools. (1995 (Reg. Sess., 1996), c. 716, s. 3; 2002-178, s. 7; 2011-145, s. 7.13(o); 2011-391, s. 14(b).)

§ 115C-105.38A. Teacher competency assurance.

(a) General Knowledge Test. -

(1) Each assistance team assigned to a low-performing school during the 1997-98 school year shall review the team's evaluations of certified staff members to determine which staff members have been designated by the team as Category 3 teachers. The assistance team shall then determine whether lack of general knowledge contributed to the Category 3 designation. If the assistance team determines that a certified staff member's lack of general knowledge contributed to that staff member being designated as a Category 3 teacher, the assistance team shall submit the staff member's name to the State Board. Upon receipt of the notification, the State Board shall require that the certified staff members identified by the assistance teams demonstrate their general knowledge by acquiring a passing score on a test designated by the

State Board. The State Board shall administer the general knowledge test required under this subdivision at the end of the 1997-98 school year.

(2) During the 1998-99 school year and thereafter, either the principal assigned to a low-performing school or the assistance team assigned to a low-performing school may recommend to the State Board that a certified staff member take a general knowledge test. A principal or an assistance team may make this recommendation if the principal or the assistance team determines that the certified staff member's performance is impaired by the staff member's lack of general knowledge. After receipt of the notification, but prior to the end of the fiscal year, the State Board shall require that all certified staff members identified under this subdivision demonstrate their general knowledge by acquiring a passing score on a test designated by the State Board.

(b) Repealed by Session Laws 1998-5, s. 1, effective June 9, 1998.

(c) Remediation. - Certified staff members who do not acquire a passing score on the test required under subsection (a) of this section shall engage in a remediation plan based upon the deficiencies identified by the test, or an assistance team, or a principal. The remediation plan for deficiencies of individual certified staff members shall consist of up to a semester of university or community college training or coursework or other similar activity to correct the deficiency. The remediation shall be developed by the State Board of Education in consultation with the Board of Governors of The University of North Carolina. The State Board shall reimburse the institution providing the remediation any tuition and fees incurred under this section. If the remediation plan requires that the staff member engage in a full-time course of study or training, the staff member shall be considered on leave with pay.

(d) (Effective until July 1, 2014) Retesting; Dismissal. - Upon completion of the remediation plan required under subsection (c) of this section, the certified staff member shall take the general knowledge test a second time. If the certified staff member fails to acquire a passing score on the second test, the State Board shall begin a dismissal proceeding under G.S. 115C-325(q)(2a).

(d) (Effective July 1, 2014, until June 30, 2018) Retesting; Dismissal. - Upon completion of the remediation plan required under subsection (c) of this section, the licensed staff member shall take the general knowledge test a second time. If the licensed staff member fails to acquire a passing score on the second test, the State Board shall begin a dismissal proceeding under G.S. 115C-325(q)(2a) or G.S. 115C-325.13.

(d) (Effective June 30, 2018) Retesting; Dismissal. - Upon completion of the remediation plan required under subsection (c) of this section, the licensed staff member shall take the general knowledge test a second time. If the licensed staff member fails to acquire a passing score on the second test, the State Board shall begin a dismissal proceeding under G.S. 115C-325.13.

(e) Repealed by Session Laws 1998-5, s. 1, effective June 9, 1998.

(f) (Effective until July 1, 2014) Other Actions Not Precluded. - Nothing in this section shall be construed to restrict or postpone the following actions:

(1) The dismissal of a principal under G.S. 115C-325(q)(1);

(2) The dismissal of a teacher, assistant principal, director, or supervisor under G.S. 115C-325(q)(2);

(3) The dismissal or demotion of a career employee for any of the grounds listed under G.S. 115C-325(e);

(4) The nonrenewal of a school administrator's or probationary teacher's contract of employment; or

(5) The decision to grant career status.

(f) (Effective July 1, 2014, until June 30, 2018) Other Actions Not Precluded. - Nothing in this section shall be construed to restrict or postpone the following actions:

(1) The dismissal of a principal under G.S. 115C-325.12.

(2) The dismissal of a teacher, assistant principal, director, or supervisor under G.S. 115C-325(q)(2) or G.S. 115C-325.13.

(3) The dismissal or demotion of an employee for any of the grounds listed under G.S. 115C-325(e) or G.S. 115C-325.4.

(4) The nonrenewal of a school administrator's or teacher's contract of employment.

(5) Repealed by Session Laws 2013-360, s. 9.7(c), effective July 1, 2014.

(f) (Effective June 30, 2018) Other Actions Not Precluded. - Nothing in this section shall be construed to restrict or postpone the following actions:

(1) The dismissal of a principal under G.S. 115C-325.12.

(2) The dismissal of a teacher, assistant principal, director, or supervisor under G.S. 115C-325.13.

(3) The dismissal or demotion of an employee for any of the grounds listed under G.S. 115C-325.4.

(4) The nonrenewal of a school administrator's or teacher's contract of employment.

(5) Repealed by Session Laws 2013-360, s. 9.7(c), effective July 1, 2014.

(g) Repealed by Session Laws 1998-5, s. 1, effective June 9, 1998. (1997-221, s. 3(a); 1998-5, s. 1; 2013-360, s. 9.7(c), (o).)

§ 115C-105.39. Dismissal or removal of personnel; appointment of interim superintendent.

(a) (Effective until July 1, 2014) Within 30 days of the initial identification of a school as low-performing, whether by the local school administrative unit under G.S. 115C-105.37(a1) or by the State Board under G.S. 115C-105.37(a), the superintendent shall take one of the following actions concerning the school's principal: (i) recommend to the local board that the principal be retained in the same position, (ii) recommend to the local board that the principal be retained in the same position and a plan of remediation should be developed, (iii) recommend to the local board that the principal be transferred, or (iv) proceed under G.S. 115C-325 to dismiss or demote the principal. The principal may be retained in the same position without a plan for remediation only if the principal was in that position for no more than two years before the school is identified as low-performing. The principal shall not be transferred to another principal position unless (i) it is in a school classification in which the principal previously demonstrated at least 2 years of success, (ii) there is a plan to evaluate and provide remediation to the principal for at least one year following the transfer to assure the principal does not impede student performance at the school to which the principal is being transferred; and (iii) the parents of the students at the school to which the principal is being transferred are notified. The principal shall not be transferred to another low-performing school in the local school administrative unit. If the superintendent intends to recommend demotion or dismissal, the superintendent shall notify the local board. Within 15 days of (i) receiving notification that the superintendent intends to proceed under G.S. 115C-325, or (ii) its decision concerning the superintendent's recommendation, but no later than September 30, the local board shall submit to the State Board a written notice of the action taken and the basis for that action. If the State Board does not assign an assistance team to that school or if the State Board assigns an assistance team to that school and the superintendent proceeds under G.S. 115C-325 to dismiss or demote the principal, then the State Board shall take no further action. If the State Board assigns an assistance team to the school and the superintendent is not proceeding under G.S. 115C-325 to dismiss or demote the principal, then the State Board shall vote to accept, reject, or modify the local board's recommendations. The State Board shall notify the local board of its action within five days. If the State Board rejects or modifies the local board's recommendations and does not recommend dismissal of the principal, the State Board's notification shall include recommended action concerning the principal's assignment or terms of employment. Upon receipt of the State Board's notification, the local board shall implement the State Board's recommended action concerning the principal's assignment or terms of employment unless the local board asks the State Board to reconsider that recommendation. The State Board shall provide an opportunity for the local board to be heard before the State Board acts on the local board's request for a reconsideration. The State Board shall vote to affirm or modify its original recommended action and shall notify the local board of its action within five days. Upon receipt of the State Board's notification, the local board shall implement the State Board's final recommended action concerning the principal's assignment or terms of employment. If the State Board rejects or modifies the local board's action and recommends dismissal of the principal, the State Board shall proceed under G.S. 115C-325(q)(1).

(a) (Effective July 1, 2014) Within 30 days of the initial identification of a school as low-performing, whether by the local school administrative unit under G.S. 115C-105.37(a1) or by the State Board under G.S. 115C-105.37(a), the superintendent shall take one of the following actions concerning the school's principal: (i) recommend to the local board that the principal be retained in the same position, (ii) recommend to the local board that the principal be retained in the same position and a plan of remediation should be developed, (iii) recommend to the local board that the principal be transferred, or (iv) proceed under G.S. 115C-325.4 to dismiss or demote the principal. The principal may be retained in the same position without a plan for remediation only if the principal was in that position for no more than two years before the school is identified as low-performing. The principal shall not be transferred to another principal position unless (i) it is in a school classification in which the principal previously demonstrated at least 2 years of success, (ii) there is a plan to evaluate and provide remediation to the principal for at least one year following the transfer to assure the principal does not impede student performance at the school to which the principal is being transferred; and (iii) the parents of the students at the school to which the principal is being transferred are notified. The principal shall not be transferred to another low-performing school in the local school administrative unit. If the superintendent intends to recommend demotion or dismissal, the superintendent shall notify the local board. Within 15 days of (i) receiving notification that the superintendent intends to proceed under G.S. 115C-325.4 or (ii) its decision concerning the superintendent's recommendation, but no later than September 30, the local board shall submit to the State Board a written notice of the action taken and the basis for that action. If the State Board does not assign an assistance team to that school or if the State Board assigns an assistance team to that school and the superintendent proceeds under G.S. 115C-325.4 to dismiss or demote the principal, then the State Board shall take no further action. If the State Board assigns an assistance team to the school and the superintendent is not proceeding under G.S. 115C-325.4 to dismiss or demote the principal, then the State Board shall vote to accept, reject, or modify the local board's recommendations. The State Board shall notify the local board of its action within five days. If the State Board rejects or modifies the local board's recommendations and does not recommend dismissal of the principal, the State Board's notification shall include recommended action concerning the principal's assignment or terms of employment. Upon receipt of the State Board's notification, the local board shall implement the State Board's recommended action concerning the principal's assignment or terms of employment unless the local board asks the State Board to reconsider that recommendation. The State Board shall provide an opportunity for the local board to be heard before the State Board acts on the local board's request for a reconsideration. The State Board shall vote to affirm or modify its original recommended action and shall notify the local board of its action within five days. Upon receipt of the State Board's notification, the local board shall implement the State Board's final recommended action concerning the principal's assignment or terms of employment. If the State Board rejects or modifies the local board's action and recommends dismissal of the principal, the State Board shall proceed under G.S. 115C-325.12.

(b) (Effective until July 1, 2014) The State Board shall proceed under G.S. 115C-325(q)(2) for the dismissal of teachers, assistant principals, directors, and supervisors assigned to a school identified as low-performing in accordance with G.S. 115C-325(q)(2).

(b) (Effective July 1, 2014, until June 30, 2018) The State Board shall proceed under G.S. 115C-325(q)(2) or G.S. 115C-325.13 for the dismissal of teachers, assistant principals, directors, and supervisors assigned to a school identified as low-performing in accordance with G.S. 115C-325(q)(2) or G.S. 115C-325.13.

(b) (Effective June 30, 2018) The State Board shall proceed under G.S. 115C-325.13 for the dismissal of teachers, assistant principals, directors, and supervisors assigned to a school identified as low-performing in accordance with G.S. 115C-325.13.

(c) The State Board may appoint an interim superintendent in a local school administrative unit:

(1) Upon the identification of more than half the schools in that unit as low-performing under G.S. 115C-105.37; or

(2) Upon the recommendation from an assistance team assigned to a school located in that unit that has been identified as low-performing under G.S. 115C-105.37. This recommendation shall be based upon a finding that the superintendent has failed to cooperate with the assistance team or has otherwise hindered that school's ability to improve.

The State Board may assign any of the powers and duties of the local superintendent and the local finance officer to the interim superintendent that the Board considers are necessary or appropriate to improve student performance in the local school administrative unit. The interim superintendent shall perform all of these assigned powers and duties. The State Board of Education may terminate the contract of any local superintendent entered into on or after July 1, 1996, when it appoints an interim superintendent. The Administrative Procedure Act shall apply to that decision. Neither party to that contract is entitled to damages.

(d) In the event the State Board has appointed an interim superintendent and the State Board determines that the local board of education has failed to cooperate with the interim superintendent or has otherwise hindered the ability to improve student performance in that local school administrative unit or in a school in that unit, the State Board may suspend any of the powers and duties of the local board of education that the State Board considers are necessary or appropriate to improve student performance in the local school administrative unit. The State Board shall perform all of these assigned powers and duties for a period of time to be specified by the State Board.

(e) If the State Board suspends any of the powers and duties of the local board of education under subsection (d) of this section and subsequently determines it is necessary to change the governance of the local school administrative unit in order to improve student performance, the State Board may recommend this change to the General Assembly, which shall consider, at its next session, the future governance of the identified local school administrative unit. (1995 (Reg. Sess., 1996), c. 716, s. 3; 1998-59, s. 2; 2013-360, s. 9.7(d), (p).)

§ 115C-105.40. Student academic performance standards.

The State Board of Education shall develop a plan to create rigorous student academic performance standards for kindergarten through eighth grade and student academic performance standards for courses in grades 9-12. The performance standards shall align, whenever possible, with the student academic performance standards developed for the National Assessment of Educational Progress (NAEP). The plan also shall include clear and understandable methods of reporting individual student academic performance to parents. (1997-221, s. 3(e).)

§ 115C-105.41. Students who have been placed at risk of academic failure; personal education plans; transition teams and transition plans.

(a) In order to implement Part 1A of Article 8 of this Chapter, local school administrative units shall identify students who are at risk for academic failure and who are not successfully progressing toward grade promotion and graduation, beginning in kindergarten. Identification shall occur as early as can reasonably be done and can be based on grades, observations, diagnostic and formative assessments, State assessments, and other factors, including reading on grade level, that impact student performance that teachers and administrators consider appropriate, without having to await the results of end-of-grade or end-of-course tests. No later than the end of the first quarter, or after a teacher has had up to nine weeks of instructional time with a student, a personal education plan for academic improvement with focused intervention and performance benchmarks shall be developed or updated for any student at risk of academic failure who is not performing at least at grade level, as identified by the State end-of-grade test and other factors noted above. Focused instructional supports and services, reading interventions, and accelerated activities should include evidence-based practices that meet the needs of students and may include coaching, mentoring, tutoring, summer school, Saturday school, and extended days. Local school administrative units shall provide these activities free of charge to students. Local school administrative units shall also provide transportation free of charge to all students for whom transportation is necessary for participation in these activities.

Local school administrative units shall give notice of the personal education plan and a copy of the personal education plan to the student's parent or guardian. Parents should be included in the implementation and ongoing review of personal education plans. If a student's school report card provides all the information required in a personal education plan, then no further personal education plan is mandated for the student.

No cause of action for monetary damages shall arise from the failure to provide or implement a personal education plan under this section.

(b) Local boards of education shall adopt and implement plans for the creation of transition teams and transition plans for students at risk, as defined by the State Board of Education, to assist them in making a successful transition between the elementary school and middle school years and between the middle school and high school years. (2001-424, s. 28.17(e); 2009-542, s. 1; 2010-162, s. 1; 2011-145, s. 7.13(ee); 2011-391, s. 14(a); 2012-77, s. 4; 2012-142, s. 7A.1(d); 2013-226, s. 2.)

§ 115C-105.42. Reserved for future codification purposes.

§ 115C-105.43. Reserved for future codification purposes.

§ 115C-105.44. Reserved for future codification purposes.

Article 8C.

Local Plans For Alternative Schools/Alternative Learning Programs and Maintaining Safe and Orderly Schools.

§ 115C-105.45. Legislative findings.

The General Assembly finds that all schools should be safe, secure, and orderly. If students are to aim for academic excellence, it is imperative that there is a climate of respect in every school and that every school is free of disruption, drugs, violence, and weapons. All schools must have plans, policies, and procedures for dealing with disorderly and disruptive behavior.

All schools and school units must have effective measures for assisting students who are at risk of academic failure or of engaging in disruptive and disorderly behavior. (1997-443, s. 8.29(r)(1).)

§ 115C-105.46. State Board of Education responsibilities.

In order to implement this Article, the State Board of Education:

(1)   through (4) Repealed by Session Laws 2011-145, s. 7.13(y), effective July 1, 2011.

(5)   Shall adopt policies that define who is an at-risk student. (1997-443, s. 8.29(r)(1); 1999-397, s. 2; 2000-140, s. 22; 2011-145, s. 7.13(y).)

§ 115C-105.47: Repealed by Session Laws 2011-145, s. 7.13(z), effective July 1, 2011.

§ 115C-105.47A. Proposals to establish alternative learning programs or alternative schools.

(a)   Before establishing any alternative learning program or alternative school, the local board of education shall develop a proposal to implement the program or school that includes all of the following:

(1)   The educational and behavioral goals for students assigned to the program or school.

(2)   The policies and procedures for the operation of the program or school based on the State Board's standards adopted under G.S. 115C-12(24). The policies and procedures shall address the assignment of students to the program or school.

(3)   Identified strategies that will be used to improve student achievement and behavior.

(4)   Documentation that similar programs and schools in or out of the State, or both, have demonstrated success in improving the academic achievement and behavior of students assigned to them.

(5)   The estimated actual cost of operating the program or school. To the extent practicable, this shall include the cost of:

a.   Staffing the program or school with teachers who have at least four years' teaching experience and who have received an overall rating of at least above standard on a formal evaluation and are certified in the areas and grade levels being taught;

b.   Providing optimum learning environments, resources and materials, and high quality, ongoing professional development that will ensure students who are placed in the program or school are provided enhanced educational opportunities in order to achieve their full potential;

c. Providing support personnel, including school counselors, psychiatrists, clinical psychologists, social workers, nurses, and other professionals to help students and their families work out complex issues and problems;

d. Maintaining safe and orderly learning environments; and

e. Providing transitional supports for students exiting the program or school and reentering the referring school.

(6) Documented support of school personnel and the community for the implementation of the program or school.

(b) After the local board completes the proposal under subsection (a) of this section, the board shall submit the proposal to the State Board of Education for its review. The State Board shall review the proposal expeditiously and, if appropriate, may offer recommendations to modify the proposal. The local board shall consider any recommendations made by the State Board before implementing the alternative learning program or alternative school. (2005-446, s. 2.)

§ 115C-105.48. Placement of students in alternative schools/alternative learning programs.

(a) Prior to referring a student to an alternative school or an alternative learning program, the referring school shall:

(1) Document the procedures that were used to identify the student as being at risk of academic failure or as being disruptive or disorderly.

(2) Provide the reasons for referring the student to an alternative school or an alternative learning program.

(3) Provide to the alternative school or alternative learning program all relevant student records, including anecdotal information.

(b) When a student is placed in an alternative school or an alternative learning program, the appropriate staff of the alternative school or alternative learning program shall meet to review the records forwarded by the referring school and to determine what support services and intervention strategies are recommended for the student. The parents shall be encouraged to provide input regarding the students' needs. (1999-397, s. 2.)

§ 115C-105.49. School safety exercises.

(a) At least every two years, each local school administrative unit is encouraged to hold a full systemwide school safety and school lockdown exercise with the local law enforcement agencies that are part of the local board of education's emergency response plan. The purpose of the exercise shall be to permit participants to (i) discuss simulated emergency situations in a low-stress environment, (ii) clarify their roles and responsibilities and the overall logistics of dealing with an emergency, and (iii) identify areas in which the emergency response plan needs to be modified.

(b) As part of a local board of education's emergency response plan, at least once a year, each school is encouraged to hold a full schoolwide school safety and lockdown exercise with local law enforcement agencies. (2013-360, s. 8.38.)

§ 115C-105.50: Reserved for future codification purposes.

§ 115C-105.51. Anonymous tip lines.

(a) Each local school administrative unit is encouraged to develop and operate an anonymous tip line, in coordination with local law enforcement and social services agencies, to receive anonymous information on internal or external risks to school buildings and school-related activities.

(b) The Department of Public Instruction, in consultation with the Department of Public Safety, may develop standards and guidelines for the development, operation, and staffing of tip lines.

(c) The Department of Public Instruction may provide information to local school administrative units on federal, State, local, and private grants available for this purpose. (2013-360, s. 8.40.)

§ 115C-105.52. School crisis kits.

The Department of Public Instruction, in consultation with the Department of Public Safety through the North Carolina Center for Safer Schools, may develop and adopt policies on the placement of school crisis kits in schools and on the contents of those kits. The kits should include, at a minimum, basic first-aid supplies, communications devices, and other items recommended by the International Association of Chiefs of Police.

The principal of each school, in coordination with the law enforcement agencies that are part of the local board of education's emergency response plan, may place one or more crisis kits at appropriate locations in the school. (2013-360, s. 8.42.)

Article 9.

Education of Children With Disabilities.

Part 1. State Policy.

§ 115C-106: Repealed by Session Laws 2006-69, s. 1, effective from and after July 1, 2006.

Part 1A. General Provisions.

§ 115C-106.1. State goal.

The goal of the State is to provide full educational opportunity to all children with disabilities who reside in the State. (1973, c. 1293, ss. 2-4; 1975, c. 563, ss. 1-5; 1977, c. 927, ss. 1, 2; 1979, 2nd Sess., c. 1295; 1981, c. 423, s. 1; 1997-443, s. 11A.47; 2006-69, s. 2.)

§ 115C-106.2. Purposes.

(a)   The purposes of this Article are to (i) ensure that all children with disabilities ages three through 21 who reside in this State have available to them a free appropriate public education that emphasizes special education and related services designed to meet their unique needs and prepares them for further education, employment, and independent living; (ii) ensure that the rights of these children and their parents are protected; and (iii) enable the State Board of Education and local educational agencies to provide for the education of all children with disabilities.

(b)   In addition to the purposes listed in subsection (a) of this section, the purpose of this Article is to enable the State Board of Education and local educational agencies to implement IDEA in this State. If this Article is silent or conflicts with IDEA, and if IDEA has specific language that is mandatory, then IDEA controls.

(c)   Notwithstanding any other section of this Article, the State Board of Education may set standards for the education of children with disabilities that are higher than those required by IDEA. (1973, c. 1293, ss. 2-4; 1975, c. 563, ss. 1-5; 1977, c. 927, ss. 1, 2; 1979, 2nd Sess., c. 1295; 1981, c. 423, s. 1; 1997-443, s. 11A.47; 2006-69, s. 2; 2007-292, s. 2.)

§ 115C-106.3. Definitions.

The following definitions apply in this Article:

(1)   "Child with a disability" means a child with at least one disability who because of that disability requires special education and related services.

(2)   "Disability" includes mental retardation; hearing impairment, including deafness; speech or language impairment; visual impairment, including blindness; serious emotional disturbance; orthopedic impairment; autism; traumatic brain injury; other health impairments, specific learning disability, or other disability as may be required to be included under IDEA. For a child ages three through seven, this term also includes developmental delay.

(3)   "Dispute" means a disagreement between the parties.

(3a)   "Educational services" means all of the following:

a.   The necessary instructional hours per week in the form and format as determined by the child's IEP team and consistent with federal and State law. The instruction shall be delivered by an appropriately qualified teacher to the extent required by federal and State law, which requires a free appropriate public education and the opportunity for a sound basic education.

b.   Related services included in the child's IEP.

c.   Behavior intervention services to the extent required by federal law.

(4)   "Free appropriate public education" means special education and related services that:

a.   Are provided at public expense, under public supervision and direction, and without charge;

b.   Meet the standards of the State Board;

c.   Include an appropriate preschool, elementary school, or secondary school education in the State; and

d.   Are provided in conformity with an individualized education program.

(5)   "Hearing officers" include administrative law judges as defined in G.S. 150B-2(1) and hearing review officers.

(5a)   "Homebound instruction" means educational services provided to a student outside the school setting.

(6)   "IDEA" means The Individuals with Disabilities Education Improvement Act, 20 U.S.C. § 1400, et seq., (2004), as amended, and federal regulations adopted under this act.

(7)   "IEP Team" is as defined in IDEA.

(8) "Individualized education program" or "IEP" means a written statement for each child with a disability that is developed, reviewed, implemented, and revised consistent with IDEA and State law.

(9) "Infant or toddler with a disability" is as defined in IDEA.

(10) "Least restrictive environment" means to the maximum extent appropriate, children with disabilities are educated with children who are not disabled, and special classes, separate schooling, or other removal of children with disabilities from the regular educational environment occurs only when the nature of the disability is such that education in regular classes with the use of supplementary aids and services cannot be achieved satisfactorily.

(11) "Local educational agency" includes any of the following that provides special education and related services to children with disabilities:

a. A local school administrative unit.

b. A charter school.

c. The Department of Health and Human Services.

d. The Division of Adult Correction of the Department of Public Safety.

e. The Division of Juvenile Justice of the Department of Public Safety.

f. Any other State agency or unit of local government.

(12) "Mediation" means an informal process conducted by a mediator with the objective of helping parties voluntarily settle their dispute.

(13) "Mediator" means a neutral person who acts to encourage and facilitate a resolution of a dispute.

(14) "Parent" means:

a. A natural, adoptive, or foster parent;

b. A guardian, but not the State if the child is a ward of the State;

c. An individual acting in the place of a natural or adoptive parent, including a grandparent, stepparent, or other relative, and with whom the child lives;

d. An individual who is legally responsible for the child's welfare; or

e. A surrogate if one is appointed under G.S. 115C-109.2.

(15) "Party" or "Parties" means the local educational agency or the parents, or both.

(16) "Petition" means a request for a due process hearing as provided for under IDEA.

(17) "Preschool child with a disability" means a child with one or more disabilities who meets all of the following criteria:

a. Has reached his or her third birthday and whose parents have requested services from the public schools.

b. Is not eligible to enroll in public kindergarten.

c. Because of the disability, needs special education and related services in order to prepare the child to benefit from the educational programs provided by the public schools, beginning with kindergarten.

(18) "Related services" is as defined in IDEA.

(18a) "Residence" or "reside" means the place where a child with a disability is entitled to be enrolled in a North Carolina public school under G.S. 115C-366 except for the age requirements of that section. This definition shall not apply to children with disabilities who were (i) enrolled in a particular local school administrative unit on the last day of school for the 2006-2007 school year, or (ii) enrolled in and attending a school in a particular local school administrative unit on August 1, 2007, for the 2007-2008 school year for as long as they live within and are continuously enrolled in that local school administrative unit.

(19) "Rules" includes rules, policies, and procedures. Rules as defined in G.S. 150B-2(8a) shall be adopted in accordance with Article 2A of Chapter 150B of the General Statutes.

(20) "Special education" means specially designed instruction, at no cost to parents, to meet the unique needs of a child with a disability. The term includes instruction in physical education and instruction conducted in a classroom, the home, a hospital or institution, and other settings. (1977, c. 927, s. 1; 1981, c. 423, s. 1; 1983, c. 247, ss. 1, 2; 1983 (Reg. Sess., 1984), c. 1034, ss. 23, 24; 1985, c. 479, s. 26(a);1985, c. 780, ss. 3, 4; 1989(Reg. Sess., 1990), c. 1003, s. 5; 1996, 2nd Ex. Sess., ch. 18, s. 18.24(b); 2006-69, s. 2; 2007-292, s. 1; 2007-429, s. 1; 2008-90, s. 1; 2011-145, s. 19.1(h), (l).)

§ 115C-107: Repealed by Session Laws 2006-69, s. 1, effective from and after July 1, 2006.

Part 1B. Provision of Free Appropriate Public Education.

§ 115C-107.1. Free appropriate public education; ages.

(a) A free appropriate public education shall be made available to the following:

(1) All children with disabilities who reside in the State, who are the ages of three through 21, who have not graduated from high school, and who require special education and related services.

(2) Any child with a disability who is receiving special education and related services and who has not graduated from high school until the end of the school year in which that child reaches the age of 22.

(3) Children with disabilities who require special education and related services and who are suspended or expelled from school and entitled to continuing education services as provided in IDEA.

(b) A free appropriate public education is not required to be provided to infants and toddlers with disabilities. However, early intervention services shall be made available to these children under G.S. 143B-139.6A.

(c) If funds are made available, the State Board and the Secretary of Health and Human Services may adopt an agreement to allow the continuation of early intervention services for children with a disability who are at least three years old but before they enter kindergarten or are eligible to enter kindergarten. If an agreement is adopted under this subsection, then a free appropriate public education is not required to be provided to any child with a disability who continues to receive early intervention services in accordance with that agreement.

(d) Nothing in this Article requires a free appropriate public education to be made available to any individual aged 18 through 21 who, in the educational placement immediately before that individual's incarceration in an adult correctional facility, was not actually identified as being a child with a disability and did not have an IEP. (1977, c. 927, s. 1; 1981, c. 423, s. 1; 1989 (Reg. Sess., 1990), c. 1003, s. 5; 1997-443, s. 11A.118(a); 1998-202, s. 4(h); 2000-137, s. 4(k); 2006-69, s. 2.)

§ 115C-107.2. Duties of State Board of Education.

(a) The State Board of Education shall adopt rules to ensure that:

(1) The requirements of this Article and IDEA are met.

(2) All educational programs under the supervision of any local educational agency for children with disabilities meet all of the following requirements:

a. The programs are under the general supervision of individuals in the State who are responsible for educational programs for children with disabilities.

b. The programs meet the State Board's educational standards.

c. With respect to homeless children, the programs meet the requirements of 20 U.S.C. § 1431, McKinney-Vento Homeless Assistance Act.

(b) The rules adopted under subsection (a) of this section shall include rules that:

(1) Establish standards for the programs of special education to be administered by local educational agencies and by the State Board.

(2) Ensure that children with disabilities are educated in the least restrictive environment.

(3) Ensure that local school administrative units make available special education and related services to all preschool children with disabilities whose parents request these services.

(4) Provide for public hearings, adequate notice of these hearings, and an opportunity for comment from the general public before the adoption of the rules required by this Article.

(5) Are required in order to receive federal funding under IDEA.

(6) Provide that, where a local educational agency finds that appropriate services are available from other public agencies or private organizations, the local educational agency may contract for those services rather than provide them directly.

(7) Enable local educational agencies to identify, evaluate, place, and make other educational decisions for children with disabilities.

(8) Provide procedural safeguards for children with disabilities and their parents.

(9) Designate a person in the Department of Public Instruction who is charged with receiving and responding to notices or other legal documents under Part 1D of this Article.

(10) Support and facilitate local educational agency and school-level system improvement designed to enable children with disabilities to meet the challenging State student academic achievement standards.

(c) Rules adopted under this section shall be consistent with IDEA and shall comply with G.S. 115C-12(19). Local educational agencies, parents, and other individuals concerned with the education of children with disabilities shall be consulted in the development of rules adopted under this Article.

(d) The State Board shall develop forms for local educational agencies to use in order to comply with this Article. The forms shall comply with G.S. 115C-12(19), and whenever practicable, (i) limit the requirement for narrative reporting to essential components requiring personalized student information and (ii) be in an electronic format.

(e) The State Board shall provide technical assistance to local educational agencies at their request.

(f) The State Board shall develop any plans that meet the criteria of IDEA and are required to be submitted to the United States Department of Education.

(g) The State Board shall make available to hearing officers training related to IDEA and its legal interpretations in order to facilitate hearings and reviews under G.S. 115C-109.6. (1977, c. 927, s. 1; 1981, c. 423, s. 1; 1983, c. 247, ss. 3, 4; 1989, c. 585, s. 3; 1989 (Reg. Sess., 1990), c. 1003, s. 5; 1996, 2nd Ex. Sess., c. 18, ss. 18.24(c), (d); 1997-443, s. 11A.118(a); 1998-202, s. 4(g); 2000-137, s. 4(j); 2006-69, s. 2; 2013-226, s. 10.)

§ 115C-107.3. Child find.

(a) The Board shall require an annual census of all children with disabilities residing in the State, subdivided for "identified" and "suspected" children with disabilities, to be taken in each school year. Suspected children are those in the formal process of being evaluated or identified as children with disabilities. The census shall be conducted annually and shall be completed by October 15, submitted to the Governor and General Assembly and made available to the public by January 15 annually.

(b) In taking the census, the Board requires the cooperation, participation, and assistance of all local educational agencies. Therefore, each local educational agency shall cooperate and participate with and assist the Board in conducting the census.

(c) The census shall include the number of children identified and suspected with disabilities, their age, the nature of their disability, their county or city of residence, their local school administrative unit residence, whether they are being provided special educational or related services and if so by what local educational agency, the identity of each local educational agency having children with disabilities in its care, custody, management, jurisdiction, control, or programs, the number of children with disabilities being served by each local educational agency, and any other information or data that the Board requires.

The census shall be of children with disabilities between the ages three through 21 but is not required to include children with disabilities that have graduated from high school. (1977, c. 927, s. 1; 1981, c. 423, s. 1; 1983, c. 247, ss. 3, 4; 1989, c. 585, s. 3; 1996, 2nd Ex. Sess., c. 18, ss. 18.24(c), (d); 1997-443, s. 11A.118(a); 1998-202, s. 4(g); 2000-137, s. 4(j); 2006-69, s. 2; 2007-292, s. 3.)

§ 115C-107.4. Monitoring and enforcement.

(a)   The State Board shall monitor all local educational agencies to determine compliance with this Article and IDEA. The State Board also shall monitor the effectiveness of IEPs in meeting the educational needs of children with disabilities.

(b)   The State Board shall implement an effective and efficient system of incentives and sanctions for local educational agencies in order to improve results for children with disabilities and meet the requirements of this Article and IDEA. The system, which must be based on a continuum of recognition and sanctions, shall:

(1)   Identify and recognize local educational agencies that achieve or exceed targets and indicators as determined by the State Board, demonstrate significant improvement over time, and show growth on targets and indicators as determined by each local educational agency.

(2)   Provide consequences for local educational agencies that are substantially noncompliant with statutory and regulatory requirements under this Article and IDEA.

(c)   The system of incentives developed under subsection (b) of this section may include commendations, public recognition, allocation of grant funds if available, and any other incentives as considered appropriate by the State Board.

(d)   The system of sanctions developed under subsection (b) of this section shall include the following:

(1)   Level One - Needs Assistance: When the State Board determines (i) a local school educational agency has been in noncompliance for two years and (ii) that agency needs assistance in implementing the requirements of this

Article and IDEA, the State Board shall take one or more of the following actions:

a. The Board may direct the local educational agency to allocate additional time and resources for technical assistance and guidance related to areas of noncompliance.

b. The Board may impose special conditions on that agency's application for IDEA funds and receipt of State funds.

c. The Board may direct how that local educational agency utilizes IDEA and State funds to address the remaining findings of noncompliance. The local educational agency must track the use of these funds to show how the funds are targeted to address areas of noncompliance.

(2) Level Two - Needs Intervention: If the State Board determines (i) that the local educational agency has been in noncompliance for three years and (ii) that agency needs assistance in implementing this Article and IDEA, the following apply:

a. The Board may take any of the actions described in subdivision (1) of this subsection.

b. The Board shall withhold, in whole or in part, any further payments of IDEA and State funds to the agency.

c. The Board shall require the agency to enter into a compliance agreement.

(3) Level Three - Needs Substantial Intervention: In addition to the sanctions described in subdivisions (1) and (2) of this subsection, if at any time the State Board determines a local educational agency (i) needs substantial intervention in implementing the requirements of this Article and IDEA, or (ii) has established a substantial failure to comply with this Article and IDEA, the Board shall take one or more of the following actions:

a. The Board shall direct the agency to implement a compliance agreement, billed to that agency.

b. The Board shall recover IDEA and State funds.

c.   The Board shall refer the agency for appropriate enforcement under State or federal law.

(e)   In addition to the consequences required under subsections (b) and (d) of this section, the State Board shall develop sanctions for local educational agencies that fail to implement a corrective action or hearing decision. (1977, c. 927, s. 1; 1981, c. 423, s. 1; 1983, c. 247, ss. 3, 4; 1989, c. 585, s. 3; 1996, 2nd Ex. Sess., c. 18, ss. 18.24(c), (d); 1997-443, s. 11A.118(a); 1998-202, s. 4(g); 2000-137, s. 4(j); 2006-69, s. 2.)

§ 115C-107.5. Annual reports.

The State Board shall report annually to the Joint Legislative Education Oversight Committee on the implementation of this Article and the educational performance of children with disabilities. Each annual report shall include a copy of the following documents that were submitted, received, or made public during the year: (i) the most recent State performance plan and any amendments to that plan submitted to the Secretary of Education, (ii) compliance and monitoring reports submitted to the Secretary of Education, (iii) the annual report submitted to the Secretary of Education on the performance of the State under its performance plan, and (iv) any other information required under IDEA to be made available to the public. In addition, the annual report shall include an analysis of the educational performance of children with disabilities in the State and a summary of disputes under Part 1D of this Chapter. The report shall be filed no later than October 15 each year and may be filed electronically. (1977, c. 927, s. 1; 1981, c. 423, s. 1; 1983, c. 247, ss. 3, 4; 1989, c. 585, s. 3; 1996, 2nd Ex. Sess., c. 18, ss. 18.24(c), (d); 1997-443, s. 11A.118(a); 1998-202, s. 4(g); 2000-137, s. 4(j); 2006-69, s. 2.)

§ 115C-107.6. Duties of local educational agencies.

(a)   Each local educational agency, in providing for the education of children with disabilities within its jurisdiction, must comply with IDEA and the rules adopted by the State Board under this Article. In addition, each local educational agency shall have in effect policies, procedures, and programs that are consistent with this Article, IDEA, and rules adopted by the State Board.

(b) No child with disabilities shall be prevented from attending the public schools of the local educational agency in which the child resides or from which the child receives services or from attending any other public program of free appropriate public education based solely on the fact that the child has a disability. If it appears the child should receive a program of free appropriate public education in a program operated by or under the supervision of the Department of Health and Human Services or the Division of Juvenile Justice of the Department of Public Safety, the local school administrative unit shall confer with the appropriate Department of Health and Human Services or Division of Juvenile Justice of the Department of Public Safety staff for their participation and determination of the appropriateness of placement in that program and development of the child's individualized education program.

(c) No matriculation or tuition fees or other fees or charges shall be required or asked of children with disabilities or their parents except those fees or charges that are required uniformly of all public school pupils. The provision of a free appropriate public education within the facilities of the Department of Health and Human Services and the Division of Juvenile Justice of the Department of Public Safety may not prevent that Department from charging for other services or treatment.

(d) Each child with a disability shall be educated in accordance with that child's IEP and in the least restrictive environment for that child.

(e) Each local educational agency may use the forms developed under G.S. 115C-107.2(d). (1977, c. 927, s. 1; 1981, c. 423, s. 1; 1983, c. 247, ss. 3, 4; 1989, c. 585, s. 3; 1996, 2nd Ex. Sess., c. 18, ss. 18.24(c), (d); 1997-443, s. 11A.118(a); 1998-202, s. 4(g); 2000-137, s. 4(j); 2006-69, s. 2; 2007-292, s. 4; 2011-145, s. 19.1(l).)

§ 115C-107.7. Discipline, corporal punishment, and homebound instruction.

(a) The policies and procedures for the discipline of students with disabilities shall be consistent with federal laws and regulations.

(a1) Any corporal punishment administered on students with disabilities shall be consistent with the requirements of G.S. 115C-390.4.

(b) If a change of placement occurs under the discipline regulations of IDEA, a local educational agency shall not assign a student to homebound instruction without a determination by the student's IEP team that the homebound instruction is the least restrictive alternative environment for that student. If it is determined that the homebound instruction is the least restrictive alternative environment for the student, the student's IEP team shall meet to determine the nature of the homebound educational services to be provided to the student. In addition, the continued appropriateness of the homebound instruction shall be evaluated monthly by the designee or designees of the student's IEP team.

(c) A local educational agency shall be deemed to have a "basis of knowledge" that a child is a child with a disability if, prior to the behavior that precipitated the disciplinary action, the behavior and performance of the child clearly and convincingly establishes the need for special education. Prior disciplinary infractions shall not, standing alone, constitute clear and convincing evidence. (2006-69, s. 2; 2007-425, s. 1; 2008-90, ss. 2, 3; 2010-36, s. 1; 2010-159, s. 1; 2012-77, s. 5; 2012-149, s. 11.5; 2012-194, ss. 48, 52.)

§ 115C-108: Repealed by Session Laws 2006-69, s. 1, effective from and after July 1, 2006.

Part 1C. Interagency Coordination.

§ 115C-108.1. State Board lead agency.

(a) The Board shall cause all local educational agencies to provide special education and related services to children with disabilities in their care, custody, management, jurisdiction, control, or programs.

(b) The jurisdiction of the Board with respect to the design and content of special education programs or related services for children with disabilities extends to and over the Department of Health and Human Services, the Division of Juvenile Justice of the Department of Public Safety, and the Division of Adult Correction of the Department of Public Safety.

(c) All provisions of this Article that are specifically applicable to local school administrative units also are applicable to the Department of Health and Human Services, the Division of Juvenile Justice of the Department of Public Safety, and the Division of Adult Correction of the Department of Public Safety, and their divisions and agencies; all duties, responsibilities, rights, and privileges specifically imposed on or granted to local school administrative units by this Article also are imposed on or granted to the Department of Health and Human Services, the Division of Juvenile Justice of the Department of Public Safety, and the Division of Adult Correction of the Department of Public Safety, and their divisions and agencies. However, with respect to children with disabilities who are residents or patients of any State-operated or State-supported residential treatment facility, including a school for the deaf, school for the blind, mental hospital or center, mental retardation center, or in a facility operated by the Division of Juvenile Justice of the Department of Public Safety, the Division of Adult Correction of the Department of Public Safety, or any of their divisions and agencies, the Board may contract with the Department of Health and Human Services, the Division of Juvenile Justice of the Department of Public Safety, and the Division of Adult Correction of the Department of Public Safety for the provision of special education and related services and the power to review, revise, and approve any plans for special education and related services to those residents.

(d) The Departments of Health and Human Services, Correction, and Juvenile Justice and Delinquency Prevention shall submit to the Board their plans for the education of children with disabilities in their care, custody, or control. The Board may grant specific exemptions for programs administered by the Department of Health and Human Services, the Division of Juvenile Justice of the Department of Public Safety, or the Division of Adult Correction of the Department of Public Safety when compliance by them with the Board's standards would, in the Board's judgment, impose undue hardship on that department or division and when other procedural due process requirements, substantially equivalent to those required under this Article and IDEA, are assured in programs of special education and related services furnished to children with disabilities served by that department. Further, the Board shall recognize that inpatient and residential special education programs within the Departments of Health and Human Services, the Division of Juvenile Justice of the Department of Public Safety, or the Division of Adult Correction of the Department of Public Safety may require more program resources than those necessary for optimal operation of these programs in local school administrative units.

(e) The Board shall support and encourage joint and collaborative special education planning and programming at local levels to include local school administrative units and the programs and agencies of the Departments of Health and Human Services, the Division of Juvenile Justice of the Department of Public Safety, or the Division of Adult Correction of the Department of Public Safety. (2006-69, s. 2; 2011-145, s. 19.1(h), (l); 2012-83, ss. 38, 39.)

§ 115C-108.2. Interlocal cooperation.

The Board, any two or more local educational agencies, and any other agency and any State department, agency, or division having responsibility for the education, treatment, or habilitation of children with disabilities may enter into interlocal cooperative undertakings under Part 1 of Article 20 of Chapter 160A of the General Statutes or into undertakings with a State agency such as the Departments of Public Instruction, Health and Human Services, Juvenile Justice and Delinquency Prevention, or Correction, or their divisions, agencies, or units, for the purpose of providing for the special education and related services, treatment, or habilitation of these children within the jurisdiction of the agency or unit, and shall do so when it is unable to provide the appropriate public special education or related services for these children. In entering into such undertakings, the local agency and State department, agency, or division shall also contract to provide the special education or related services that are educationally appropriate to the children with disabilities for whose benefit the undertaking is made and provide these services by or in the local agency unit or State department, agency, or division located in the place most convenient to these children. (1977, c. 927, s. 1; 1981, c. 423, s. 1; 1997-443, s. 11A.118(a); 1998-202, s. 4(m); 2000-137, s. 4(p); 2006-69, s. 2.)

§ 115C-109: Repealed by Session Laws 2006-69, s. 1, effective from and after July 1, 2006.

Part 1D. Procedural Safeguards.

§ 115C-109.1. Handbook for parents.

The State Board of Education shall make available to parents a handbook of procedural safeguards. This handbook for parents shall be made available at least once each school year, except that a copy also shall be given to the parent (i) upon the initial referral or parental request for an evaluation; (ii) upon the first occurrence of the filing of a petition under G.S. 115C-109.6 and IDEA; (iii) upon the parent's request; and (iv) upon any revision to the content of the handbook. This handbook for parents shall include a full explanation of the procedural safeguards under this Article and IDEA, be written in the native language of the parent unless it clearly is not feasible to do so, be written in an easily understood manner, and include information required under IDEA to be included.

The State Board shall place a current copy of the handbook for parents on its Internet Web site. (2006-69, s. 2.)

§ 115C-109.2. Adult children with disabilities; surrogate parents.

(a)   When a child with a disability reaches the age of 18, all of the following apply:

(1)   Notices required under this Article shall be provided to both the child and the child's parent.

(2)   All other rights accorded to parents under this Article and IDEA transfer to the child.

(3)   The local educational agency shall notify the child and the child's parent of these transfer rights.

(b)   Notwithstanding subsection (a) of this section, for a child with a disability who has reached the age of majority under State law and who has not been determined to be incompetent but is determined to not have the ability to provide informed consent with respect to his or her education program, the State Board shall establish procedures for appointing the parent of the child, or if the parent is not available, another appropriate individual, to represent the educational interests of the child throughout the period of eligibility under this section.

(c)   A reasonable effort must be made to appoint a surrogate for a child with a disability within 30 days of a determination that one of the following conditions exists and that the child needs a surrogate:

(1)   The parents of that child are not known;

(2) The parents, after reasonable efforts, cannot be located; or

(3) The child is a ward of the State.

(d) A person must be eligible under IDEA to be appointed as a child's surrogate. (1987 (Reg. Sess., 1988), c. 1079, s. 2; 1997-443, s. 11A.118(a); 1998-202, s. 4(j); 2000-137, s. 4(m); 2006-69, s. 2.)

§ 115C-109.3. Access to records; opportunity for parents to participate in meetings.

(a) Each local educational agency shall provide an opportunity for the parents of a child with a disability to examine all records relating to that child and to participate in meetings with respect to the identification, evaluation, and educational placement of the child, and the provision of a free appropriate public education to that child.

(b) Local educational agencies may release the records of a child with a disability only as permitted under State or federal law. The parents of a child with a disability may have access to the child's records and may read, inspect, and copy all and any records, data, and information maintained by a local educational agency with respect to that child. Parents, upon their request, are entitled to have those records, data, and information fully explained, interpreted, and analyzed for them by the staff of the agency, unless specifically prohibited by court order. If a request is made under this subsection, the local educational agency shall honor the request within not more than 45 days after it is made or in time for the individual who made the request to prepare for a meeting under subsection (a) of this section, whichever is sooner.

(c) The student and the student's parents may add written explanations or clarifications to the records, data, and information and may request the expunction of incorrect, outdated, misleading, or irrelevant entries. If a local educational agency refuses to expunge incorrect, outdated, misleading, or irrelevant entries after having been asked to do so by the parent, the parent may appeal that decision under G.S. 115C-45(c)(2). (1977, c. 927, s. 1; 1981, c. 423, s. 1; 2006-69, s. 2.)

§ 115C-109.4. Mediation.

(a) It is the policy of this State to encourage local educational agencies and parents to seek mediation involving any dispute under this Article, including matters arising before or after filing a petition under G.S. 115C-109.6.

(b) Mediation under this section must meet the following requirements:

(1) The mediation must be voluntary on the part of both parties.

(2) Mediation shall not be used to deny or delay a parent's right to an impartial hearing under G.S. 115C-109.6, or to deny any other rights afforded under this Article or IDEA.

(3) The mediation shall be conducted by a qualified and impartial mediator who is trained in effective mediation techniques.

(c) The State Board may establish procedures to offer to parties that do not choose to use the mediation process an opportunity to meet with a disinterested party, as provided under IDEA, who can encourage the use and explain the benefits of the mediation process to the parties. This meeting must be at a time and location convenient to the parents.

(d) The State Board shall maintain a list of qualified mediators who are knowledgeable in laws and regulations relating to the provision of special education and related services. When mediation is requested, the Exceptional Children Division of the Department of Public Instruction shall assign a mediator from this list of mediators.

(e) The State shall bear the cost of the mediation process, including the costs of meetings described under subsection (c) of this section, unless the parties opt to select a mediator other than the mediator assigned under subsection (d) of this section or if the parties opt to use an alternative method of dispute resolution.

(f) Each session in the mediation process shall be scheduled in a timely manner and shall be held in a location that is convenient to the parties to the dispute.

(g) Evidence of statements made and conduct occurring in a mediation are confidential, are not subject to discovery, and are inadmissible in any proceeding in the action or other actions on the same claim. However, no evidence otherwise discoverable is inadmissible merely because it is presented or discussed in a mediation. Mediators shall not be compelled in any civil proceeding to testify or produce evidence concerning statements made and conduct occurring in a mediation.

(h) When resolution is reached to resolve the dispute through the mediation process, the parties shall execute a legally binding agreement that:

(1) Sets forth the agreement.

(2) States that all discussions that occurred during the mediation process are confidential and may not be used as evidence in any subsequent impartial hearing under G.S. 115C-109.6 or in any civil proceeding.

(3) Is signed by both the parent and a representative of the local educational agency who has the authority to bind that agency.

(4) Is enforceable in any State administrative forum provided for in IDEA, any State court of competent jurisdiction, or in a district court of the United States.

(i) In addition to mediation as provided by this section, the parties may participate in a mediated settlement conference as provided by G.S. 150B-23.1. In addition, the parties may agree to use other dispute resolution methods or to use mediation in other circumstances, including after a request for formal administrative review is filed, to the extent permitted under State and federal law. (1973, c. 1293, s. 10; 1975, c. 151, ss. 1, 2; c. 563, ss. 8, 9; 1975, 2nd Sess., c. 983, ss. 79, 80; 1981, c. 423, s. 1; c. 497, ss. 1, 2; 1983, c. 247, s. 6; 1985, c. 412, s. 2; 1987, c. 827, s. 1; 1987 (Reg. Sess., 1988), c. 1079, s. 1; 1989, c. 362; 1989 (Reg. Sess., 1990), c. 1058; 1991, c. 540, s. 1; 1991 (Reg. Sess., 1992), c. 1030, s. 27; 1993, c. 270, s. 1; 1997-115, s. 1; 2006-69, s. 2.)

§ 115C-109.5. Prior written notice.

(a) The local educational agency shall provide prompt written notice to parents whenever that agency proposes to initiate or change, or refuses to initiate or change (i) the identification, evaluation, or educational placement of a child, or (ii) the provision of a free appropriate public education to a child with a disability. The local educational agency shall document that all required notices have been sent to and received by parents.

(b) This prior written notice shall be in the native language of the parents, unless it clearly is not feasible to translate it, and shall contain all of the following information:

(1) A description of the action proposed or refused by the local educational agency.

(2) An explanation of why the local educational agency proposes or refuses to take the action and a description of each evaluation procedure, assessment, record, or report that agency used as a basis for the proposed or refused action.

(3) A statement that the parent of a child with a disability has protection under the procedural safeguards of this Article and IDEA and, if this notice is not the initial referral for evaluation, the means by which a copy of the procedural safeguards can be obtained.

(4) Sources for parents to contact to obtain assistance in understanding this Article and IDEA.

(5) A description of other options considered by the IEP Team and the reason why those options were rejected.

(6) A description of the factors that are relevant to the local educational agency's proposal or refusal.

(7) Any other information required to be included under IDEA. (1973, c. 1293, s. 10; 1975, c. 151, ss. 1, 2; c. 563, ss. 8, 9; 1975, 2nd Sess., c. 983, ss. 79, 80; 1981, c. 423, s. 1; c. 497, ss. 1, 2; 1983, c. 247, s. 6; 1985, c. 412, s. 2; 1987, c. 827, s. 1; 1987 (Reg. Sess., 1988), c. 1079, s. 1; 1989, c. 362; 1989 (Reg. Sess., 1990), c. 1058; 1991, c. 540, s. 1; 1991 (Reg. Sess., 1992), c. 1030, s. 27; 1993, c. 270, s. 1; 1997-115, s. 1; 2006-69, s. 2.)

§ 115C-109.6. Impartial due process hearings.

(a) Any party may file with the Office of Administrative Hearings a petition to request an impartial hearing with respect to any matter relating to the identification, evaluation, or educational placement of a child, or the provision of a free appropriate public education of a child, or a manifestation determination. The party filing the petition must notify the other party and the person designated under G.S. 115C-107.2(b)(9) by simultaneously serving them with a copy of the petition.

(b) Notwithstanding any other law, the party shall file a petition under subsection (a) of this section that includes the information required under IDEA and that sets forth an alleged violation that occurred not more than one year before the party knew or reasonably should have known about the alleged action that forms the basis of the petition. The issues for review under this section are limited to those set forth in subsection (a) of this section. The party requesting the hearing may not raise issues that were not raised in the petition unless the other party agrees otherwise.

(c) The one-year restriction in subsection (b) of this section shall not apply to a parent if the parent was prevented from requesting the hearing due to (i) specific misrepresentations by the local educational agency that it had resolved the problem forming the basis of the petition, or (ii) the local educational agency's withholding of information from the parent that was required under State or federal law to be provided to the parent.

(d) The hearing shall be conducted in the county where the child attends school or is entitled to enroll under G.S. 115C-366, unless the parties mutually agree to a different venue.

(e) The hearing shall be closed to the public unless the parent requests in writing that the hearing be open to the public.

(f) Subject to G.S. 115C-109.7, the decision of the administrative law judge shall be made on substantive grounds based on a determination of whether the child received a free appropriate public education. Following the hearing, the administrative law judge shall issue a written decision regarding the issues set forth in subsection (a) of this section. The decision shall contain findings of fact and conclusions of law. Notwithstanding Chapter 150B of the General Statutes, the decision of the administrative law judge becomes final and is not subject to further review unless appealed to the Review Officer under G.S. 115C-109.9.

(g) A copy of the administrative law judge's decision shall be served upon each party and a copy shall be furnished to the attorneys of record. The written notice shall contain a statement informing the parties of the availability of appeal and the 30-day limitation period for appeal as set forth in G.S. 115C-109.9.

(h)   In addition to the petition, the parties shall simultaneously serve a copy of all pleadings, agreements, and motions under this Part with the person designated by the State Board under G.S. 115C-107.2(b)(9). The Office of Administrative Hearings shall simultaneously serve a copy of all orders and decisions under this Part with the person designated by the State Board under G.S. 115C-107.2(b)(9).

(i)   Nothing in this section shall be construed to preclude a parent from filing a separate due process petition on an issue separate from a petition already filed.

(j)   The State Board, through the Exceptional Children Division, and the State Office of Administrative Hearings shall develop and enter into a binding memorandum of understanding to ensure compliance with the statutory and regulatory procedures and timelines applicable under IDEA to due process hearings and to hearing officers' decisions, and to ensure the parties' due process rights to a fair and impartial hearing. This memorandum of understanding shall be amended if subsequent changes to IDEA are made. The procedures and timelines shall be made part of the Board's procedural safeguards that are made available to parents and the public under G.S. 115C-109.1 and G.S. 115C-109.5. (1973, c. 1293, s. 10; 1975, c. 151, ss. 1, 2; c. 563, ss. 8, 9; 1975, 2nd Sess., c. 983, ss. 79, 80; 1981, c. 423, s. 1; c. 497, ss. 1, 2; 1983, c. 247, s. 6; 1985, c. 412, s. 2; 1987, c. 827, s. 1; 1987 (Reg. Sess., 1988), c. 1079, s. 1; 1989, c. 362; 1989 (Reg. Sess., 1990), c. 1058; 1991, c. 540, s. 1; 1991 (Reg. Sess., 1992), c. 1030, s. 27; 1993, c. 270, s. 1; 1997-115, s. 1; 2006-69, s. 2.)

§ 115C-109.7. Resolution session.

(a)   Within 15 days of receiving notice of the parent's petition filed under G.S. 115C-109.6 and before the opportunity for an impartial hearing, the local educational agency shall convene a meeting with the parent and the relevant members of the IEP Team who have specific knowledge of the facts identified in the petition. This meeting shall include a representative of the agency who has decision-making authority on behalf of that agency and may not include an attorney of the local educational agency unless the parent is accompanied by an attorney. If the parent plans to be accompanied by an attorney under this section, the parent must give prior written notice of this fact to the agency. The purposes of the meeting are (i) for the parent to have an opportunity to discuss the petition and the facts that form the basis of the petition and (ii) for the local educational agency to have the opportunity to resolve the dispute.

(b) The parent and the local educational agency jointly may agree in writing to waive the meeting under subsection (a) of this section or to use the mediation process described in G.S. 115C-109.4.

(c) If the local educational agency does not resolve the dispute to the satisfaction of the parents within 30 days of the agency's receipt of the petition, the impartial hearing under G.S. 115C-109.6 may occur and all of the applicable timelines for that hearing shall commence.

(d) If a resolution is reached to resolve the dispute at a meeting under subsection (a) of this section, the parties shall execute a legally binding agreement that is:

(1) Signed by both the parent and a representative of the local educational agency who has the authority to bind the agency;

(2) Enforceable in any State administrative forum provided for in IDEA, any State court of competent jurisdiction, or in a district court of the United States; and

(3) Filed with the person designated by the State Board to receive notices and with the Office of Administrative Hearings.

(e) If the parties execute an agreement under subsection (d) of this section, either party may void the agreement by providing written notice within three business days of the agreement's execution to the person designated by the State Board to receive notices, the Office of Administrative Hearings, and the other party. Notwithstanding subsection (c) of this section, upon receipt of this notice, the impartial hearing under G.S. 115C-109.6 may occur and all of the applicable timelines for that hearing shall commence. (1973, c. 1293, s. 10; 1975, c. 151, ss. 1, 2; c. 563, ss. 8, 9; 1975, 2nd Sess., c. 983, ss. 79, 80; 1981, c. 423, s. 1; c. 497, ss. 1, 2; 1983, c. 247, s. 6; 1985, c. 412, s. 2; 1987, c. 827, s. 1; 1987 (Reg. Sess., 1988), c. 1079, s. 1; 1989, c. 362; 1989 (Reg. Sess., 1990), c. 1058; 1991, c. 540, s. 1; 1991 (Reg. Sess., 1992), c. 1030, s. 27; 1993, c. 270, s. 1; 1997-115, s. 1; 2006-69, s. 2.)

§ 115C-109.8. Procedural issues.

(a) In matters alleging a procedural violation, the hearing officer may find that a child did not receive a free appropriate public education only if the procedural inadequacies (i) impeded the child's right to a free appropriate public education; (ii) significantly impeded the parents' opportunity to participate in the decision-making process regarding the provision of a free appropriate public education to the parents' child; or (iii) caused a deprivation of educational benefits.

(b) A hearing officer may order a local educational agency to comply with procedural requirements under this Article and IDEA. (2006-69, s. 2.)

§ 115C-109.9. Review by review officer; appeals.

(a) Any party aggrieved by the findings and decision of a hearing officer under G.S. 115C-109.6 or G.S. 115C-109.8 may appeal the findings and decision within 30 days after receipt of notice of the decision by filing a written notice of appeal with the person designated by the State Board under G.S. 107.2(b)(9) to receive notices. The State Board, through the Exceptional Children Division, shall appoint a Review Officer from a pool of review officers approved by the State Board of Education. The Review Officer shall conduct an impartial review of the findings and decision appealed under this section. The Review Officer conducting this review shall make an independent decision upon completion of the review. The decision of the Review Officer becomes final unless an aggrieved party brings a civil action under subsection (d) of this section. A copy of the decision shall be served upon each party, and a copy shall be furnished to the attorneys of record and the Office of Administrative Hearings. The written notice shall contain a statement informing the parties of the right to file a civil action and the 30-day limitation period for filing a civil action under subsection (d) of this section.

(b) A Review Officer shall be an educator or other professional who is knowledgeable about special education and who possesses other qualifications as may be established by the State Board of Education. No person may be appointed as a Review Officer if that person is an employee of the State Board of Education, the Department of Public Instruction, or the local educational agency that has been involved in the education or care of the child whose parents have filed the petition.

(c) The State Board may enforce the final decision of the administrative law judge under G.S. 115C-109.6, if not appealed under this section, or the final decision of the Review Officer, by ordering a local educational agency:

(1) To provide a child with appropriate education;

(2) To place a child in a private school that is approved to provide special education and that can provide the child an appropriate education; or

(3) To reimburse parents for reasonable private school placement costs in accordance with this Article and IDEA when it is determined that the local educational agency did not offer or provide the child with appropriate education and the private school in which the parent placed the child was an approved school and did provide the child an appropriate education.

(d) Any party that does not have the right to appeal under this Part and any party who is aggrieved by the decision of the Review Officer under this section may institute a civil action in State court within 30 days after receipt of the notice of the decision or in federal court as provided in 20 U.S.C. § 1415.

(e) Except as provided under IDEA, upon the filing of a petition under G.S. 115C-109.6 and during the pendency of any proceedings under this Part, the child must remain in the child's then-current educational placement or, if applying for initial admission to a public school, the child must be placed in the public school. Notwithstanding this subsection, the parties may agree in writing to a different educational placement for the child during the pendency of any proceedings under this Part. (2006-69, s. 2.)

§ 115C-110: Repealed by Session Laws 2006-69, s. 1, effective from and after July 1, 2006.

Part 1E. Special Education and Related Services Personnel.

§ 115C-110.1. Teacher qualifications.

The Board shall adopt rules covering the qualifications of and standards for licensure of teachers, teacher assistants, speech-language pathologists, school psychologists, and others involved in the education and training of children with disabilities. (2006-69, s. 2.)

§ 115C-110.2. Interpreters/transliterators.

Each interpreter or transliterator employed by a local educational agency to provide services to hearing-impaired students must annually complete 15 hours of job-related training that has been approved by the local educational agency. (2002-182, s. 6; 2003-56, s. 3; 2006-69, s. 2.)

§ 115C-110.3: Reserved for future codification purposes.

§ 115C-110.4: Reserved for future codification purposes.

§ 115C-110.5: Reserved for future codification purposes.

§ 115C-111: Repealed by Session Laws 2006-69, s. 1, effective from and after July 1, 2006.

Part 1F. Budgeting; Funds.

§ 115C-111.1. Out-of-state students; eligibility for State funds.

Notwithstanding any policy or rule adopted by the State Board of Education, if a local school administrative unit provides services to a student under a current IEP from another state while a determination is being made regarding the student's eligibility for services as a child with disabilities in North Carolina, the local school administrative unit is entitled to receive State funding to serve the student while the determination is being made. If the student is later determined not to qualify for services in North Carolina, the local school administrative unit is not required to repay State funds received while the determination is being made. (1997-117, s. 1; 2006-69, s. 2.)

§ 115C-111.2. Contracts with private service providers.

Local educational agencies furnishing special education and related services to children with disabilities may contract with private special education facilities or service providers to furnish any of these services that the public providers are unable to furnish. (1977, c. 927, s. 1; 1981, c. 423, s. 1; 2006-69, s. 2.)

§ 115C-111.3. Cost of education of children in group homes, foster homes, etc.

(a) Notwithstanding any other State law and without regard for the place of domicile of a parent, the cost of a free appropriate public education for a child with disabilities who is placed in or assigned to a group home or foster home, under State and federal law, shall be borne by the local board of education in which the group home or foster home is located. However, the local school administrative unit in which a child is domiciled shall transfer to the local school administrative unit in which the institution is located an amount equal to the actual local cost in excess of State and federal funding required to educate that child in the local school administrative unit for the fiscal year after all State and federal funding has been exhausted.

(b) The State Board of Education shall use State and federal funds appropriated for children with disabilities to establish a reserve fund to reimburse local boards of education for the education costs of children assigned to group homes or other facilities as provided in subsection (a) of this section. Local school administrative units may submit a Special State Reserve Program application for foster home or group home children whose special education and related services costs exceed the per child group home allocation.

(c) The Department shall review the current cost of children with disabilities served in the local school administrative units with group homes or foster homes to determine the actual cost of services. (1981, c. 859, s. 29.7; 2002-164, s. 2; 2003-294, s. 1; 2006-69, s. 2.)

§ 115C-111.4. Nonreduction.

Notwithstanding any of the other provisions of this Article, it is the intent of the General Assembly that funds appropriated by it for the operation of programs of special education and related services by local school administrative units not be reduced; rather, that adequate funding be made available to meet the special educational and related services needs of children with disabilities, without regard to which local educational agency has the child in its care, custody, control, or program. (1977, c. 927, s. 1; 1981, c. 423, s. 1; 2006-69, s. 2.)

§ 115C-111.5. Allocation of federal funds.

Whenever any federal monies for the special education and related services for children with disabilities are made available, these funds shall be allocated according to a formula designed by the Board consistent with federal laws and regulations. This formula shall ensure equitable distribution of resources and shall be implemented as funds are made available from federal and State appropriations. (1977, c. 927, s. 1; 1981, c. 423, s. 1; 2006-69, s. 2.)

§ 115C-111.6. Obligation to provide services for preschool children with disabilities.

State funds appropriated to the public schools to implement preschool services for children with disabilities under this Article and IDEA shall be used to provide special education and related services to preschool children with disabilities. These State funds shall be used to supplement and not supplant existing federal, State, and local funding for the public schools.

Preschool children with disabilities will continue to be served by all other State funds to which they are otherwise entitled. (2006-69, s. 2.)

§ 115C-112: Repealed by Session Laws 2006-69, s. 1, effective from and after July 1, 2006.

Part 1G. Council on Educational Services for Exceptional Children.

§ 115C-112.1. Establishment; organization; powers and duties.

(a) There is hereby established an Advisory Council to the State Board of Education to be called the Council on Educational Services for Exceptional Children.

(b) The Council shall consist of a minimum of 24 members to be appointed as follows: four ex officio members; one individual with a disability and one representative of a private school appointed by the Governor; one member of the Senate and one parent of a child with a disability between the ages of birth and 26 appointed by the President Pro Tempore of the Senate; one member of the House of Representatives and one parent of a child with a disability appointed by the Speaker of the House of Representatives; and 14 members appointed by the State Board of Education. The State Board shall appoint members who represent individuals with disabilities, teachers, local school administrative units, institutions of higher education that prepare special education and related services personnel, administrators of programs for children with disabilities, charter schools, parents of children with disabilities, a State or local official who carries out activities under the federal McKinney-Vento Homeless Assistance Act, vocational, community, or business organizations concerned with the provision of transition services, and others as required by IDEA. The majority of members on the Council shall be individuals with disabilities or parents of children with disabilities. The Council shall designate a chairperson from among its members. The designation of the chairperson is subject to the approval of the State Board of Education. The Board shall adopt rules to carry out this subsection.

Ex officio members of the Council shall be the following:

(1) The Secretary of Health and Human Services or the Secretary's designee.

(2) The Secretary of Public Safety or the Secretary's designee.

(3) The Secretary of Public Safety or the Secretary's designee.

(4) The Superintendent of Public Instruction or the Superintendent's designee.

The term of appointment for all members except those appointed by the State Board of Education is two years. The term for members appointed by the State Board of Education is four years. No person shall serve more than two consecutive four-year terms.

Each Council member shall serve without pay, but shall receive travel allowances and per diem in the same amount provided for members of the North Carolina General Assembly.

(c) The Council shall meet in offices provided by the Department of Public Instruction on a date to be agreed upon by the members of the Council from meeting to meeting. The Council shall meet no less than once every three months. The Department of Public Instruction shall provide the necessary secretarial and clerical staff and supplies to accomplish the objectives of the Council.

(d) The Council shall:

(1) Advise the Board with respect to unmet needs within the State in the education of children with disabilities.

(2) Comment publicly on rules, policies, and procedures proposed by the Board regarding the education of children with disabilities.

(3) Assist the Board in developing evaluations and reporting on data to the Secretary of Education under the federal Individuals with Disabilities Education Act (IDEA), as amended.

(4) Advise the State Board in developing corrective action plans to address findings identified in federal monitoring reports required under the federal Individuals with Disabilities Education Act (IDEA), as amended.

(5) Advise the State Board in developing and implementing policies relating to the coordination of services for children with disabilities.

(6) Carry out any other responsibility as designated by federal law or the State Board. (1973, c. 1079, ss. 1-4; 1977, c. 646, ss. 1-5, 1981, c. 423, s. 1; 1991, c. 739, s. 12; 1991 (Reg. Sess., 1992), c. 1038, s. 13; 1997-443, s. 11A.118(a); 1998-202, s. 4(l); 2000-137, s. 4(o); 2001-424, s. 28.29(a); 2006-69, s. 2; 2011-145, s. 19.1(i), (m).)

§ 115C-112.2: Reserved for future codification purposes.

§ 115C-112.3: Reserved for future codification purposes.

§ 115C-112.4: Reserved for future codification purposes.

Part 1H. Special Education Scholarship Grants for Children with Disabilities.

§ 115C-112.5. Definitions.

The following definitions apply in this Part:

(1)   Authority. - The North Carolina State Education Assistance Authority.

(2)   Eligible student. - A child with a disability under the age of 22 who meets all of the following criteria:

a.   Requires an Individualized Education Plan.

b.   Receives special education or related services on a daily basis.

c.   Has not been placed in a nonpublic school or facility by a public agency at public expense.

d.   Has not spent any time enrolled in a postsecondary institution as a full-time student taking at least 12 hours of academic credit.

e.   Has not received a high school diploma.

f.   Meets at least one of the following requirements:

1.   Was enrolled in a North Carolina public school during the previous semester.

2.   Received special education or related services through the North Carolina public schools as a preschool child with a disability during the previous semester.

3.   Received a scholarship grant for the previous semester.

4.   Is eligible for initial enrollment in kindergarten or the first grade in a North Carolina public school.

(3)   Nonpublic school. - A school that meets the requirements of Part 1, 2, or 3 of Article 39 of this Chapter as identified by the Division of Nonpublic Education, Department of Administration.

(4) Scholarship grants. - Grants awarded by the Authority to eligible students. (2013-364, s. 4.)

§ 115C-112.6. Scholarship grants.

(a) The Authority shall make available no later than May 1 annually applications to eligible students for the award of scholarship grants to attend any nonpublic school and to receive special education and related services in a nonpublic school setting. Information about scholarship grants and the application process shall be made available on the Authority's Web site. The Authority shall give priority in awarding scholarship grants to eligible students who received a scholarship grant during the previous semester. Except as otherwise provided by the Authority for prior scholarship grant recipients, scholarship grants shall be awarded to eligible students in the order in which the applications are received.

(b) Scholarship grants awarded to eligible students shall be for amounts of not more than three thousand dollars ($3,000) per semester per eligible student. Eligible students awarded grants may not be enrolled in a public school. Scholarship grants shall be awarded only for the reimbursement of tuition and special education and related services, including those services provided to home schooled students. Parents may only receive reimbursement for tuition if the parent provides documentation that the student was enrolled in nonpublic school for no less than 75 days of the semester for which the parent seeks reimbursement. Parents may only receive reimbursement for related services provided to home schooled students if the parent provides documentation that the student received related services for no less than 75 days of the semester for which the parent seeks reimbursement. The Authority shall notify parents in writing of their eligibility to receive scholarship grants for costs that will be incurred during the spring semester of the following year by December 1 and for costs incurred during the fall semester of that year by July 1. Following the conclusion of each school semester, the parent of an eligible student shall submit to the Authority any receipts or other documentation approved by the Authority to demonstrate the costs incurred during the semester as well as documentation that the student was enrolled in the nonpublic school for no less than 75 days of the semester for which the parent seeks reimbursement for tuition or documentation that related services were provided to a home schooled student for no less than 75 days of the semester for which the parent seeks reimbursement for related services. The Authority shall award a scholarship grant in the amount of costs demonstrated by the parent up to the maximum amount. If the costs incurred by the parent do not meet the maximum amount, the Authority shall use the remainder of those funds for the award of scholarship grants to eligible students for the following semester. The Authority shall award scholarship grants to the parents of eligible students at least semiannually.

(c) After an eligible student's initial receipt of a scholarship grant, the Authority shall ensure that the student is reevaluated at least every three years by the local educational agency in order to verify that the student continues to be a child with a disability.

(d) The Authority shall establish rules and regulations for the administration and awarding of scholarship grants. (2013-364, s. 4.)

§ 115C-112.7. Verification of eligibility.

(a) The Authority may seek verification of information on any application for scholarship grants from eligible students. If a parent fails to cooperate with verification efforts, the Authority shall revoke the award of the scholarship grant to the eligible student.

(b) Parents of applicants for scholarship grants shall authorize the Authority to access any information held by the local educational agency that is needed for verification efforts. (2013-364, s. 4.)

§ 115C-112.8. Authority reporting requirements.

(a) The Authority shall report annually, no later than October 1, to the Joint Legislative Education Oversight Committee on the Special Education Scholarship Grants for Children with Disabilities.

(b) The annual report shall include all of the following information:

(1) Total number, age, and grade level of eligible students receiving scholarship grants.

(2) Total amount of scholarship grant funding awarded.

(3) Nonpublic schools in which scholarship grant recipients are enrolled and the number of scholarship grant students at that school.

(4) The type of special education or related services for which scholarship grants were awarded. (2013-364, s. 4.)

Part 2. Nondiscrimination in Education.

§§ 115C-113 through 115C-115: Repealed by Session Laws 2006-69, s. 1, effective July 10, 2006.

Part 3. Appeals.

§ 115C-116: Repealed by Session Laws 2006-69, s. 1, effective July 10, 2006.

Part 4. Regional Educational Training Center.

§§ 115C-117 through 115C-120: Repealed by Session Laws 1997-18, s. 16.

Part 5. Council on Educational Services for Exceptional Children.

§ 115C-121: Repealed by Session Laws 2006-69, s. 1, effective July 10, 2006.

Part 6. Range of Services Available.

§ 115C-122: Repealed by Session Laws 2006-69, s. 1, effective July 10, 2006.

Part 7. State Schools for Hearing-impaired Children.

§§ 115C-123 through 115C-126.1: Recodified as §§ 143B-216.40 through 143B-216.44 by Session Laws 1997-18, s. 12.

Part 8. State School for Sight-impaired Children.

§§ 115C-127, 115C-128: Recodified as §§ 143B-164.10 and 143B-164.13.

Part 8. State School for Sight-impaired Children.

§ 115C-129: Reserved for future codification purposes.

§§ 115C-130 through 115C-133: Recodified as §§ 143B-164.14 through 143B-164.17.

Part 9. Central Orphanage of North Carolina.

§§ 115C-134 through 115C-138: Repealed by Session Laws 1997-18, s. 14.

Part 10. State and Local Relationships.

§ 115C-139: Repealed by Session Laws 2006-69, s. 1, effective July 10, 2006.

§ 115C-140: Repealed by Session Laws 2006-69, s. 1, effective July 10, 2006.

§ 115C-140.1: Repealed by Session Laws 2006-69, s. 1, effective July 10, 2006.

Part 11. Rules and Regulations.

§ 115C-141: Repealed by Session Laws 2006-69, s. 1, effective July 10, 2006.

Part 12. Nonreduction Provision.

§ 115C-142: Repealed by Session Laws 2006-69, s. 1, effective July 10, 2006.

Part 13. Budget Analysis and Departmental Funding.

§ 115C-143: Repealed by Session Laws 1981 (Regular Session, 1982), c. 1282, s. 29.

§ 115C-144: Repealed by Session Laws 1997-18, s. 7.

§ 115C-145: Repealed by Session Laws 2006-69, s. 1, effective July 10, 2006.

§ 115C-146: Reserved for future codification purposes.

Part 14. Handicapped Children, Ages Three to Five.

§§ 115C-146.1 through 115C-146.4: Repealed by Session Laws 2006-69, s. 1, effective July 10, 2006.

§ 115C-147: Reserved for future codification purposes.

§ 115C-148: Reserved for future codification purposes.

Article 9A.

Children with Chemical Dependency.

§ 115C-149. Policy. Chemically dependent children excluded from provisions of Article 9.

The General Assembly of North Carolina hereby declares that the policy of the State is to ensure that an appropriate education is provided for drug and alcohol addicted children; however, drug and alcohol addicted children are not "children with disabilities" within the meaning of G.S. 115C-106.3(1) unless because of some other condition they meet that definition. (1989, c. 316, s. 1; 2006-69, s. 3(c).)

§ 115C-150. State Board to adopt rules.

The State Board of Education shall adopt rules to ensure that local school administrative units provide an appropriate education for drug and alcohol addicted children. (1989, c. 316.)

§§ 115C-150.1 through 115C-150.4. Reserved for future codification purposes.

Article 9B.

Academically or Intellectually Gifted Students.

§ 115C-150.5. Academically or intellectually gifted students.

The General Assembly believes the public schools should challenge all students to aim for academic excellence and that academically or intellectually gifted students perform or show the potential to perform at substantially high levels of accomplishment when compared with others of their age, experience, or environment. Academically or intellectually gifted students exhibit high performance capability in intellectual areas, specific academic fields, or in both intellectual areas and specific academic fields. Academically or intellectually gifted students require differentiated educational services beyond those ordinarily provided by the regular educational program. Outstanding abilities are present in students from all cultural groups, across all economic strata, and in all areas of human endeavor. (1996, 2nd Ex. Sess., c. 18, s. 18.24(f).)

§ 115C-150.6. State Board of Education responsibilities.

In order to implement this Article, the State Board of Education shall:

(1)   Develop and disseminate guidelines for developing local plans under G.S. 115C-150.7(a). These guidelines should address identification procedures, differentiated curriculum, integrated services, staff development, program evaluation methods, and any other information the State Board considers necessary or appropriate.

(2)   Provide ongoing technical assistance to the local school administrative units in the development, implementation, and evaluation of their local plans under G.S. 115C-150.7. (1996, 2nd Ex. Sess., c. 18, s. 18.24(f).)

§ 115C-150.7. Local plans.

(a)   Each local board of education shall develop a local plan designed to identify and establish a procedure for providing appropriate educational services to each academically or intellectually gifted student. The board shall include parents, the school community, representatives of the community, and others in the development of this plan. The plan may be developed by or in conjunction with other committees.

(b)   Each plan shall include the following components:

(1)   Screening, identification, and placement procedures that allow for the identification of specific educational needs and for the assignment of academically or intellectually gifted students to appropriate services.

(2)   A clear statement of the program to be offered that includes different types of services provided in a variety of settings to meet the diversity of identified academically or intellectually gifted students.

(3)   Measurable objectives for the various services that align with core curriculum and a method to evaluate the plan and the services offered. The evaluation shall focus on improved student performance.

(4) Professional development clearly matched to the goals and objectives of the plan, the needs of the staff providing services to academically or intellectually gifted students, the services offered, and the curricular modifications.

(5) A plan to involve the school community, parents, and representatives of the local community in the ongoing implementation of the local plan, monitoring of the local plan, and integration of educational services for academically or intellectually gifted students into the total school program. This should include a public information component.

(6) The name and role description of the person responsible for implementation of the plan.

(7) A procedure to resolve disagreements between parents or guardians and the local school administrative unit when a child is not identified as an academically or intellectually gifted student or concerning the appropriateness of services offered to the academically or intellectually gifted student.

(8) Any other information the local board considers necessary or appropriate to implement this Article or to improve the educational performance of academically or intellectually gifted students.

(c) Upon its approval of the plan developed under this section, the local board shall submit the plan to the State Board of Education for its review and comments. The local board shall consider the comments it receives from the State Board before it implements the plan.

(d) A plan shall remain in effect for no more than three years; however, the local board may amend the plan as often as it considers necessary or appropriate. Any changes to a plan shall be submitted to the State Board of Education for its review and comments. The local board shall consider the State Board's comments before it implements the changes. (1996, 2nd Ex. Sess., c. 18, s. 18.24(f).)

§ 115C-150.8. Review of Disagreements.

In the event that the procedure developed under G.S. 115C-150.7(b)(7) fails to resolve a disagreement, the parent or guardian may file a petition for a contested case hearing under Article 3 of Chapter 150B of the General Statutes. The scope of review shall be limited to (i) whether the local school administrative unit improperly failed to identify the child as an academically or intellectually gifted student, or (ii) whether the local plan developed under G.S. 115C-150.7 has been implemented appropriately with regard to the child. Following the hearing, the administrative law judge shall make a decision that contains findings of fact and conclusions of law. Notwithstanding the provisions of Chapter 150B of the General Statutes, the decision of the administrative law judge becomes final, is binding on the parties, and is not subject to further review under Article 4 of Chapter 150B of the General Statutes. (1996, 2nd Ex. Sess., c. 18, s. 18.24(f).)

§ 115C-150.9: Reserved for future codification purposes.

§ 115C-150.10: Reserved for future codification purposes.

Article 9C.

Schools for Students with Visual and Hearing Impairments.

§ 115C-150.11. State Board of Education as governing agency.

The State Board of Education shall be the sole governing agency for the Governor Morehead School for the Blind, the Eastern North Carolina School for the Deaf, and the North Carolina School for the Deaf. The Department of Public Instruction shall be responsible for the administration and oversight of a school governed by this Article. (2013-247, s. 2.)

§ 115C-150.12. Applicability of Chapter.

Except as otherwise provided, the requirements of this Chapter shall apply to the schools governed by this Article. (2013-247, s. 2.)

§ 115C-150.13. Rule making.

(a) The State Board of Education shall adopt rules necessary for the Department of Public Instruction to implement this Article, including, at a minimum, rules to address eligibility for admission criteria. In determining rules for admission criteria, the State Board of Education shall take into account the following factors:

(1) State and federal laws.

(2) Optimal academic and communicative outcomes for the child.

(3) Parental input and choice.

(4) Recommendations in a child's Individualized Education Program (IEP).

(b) Rules shall be adopted in accordance with Chapter 150B of the General Statutes. (2013-247, s. 2.)

§ 115C-150.14. Tuition and room and board.

Only children who are residents of North Carolina are entitled to free tuition and room and board at a school governed by this Article. (2013-247, s. 2.)

Article 10.

Vocational and Technical Education.

Part 1. Vocational and Technical Education Programs.

§ 115C-151. Statement of purpose.

It is the intent of the General Assembly that vocational and technical education be an integral part of the educational process. The State Board of Education shall administer through local boards of education a comprehensive program of vocational and technical education that shall be available to all students, with priority given to students in grades eight through 12, who desire it in the public secondary schools and middle schools of this State. The purposes of vocational and technical education in North Carolina public secondary schools shall be:

(1) Occupational Skill Development. - To prepare individuals for paid or unpaid employment in recognized occupations, new occupations, and emerging occupations.

(2) Preparation for Advanced Education. - To prepare individuals for participation in advanced or highly skilled vocational and technical education.

(3) Career Development; Introductory. - To assist individuals in the making of informed and meaningful occupational choices.

It is also legislative intent to authorize the State Board of Education to support appropriate vocational and technical education instruction and related services for individuals who have special vocational and technical education needs which can be fulfilled through a comprehensive vocational and technical education program as designated by State Board of Education policy or federal vocational and technical education legislation. (1977, c. 490, s. 2; 1981, c. 423, s. 1; 1987, c. 738, s. 183; 1993, c. 180, s. 3; 2004-124, s. 7.15(b).)

§ 115C-152. Definitions.

The State Board of Education shall provide appropriate definitions to vocational and technical education programs, services, and activities in grades 6-12 not otherwise included in this Part. As used in this Part, unless the context requires otherwise:

(1) "Career development; introductory" means an instructional program, service, or activity designed to familiarize individuals with the broad range of occupations for which special skills are required and the requisites for careers in such occupations.

(2)   "Comprehensive vocational and technical education" means instructional programs, services, or activities directly related to preparation for and placement in employment, for advanced technical preparation, or for the making of informed and meaningful educational and occupational choices.

(3)   "Occupational skill development" means a program, service, or activity designed to prepare individuals for paid or unpaid employment as semiskilled or skilled workers, technicians, or professional-support personnel in recognized occupations and in new and emerging occupations including occupations or a trade, technical, business, health, office, homemaking, homemaking-related, agricultural, marketing, and other nature. Instruction is designed to fit individuals for initial employment in a specific occupation or a cluster of closely related occupations in an occupational field. This instruction includes education in technology, manipulative skills, theory, auxiliary information, application of academic skills, and other associated knowledges.

(4)   "Preparation for advanced education" means a program, service, or activity designed to prepare individuals for participation in advanced or highly skilled post-secondary and technical education programs leading to employment in specific occupations or a cluster of closely related occupations and for participation in vocational and technical education teacher education programs. (1977, c. 490, s. 2; 1981, c. 423, s. 1; 1987, c. 738, s. 184; 1993, c. 180, s. 3.)

§ 115C-153. Administration of vocational and technical education.

The State Board of Education shall be the sole State agency for the State administration of vocational and technical education at all levels, shall be designated as the State Board of Vocational and Technical Education, and shall have all necessary authority to cooperate with any and all federal agencies in the administration of national acts assisting vocational and technical education, to administer any legislation pursuant thereto enacted by the General Assembly of North Carolina, and to cooperate with local boards of education in providing vocational and technical education programs, services, and activities for youth and adults residing in the areas under their jurisdiction. (1977, c. 490, s. 2; 1981, c. 423, s. 1; 1993, c. 180, s. 3.)

§ 115C-154. Duties of the State Board of Education.

In carrying out its duties, the State Board of Education shall develop and implement any policies, rules, regulations, and procedures as necessary to ensure vocational and technical education programs of high quality. The State Board of Education shall prepare a Master Plan for Vocational and Technical Education. The plan, to be updated periodically, shall ensure minimally that:

(1)   Articulation shall occur with institutions, agencies, councils, and other organizations having responsibilities for work force preparedness.

(2)   Business, industrial, agricultural, and lay representatives, including parents of students enrolled in Vocational and Technical Education courses, organized as advisory committees have been utilized in the development of decisions affecting vocational and technical education programs and services.

(3)   Public hearings are conducted annually to afford the public an opportunity to express their views concerning the State Board's plan and to suggest changes in the plan.

(4)   The plan describes the State's policy for vocational and technical education and the system utilized for the delivery of vocational and technical education programs, services, and activities. The policy shall include priorities of curriculum, integration of vocational and academic education, technical preparation, and youth apprenticeships.

(5)   A professionally and occupationally qualified staff is employed and organized in a manner to assure efficient and effective State leadership for vocational and technical education. Provisions shall be made for such functions as: planning, administration, supervision, personnel development, curriculum development, vocational student organization and coordination research and evaluation, and such others as the State Board may direct.

(6)   An appropriate supply of qualified personnel is trained for program expansion and replacements through cooperative arrangements with institutions of higher education and other institutions or agencies, including where necessary financial support of programs and curriculums designed for the preparation of vocational administrators, supervisors, coordinators, instructors, and support personnel.

(7)   Minimum standards shall be prescribed for personnel employed at the State and local levels.

(8) Local boards of education submit to the State Board of Education a local plan for vocational and technical education that has been prepared in accordance with the procedures set forth in the Master Plan for Vocational and Technical Education.

(9) Appropriate minimum standards for vocational and technical education programs, services, and activities shall be established, promulgated, supervised, monitored, and maintained. These standards shall specify characteristics such as program objectives, competencies, course sequence, program duration, class size, supervised on-the-job experiences, vocational student organization, school-to-work transition programs, qualifications of instructors, and all other standards necessary to ensure that all programs conducted by local school administrative units shall be of high quality, relevant to student needs, and coordinated with employment opportunities.

(10) A system of continuing qualitative and quantitative evaluation of all vocational and technical education programs, services, and activities supported under the provisions of this Part shall be established, maintained, and utilized periodically. One component of the system shall be follow-up studies of employees and former students of vocational and technical education programs who have been out of school for one year, and for five years to ascertain the effectiveness of instruction, services, and activities. (1977, c. 490, s. 2; 1981, c. 423, s. 1; 1983, c. 750, s. 1; 1993, c. 180, s. 3.)

§ 115C-154.1. Approval of local vocational and technical education plans or applications.

The State Board of Education shall not approve any local vocational and technical education plans or applications unless:

(1) The programs are in accordance with the purposes of G.S. 115C-151;

(2) The vocational programs and courses are not duplicated within a local school administrative unit, unless the unit has data to justify the duplication or the unit has a plan to redirect the duplicative programs within three years;

(3) For all current job skill programs, there is a documented need, based on labor market data or follow-up data, or there is a plan to redirect the program within two years;

(4) New vocational programs show documented need based on student demand, or for new job skill programs, based on student and labor market demand; and

(5) All programs are responsive to technological advances, changing characteristics of the work force, and the academic, technical, and attitudinal development of students.

Local programs using the cooperative vocational and technical education method shall be approved subject to students enrolled being placed in employment commensurate with the respective program criteria. (1987, c. 738, s. 185; 1993, c. 180, s. 3.)

§ 115C-154.2. Vocational and technical education equipment standards.

The State Board of Education shall develop equipment standards for each vocational and technical education program level and shall assist local school administrative units in determining the adequacy of equipment for each vocational and technical education program available in each local school administrative unit.

The State Board shall also develop a plan to assure that minimum equipment standards for each program are met to the extent that State, local, and federal funds are available for that purpose. The State Board shall consider all reasonable and prudent means to meet these minimum equipment standards and to ensure a balanced vocational and technical education program for students in the public schools. (1991, c. 570; 1993, c. 180, s. 3.)

§ 115C-155. Acceptance of benefits of federal vocational acts.

The State of North Carolina, through the State Board of Education, may accept all the provisions and benefits of acts passed by the Congress of the United States providing federal funds for vocational and technical education programs: Provided, however, that the State Board of Education shall not accept those funds upon any condition that the public schools of this State shall be operated contrary to any provision of the Constitution or statutes of this State. (1977, c. 490, s. 2; 1981, c. 423, s. 1; 1993, c. 180, s. 3.)

§ 115C-156. State funds for vocational and technical education.

It is the intent of the General Assembly of North Carolina to appropriate funds for each fiscal year to support the purposes of vocational and technical education as set forth in G.S. 115C-151. From funds appropriated, the State Board of Education shall establish a sum of money for State administration of vocational and technical education and shall allocate the remaining sum on an equitable basis to local school administrative units, except that a contingency fund is established to correct excess deviations that may occur during the regular school year. In the administration of State funds, the State Board of Education shall adopt such policies and procedures as necessary to ensure that the funds appropriated are used for the purpose stated in this Part and consistent with the policy set forth in the Master Plan for Vocational Education. (1977, c. 490, s. 2; 1981, c. 423, s. 1; 1993, c. 180, s. 3.)

§ 115C-156.1: Repealed by Session Laws 1993, c. 180, s. 3.

§ 115C-156.2. Industry certifications and credentials program.

(a)   It is the intent of the State to encourage students to enroll in and successfully complete rigorous coursework and credentialing processes in career and technical education to enable success in the workplace. To attain this goal, to the extent funds are made available for this purpose, students shall be supported to earn approved industry certifications and credentials:

(1)   Students enrolled in public schools and in career and technical education courses shall be exempt from paying any fees for one administration of examinations leading to industry certifications and credentials pursuant to rules adopted by the State Board of Education.

(2)   Each school year, at such time as agreed to by the Department of Commerce and the State Board of Education, the Department of Commerce shall provide the State Board of Education with a list of those occupations in high need of additional skilled employees. If the occupations identified in such list are not substantially the same as those occupations identified in the list from the prior year, reasonable notice of such changes shall be provided to local school administrative units.

(3) Local school administrative units shall consult with their local industries, employers, and workforce development boards to identify industry certification and credentials that the local school administrative unit may offer to best meet State and local workforce needs.

(b) Beginning in 2014, the State Board of Education shall report to the Joint Legislative Education Oversight Committee by September 1 of each year on the number of students in career and technical education courses who earned (i) community college credit and (ii) related industry certifications and credentials. (2013-360, s. 8.28(b).)

§ 115C-157. Responsibility of local boards of education.

Each local school administrative unit, shall provide free appropriate vocational and technical education instruction, activities, and services in accordance with the provisions of this Part for all youth, with priority given to youth in grades eight through 12, who elect the instruction and shall have responsibility for administering the instruction, activities, and services in accordance with federal and State law and State Board of Education policies. (1977, c. 490, s. 2; 1981, c. 423, s. 1; 1993, c. 180, s. 3; 2004-124, s. 7.15(c).)

§ 115C-158. Federal funds division.

The division between secondary and post-secondary educational systems and institutions of federal funds for which the State Board of Vocational and Technical Education has responsibility shall, within discretionary limits established by law, require the concurrence of the State Board of Education and the State Board of Community Colleges on and after January 1, 1981. The portion of the approved State Plan for post-secondary vocational and technical education required by G.S. 115C-154 shall be as approved by the State Board of Community Colleges. (1979, 2nd Sess., c. 1130, s. 4; 1981, c. 423, s. 1; 1993, c. 180, s. 3.)

Part 2. Vocational and Technical Education Production Work Activities.

§ 115C-159. Statement of purpose.

It is the intent of the General Assembly that practical work experiences within the school and outside the school, which are valuable to students and which are under the supervision of a teacher, should be encouraged as a part of vocational and technical education instruction in the public secondary schools and middle schools when those experiences are organized and maintained to the best advantage of the vocational programs. Those activities are a part of the instructional activities in the vocational programs and are not to be construed as engaging in business. Those services, products, and properties generated through these instructional activities are exempt from the requirements of G.S. 115C-518; the local board shall adopt rules for the disposition of these services, products, and properties. Local boards of education may use available financial resources to support that instruction. (1977, c. 490, s. 4; 1981, c. 423, s. 1; 1983, c. 750, s. 2; 1985, c. 479, s. 32; 1987, c. 738, s. 184; 1993, c. 180, s. 3.)

§ 115C-160. Definitions.

The State Board of Education shall provide appropriate definitions necessary to this part of vocational and technical education instruction not otherwise included in this Part. As used in this Part, unless the context requires otherwise:

(1) The term "building trades training" means the development of vocational skills through the construction of dwellings or other buildings and related activities by students in vocational and technical education programs.

(2) The term "production work" means production activities and services performed by vocational and technical education classes under contract with a second party for remuneration. (1977, c. 490, s. 4; 1981, c. 423, s. 1; 1993, c. 180, s. 3.)

§ 115C-161. Duties of the State Board of Education.

The State Board of Education is authorized and directed to establish, maintain, and implement such policies, rules, regulations, and procedures not in conflict with State law or other State Board policies as necessary to assist local boards of education in the conduct of production work experiences performed in connection with approved State Board of Education vocational and technical education programs. (1977, c. 490, s. 4; 1981, c. 423, s. 1; 1993, c. 180, s. 3.)

§ 115C-162. Use of proceeds derived from production work.

Unless elsewhere authorized in these statutes, local boards of education shall deposit to the appropriate school account, no later than the end of the next business day after receipt of funds, all proceeds derived from the sale of products or services from production work experiences. These proceeds shall be established as a revolving fund to be used solely in operating and improving vocational and technical education programs. (1977, c. 490, s. 4; 1981, c. 423, s. 1; 1993, c. 180, s. 3.)

§ 115C-163. Acquisition of land for agricultural education instructional programs.

Local boards of education may acquire by gift, purchase, or lease for not less than the useful life of any project to be conducted upon the premises, a parcel of land suitable for a land laboratory to provide students with practical instruction in soil science, plant science, horticulture, forestry, animal husbandry, and other subjects related to the agriculture curriculum.

Each deed, lease, or other agreement for land shall be made to the respective local board of education in which the school offering instruction in agriculture is located; and title to such land shall be examined and approved by the school attorney.

Any land laboratory thus acquired shall be assigned to the agricultural education program of the school, to be managed with the advice of an agricultural education advisory committee.

The products of the land laboratory not needed for public school purposes may be sold to the public: Provided, however, that all proceeds from the sale of products shall be deposited in the appropriate school account no later than the end of the next business day after receipt of funds. The proceeds shall be established as a revolving fund to be used solely in operating and improving vocational and technical education programs. (1977, c. 490, s. 4; 1981, c. 423, s. 1; 1993, c. 180, s. 3.)

§ 115C-164. Building trades training.

In the establishment and implementation of production work experience policies, the State Board of Education shall be guided as follows:

(1) Local boards of education may use supplementary tax funds or other local funds available for the support of vocational and technical education to purchase and develop suitable building sites on which dwellings or other buildings are to be constructed by vocational and technical education trade classes of each public school operated by local boards of education. Local boards of education may use these funds for each school to pay the fees necessary in securing and recording deeds to these properties for each public school operated by local boards of education and to purchase all materials needed to complete the construction of buildings by vocational and technical education trade classes and for development of site and property by other vocational and technical education classes. Local boards of education may use these funds to acquire skilled services, including electrical, plumbing, heating, sewer, water, transportation, grading, and landscaping needed in the construction and completion of buildings, that cannot be supplied by the students in vocational and technical education trade classes.

(2) Local boards of education may, in conjunction with or in lieu of subdivision (1) of this section, contract with recognized building trades educational foundations or associations in the purchase of land for the construction and development of buildings: Provided however, that all contracts shall be in accordance with the requirements set forth by the State Board of Education. (1977, c. 490, s. 4; 1981, c. 423, s. 1; 1993, c. 180, s. 3.)

§ 115C-165. Advisory committee on production work activities.

The board of education of each local school administrative unit in which the proposed production work activities are to be undertaken shall appoint appropriate advisory committees of no less than three persons residing within that administrative unit for each program (or in the case of Trade and Industrial

Education, for each specialty) for the purpose of reviewing and making recommendations on such production work activities. Respective advisory committee members shall be lay persons who are actively involved in the appropriate business or trade. No production work activity shall be undertaken without the involvement of the appropriate advisory committee. (1977, c. 490, s. 4; 1981, c. 423, s. 1; 1983, c. 750, s. 3.)

Part 3. Eye Safety Devices Required.

§ 115C-166. Eye protection devices required in certain courses.

The governing board or authority of any public or private school or educational institution within the State, wherein shops or laboratories are conducted providing instructional or experimental programs involving:

(1)   Hot solids, liquids or molten metals;

(2)   Milling, sawing, turning, shaping, cutting, or stamping of any solid materials;

(3)   Heat treatment, tempering, or kiln firing of any metal or other materials;

(4)   Gas or electric arc welding;

(5)   Repair or servicing of any vehicle; or

(6)   Caustic or explosive chemicals or materials,

shall provide for and require that every student and teacher wear industrial-quality eye protective devices at all times while participating in any such program. These industrial-quality eye protective devices shall be furnished free of charge to the student and teacher. (1969, c. 1050, s. 1; 1981, c. 423, s. 1.)

§ 115C-167. Visitors to wear eye safety devices.

Visitors to such shops and laboratories shall be furnished with and required to wear such eye safety devices while such programs are in progress. (1977, c. 1050, s. 2; 1981, c. 423, s. 1.)

§ 115C-168. "Industrial-quality eye protective devices" defined.

"Industrial-quality eye protective devices", as used in G.S. 115C-166, means devices meeting the standards of the U.S.A. Standard Practice for Occupational and Educational Eye and Face Protection, Z 87.1-1968 approved by the U.S.A. Standards Institute, Inc. (1969, c. 1050, s. 3; 1981, c. 423, s. 1.)

§ 115C-169. Corrective-protective devices.

In those cases where corrective-protective devices that require prescription ophthalmic lenses are necessary, such devices shall only be supplied by those persons licensed by the State to prescribe or supply corrective-protective devices. (1969, c. 1050, s. 4; 1981, c. 423, s. 1.)

§§ 115C-170 through 115C-174. Reserved for future codification purposes.

Article 10A.

Testing.

Part 1. Commission on Testing.

§§ 115C-174.1 through 115C-174.6: Repealed by Session Laws 1995, c. 524, s. 1.

§ 115C-174.7. Reserved for future codification purposes.

§ 115C-174.8. Reserved for future codification purposes.

§ 115C-174.9. Reserved for future codification purposes.

Part 2. Statewide Testing Program.

§ 115C-174.10. Purposes of the Statewide Testing Program.

The testing programs in this Article have three purposes: (i) to assure that all high school graduates possess those minimum skills and that knowledge thought necessary to function as a member of society; (ii) to provide a means of identifying strengths and weaknesses in the education process in order to improve instructional delivery; and (iii) to establish additional means for making the education system at the State, local, and school levels accountable to the public for results. (1977, c. 522, s. 1; 1981, c. 423, s. 1; 1985 (Reg. Sess., 1986), c. 1014, s. 74(a); 1995, c. 524, s. 2; 2009-451, s. 7.20(a).)

§ 115C-174.11. Components of the testing program.

(a)   Assessment Instruments for Kindergarten, First, Second, and Third Grades. - The State Board of Education shall develop, adopt, and provide to the local school administrative units developmentally appropriate individualized assessment instruments consistent with the Basic Education Program and Part 1A of Article 8 of this Chapter for the kindergarten, first, second, and third grades. Local school administrative units shall use these assessment instruments provided to them by the State Board for kindergarten, first, second, and third grade students to assess progress, diagnose difficulties, and inform instruction and remediation needs. Local school administrative units shall not use standardized tests for summative assessment of kindergarten, first, and second grade students except as required as a condition of receiving federal grants.

(b)   Repealed by Session Laws 2009-451, s. 7.20(c), effective July 1, 2009.

(c)   Annual Testing Program. -

(1) The State Board of Education shall adopt the tests for grades three through 12 that are required by federal law or as a condition of a federal grant. These tests shall be designed to measure progress toward reading, communication skills, and mathematics for grades three through eight, and toward competencies for grades nine through 12. Students who do not pass the tests adopted for eighth grade shall be provided remedial instruction in the ninth grade.

(2) If the State Board of Education finds that additional testing in grades three through 12 is desirable to allow comparisons with national indicators of student achievement, that testing shall be conducted with the smallest size sample of students necessary to assure valid comparisons with other states.

(3) The State Board of Education shall continue to participate in the development of the Common Core State Standards in conjunction with the consortium of other states, review all national assessments developed by both multistate consortia, and implement the assessments that the State Board deems most appropriate to assess student achievement on the Common Core State Standards.

(4) To the extent funds are made available, the State Board of Education shall plan for and require the administration of the ACT test for all students in the eleventh grade unless the student has already taken a comparable test and scored at or above a level set by the State Board. The State Board of Education shall require the administration of an alternate to the ACT or an alternate to the PLAN precursor test to the ACT to a student who (i) exhibits severe and pervasive delays in all areas of conceptual, linguistic, and academic development and in adaptive behaviors, including communication, daily living skills, and self-care, (ii) is following the extended content standards of the Standard Course of Study as provided in G.S. 115C-81, or is following a course of study that, upon completing high school, may not lead to admission into a college-level course of study resulting in a college degree, and (iii) has a written parental request for an alternate assessment.

The State Board of Education shall ensure that parents of students enrolled in all public schools, including charter and regional schools, have the necessary information to make informed decisions regarding participation in the ACT and the PLAN precursor test to the ACT.

Alternate assessment and ACT assessment results of students with disabilities shall be included in school accountability reports, including charter and regional schools, provided by the State Board of Education.

(d) Except as provided in subsection (c) of this section, the State Board of Education shall not require the public schools to administer any standardized tests except for those required by federal law or as a condition of a federal grant.

The State Board of Education shall adopt and provide to local school administrative units all tests required by federal law or as a condition of a federal grant. (1977, c. 522, s. 1; c. 541, s. 1; 1981, c. 423, s. 1; 1983, c. 627, s. 1; 1985, c. 409, ss. 1, 2; 1985 (Reg. Sess., 1986), c. 1014, s. 74(a); 1987, c. 738, s. 180(a); 1987 (Reg. Sess., 1988), c. 1086, s. 77(a); 1989, c. 778, ss. 4, 5; 1995, c. 524, s. 3; 1996, 2nd Ex. Sess., c. 18, s. 18.14; 1998-212, s. 9.15(b); 1998-220, ss. 6, 11; 2000-140, s. 21(a), (b); 2003-275, s. 1; 2004-124, ss. 7.11, 7.27; 2005-458, s. 3; 2009-451, s. 7.20(c); 2010-31, s. 7.30; 2011-8, s. 1; 2011-145, s. 7.30(a); 2011-280, ss. 1, 2.1; 2012-142, s. 7A.1(e); 2013-208, s. 1.)

§ 115C-174.12. Responsibilities of agencies.

(a) The State Board of Education shall establish policies and guidelines necessary for minimizing the time students spend taking tests administered through State and local testing programs, for minimizing the frequency of field testing at any one school, and for otherwise carrying out the provisions of this Article. These policies and guidelines shall include the following:

(1) Schools shall devote no more than two days of instructional time per year to the taking of practice tests that do not have the primary purpose of assessing current student learning;

(2) Students in a school shall not be subject to field tests or national tests during the two-week period preceding the administration of end-of-grade tests, end-of-course tests, or the school's regularly scheduled final exams; and

(3) No school shall participate in more than two field tests at any one grade level during a school year; [and]

(4) All annual assessments of student achievement adopted by the State Board of Education pursuant to G.S. 115C-174.11(c)(1) and (3) and all final exams for courses shall be administered within the final 10 instructional days of the school year for year-long courses and within the final five instructional days of the semester for semester courses. Exceptions shall be permitted to accommodate a student's individualized education program and section 504 (29 U.S.C. § 794) plans and for the administration of final exams for courses with national or international curricula required to be held at designated times.

These policies shall reflect standard testing practices to insure reliability and validity of the sample testing. The results of the field tests shall be used in the final design of each test. The State Board of Education's policies regarding the testing of children with disabilities shall (i) provide broad accommodations and alternate methods of assessment that are consistent with a student's individualized education program and section 504 (29 U.S.C. § 794) plans, (ii) prohibit the use of statewide tests as the sole determinant of decisions about a student's graduation or promotion, and (iii) provide parents with information about the Statewide Testing Program and options for children with disabilities. The State Board shall report its proposed policies and proposed changes in policies to the Joint Legislative Education Oversight Committee prior to adoption.

The State Board of Education may appoint an Advisory Council on Testing to assist in carrying out its responsibilities under this Article.

(b) The Superintendent of Public Instruction shall be responsible, under policies adopted by the State Board of Education, for the statewide administration of the testing program provided by this Article.

(b1) The Superintendent shall notify local boards of education by October 1 of each year of any field tests that will be administered in their schools during the school year, the schools at which the field tests will be administered, and the specific field tests that will be administered at each school.

(c) Local boards of education shall cooperate with the State Board of Education in implementing the provisions of this Article, including the regulations and policies established by the State Board of Education. Local school administrative units shall use the annual tests to fulfill the purposes set out in this Article. Local school administrative units are encouraged to continue to develop local testing programs designed to diagnose student needs. (1977, c. 522, ss. 4-6; c. 541, ss. 2, 5-7; 1981, c. 423, s. 1; 1985 (Reg. Sess., 1986), c.

1014, s. 74(a); 1995, c. 524, s. 4; 2001-424, s. 28.17(f); 2002-126, s. 7.30; 2002-159, s. 70; 2005-276, s. 7.37; 2009-451, s. 7.20(d); 2011-145, s. 7.13(q); 2011-391, s. 14(b); 2013-360, s. 9.2(a).)

§ 115C-174.13. Public records exemption.

Any written material containing the identifiable scores of individual students on any test taken pursuant to the provisions of this Article is not a public record within the meaning of G.S. 132-1 and shall not be made public by any person, except as permitted under the provisions of the Family Educational and Privacy Rights Act of 1974, 20 U.S.C. 1232g. (1977, c. 522, s. 7; c. 541, s. 8; 1981, c. 423, s. 1; 1985 (Reg. Sess., 1986), c. 1014, s. 74(a).)

§ 115C-174.14. Provisions for nonpublic schools.

All components of the Statewide Testing Program shall be made available to nonpublic schools in the manner prescribed in G.S. 115C-551 and G.S. 115C-559. (1977, c. 522, s. 8; c. 541, s. 9; 1981, c. 423, s. 1; 1985 (Reg. Sess., 1986), c. 1014, s. 74(a).)

§ 115C-174.15. Reserved for future codification purposes.

§ 115C-174.16. Reserved for future codification purposes.

§ 115C-174.17. Reserved for future codification purposes.

Part 3. Preliminary Scholastic Aptitude Test Opportunities Encouraged.

§ 115C-174.18. Opportunity to take Preliminary SAT/National Merit Scholarship Qualifying Test (PSAT/NMSQT).

Every student in the eighth through tenth grades who has completed Algebra I or who is in the last month of Algebra I shall be given an opportunity to take a version of either the Preliminary SAT/National Merit Scholarship Qualifying Test (PSAT/NMSQT) or the PLAN precursor test to the ACT, at the discretion of the local school administrative unit, one time at no cost to the student. The maximum amount of State funds used for this purpose shall be the cost of the PSAT/NMSQT. (1989, c. 752, s. 77(a); 2005-154, s. 1; 2013-360, s. 8.27(c); 2013-363, s. 3.18.)

§ 115-174.19: Repealed by Session Laws 1993 (Reg. Sess., 1994), c. 677, s. 5.

§ 115C-174.20: Reserved for future codification purposes.

§ 115C-174.21: Reserved for future codification purposes.

Part 4. Student Diagnostic Tests.

§ 115C-174.22. Tools for student learning.

To the extent funds are made available for this purpose, and except as otherwise provided in G.S. 115C-174.11(c)(4), the State Board shall plan for and require the administration of diagnostic tests in the eighth and tenth grades that align to the ACT test in order to help diagnose student learning and provide for students an indication of whether they are on track to be remediation-free at a community college or university. (2011-145, s. 7.30(b); 2011-280, ss. 2, 2.1; 2013-208, s. 2.)

§ 115C-174.23: Reserved for future codification purposes.

§ 115C-174.24: Reserved for future codification purposes.

Part 5. Career Readiness.

§ 115C-174.25. WorkKeys.

To the extent funds are made available for this purpose, the State Board shall plan for and require local school administrative units to make available the appropriate WorkKeys tests for all students who complete the second level of vocational/career courses. (2011-145, s. 7.30(b); 2011-280, ss. 2, 2.1.)

Article 11.

High School Competency Testing.

§§ 115C-175 through 115C-188: Repealed by Session Laws 1985 (Regular Session, 1986), c. 1014, s. 74(a).

Article 12.

Statewide Testing Program.

§§ 115C-189 through 115C-202: Repealed by Session Laws 1985 (Reg. Sess., 1986), c. 1014, s. 74(a).

Article 13.

Community Schools Act.

§ 115C-203. Title of Article.

This Article shall be known and may be cited as the "Community Schools Act." (1977, c. 682; 1981, c. 423, s. 1.)

§ 115C-204. Purpose of Article.

The purpose of this Article is to encourage greater community involvement in the public schools and greater community use of public school facilities. To this end it is declared to be the policy of this State:

(1)   To provide for increased involvement by citizens in their local schools through community schools advisory councils.

(2)   To assure maximum use of public school facilities by the citizens of each community in this State.

It is further declared to be the policy of this State that, to the extent sufficient funds are made available, each local board of education shall comply with the provisions of this Article. (1977, c. 682; 1981, c. 423, s. 1.)

§ 115C-205. Definitions.

As used in this Article:

(1) The term "community schools advisory council" means a committee of citizens organized to advise community school coordinators, administrators, and local boards of education in the involvement of citizens in the educational process and in the use of public school facilities.

(2) The term "community schools coordinator" means an employee of a local board of education whose responsibility it is to promote and direct maximum use of the public schools and public school facilities as centers for community development.

(3) The term "interagency council" means a committee of agency and organizational representatives appointed by the Governor to work with the Superintendent of Public Instruction concerning the involvement of statewide agencies and organizations with the public schools.

(4) The term "public school facility" means any education facility under the jurisdiction of a local board of education, whether termed an elementary school, middle school, junior high school, high school or union school. (1977, c. 682; 1981, c. 423, s. 1.)

§ 115C-206. State Board of Education; duties; responsibilities.

The Superintendent of Public Instruction shall prepare and present to the State Board of Education recommendations for general guidelines for encouraging increased community involvement in the public schools and use of public school facilities. These recommendations shall include, but shall not be limited to provisions for:

(1) The use of public school facilities by governmental, charitable or civic organizations for activities within the community.

(2) The utilization of the talents and abilities of volunteers within the community for the enhancement of public school programs including tutoring, counseling and cultural programs and projects.

(3) Increased communications between the staff and faculty of the public schools, other community institutions and agencies, and citizens in the community.

Based on the recommendations of the Superintendent of Public Instruction, the State Board of Education shall adopt appropriate policies and guidelines for encouraging increased community involvement in the public schools and use of the public school facilities. (1977, c. 682; 1981, c. 423, s. 1; 1995, c. 450, s. 8.)

§ 115C-207. Authority and responsibility of local boards of education.

Every local board of education that uses State funds to implement programs under this Article shall:

(1) Develop programs and plans for increased community involvement in the public schools based upon policies and guidelines adopted by the State Board of Education.

(1a) Develop policies and programs designed to encourage the use of community-based academic booster organizations, which may be known as Community Achievement Network - Developing Our Educational Resources (CAN DOER) organizations, to provide tutoring and other appropriate services to encourage and support student academic achievement.

(1b) Develop policies and/or procedures for approving the use of volunteer organizations and for approving the use of individual volunteers.

(1c) Develop policies and/or procedures designed to make information available to parents and students about what tutoring and other academic support services are available to students in the community or through school volunteers or other community organizations.

(2) Develop programs and plans for increased community use of public school facilities based upon policies and guidelines adopted by the State Board of Education.

(3) Establish rules governing the implementation of such programs and plans in its public schools and submit these rules along with adopted programs and plans to the State Board of Education for approval by the State Board of Education.

Programs and plans developed by a local board of education may provide for the establishment of one or more community schools advisory councils for the public schools under the board's jurisdiction and for the employment of one or more community schools coordinators. The local board of education shall establish the terms and conditions of employment for the community schools coordinators.

Every local board of education using State funds to implement a community schools program under this Article may enter into agreements with other local boards of education, agencies and institutions for the joint development of plans and programs and the joint expenditure of these State funds. (1977, c. 682; 1981, c. 423, s. 1; 1995, c. 450, s. 9; 2009-453, s. 1.)

§ 115C-208. Community schools advisory councils; duties; responsibilities; membership.

Every local board of education that establishes a community schools program under this Article may establish one or more community schools advisory councils which may become involved in matters affecting the educational process in accordance with rules established by the local board of education and approved by the State Board of Education and further may consider ways of increasing community involvement in the public schools and utilization of public school facilities. Community schools advisory councils may assist local boards of education in the development and preparation of the plans and programs to achieve such goals, may assist in the implementation of such plans and programs and may provide such other assistance as may be requested by the local boards of education.

Community schools advisory councils may work with local school officials and personnel, parent-teacher organizations, and community groups and agencies in providing maximum opportunities for public schools to serve the communities, and may encourage the maximum use of volunteers in the public schools.

At least one half of the members of each community schools advisory council should be the parents of students in the particular public school system: Provided, that less than twenty-five percent (25%) of the pupils attending a particular school reside outside the immediate community of the school, at least one half of the members should be parents of students in the particular school for which the advisory council is established. Wherever possible the local board of education is encouraged to include at least one high school student. The size of the councils and the terms of membership on the councils shall be determined by the local board of education in accordance with the State guidelines. (1977, c. 682; 1979, c. 828; 1981, c. 423, s. 1; 1995, c. 450, s. 10.)

§ 115C-209. Community schools coordinators.

Every local board of education may employ one or more community schools coordinators and shall establish the terms and conditions of their employment. Community schools coordinators shall be responsible for:

(1) Providing support to the community schools advisory councils and public school officials.

(2) Fostering cooperation between the local board of education and appropriate community agencies.

(3) Encouraging maximum use of community volunteers in the public schools.

(4) Performing any other duties as may be assigned by the local superintendent and the local board of education, consistent with the purposes of this Article. (1977, c. 682; 1981, c. 423, s. 1; 1995, c. 450, s. 11.)

§ 115C-209.1. Nondisclosure of certain volunteer records.

(a) The records comprising a volunteer file of a local school administrative unit are not public records as provided in Chapter 132 of the General Statutes. These records shall be open for inspection only to the following individuals:

(1) The volunteer, former volunteer, individual who applied to be a volunteer, or that individual's properly authorized agent who may examine the individual's file in its entirety at any reasonable time.

(2) The superintendent and other supervisory personnel.

(3) The parent or guardian of any student with whom the volunteer has or had contact.

(4) Members of the local board of education and the board's attorney.

(5) A party to a lawsuit, by authority of a subpoena or proper court order, only to the extent authorized by and in accordance with that subpoena or court order.

(b) A local board of education shall also release or permit the inspection of a volunteer file, except as prohibited by State or federal law, if prior to the release of the information or inspection of the file:

(1) The local board of education determines that the release of the information or inspection of the file is essential (i) to maintaining the integrity of the local board of education or (ii) to maintaining the level or quality of services provided by the local board of education; or

(2) The local board of education makes a written finding that there is a substantial showing of the criteria set forth in subdivision (1) of this subsection. The local board of education's written finding shall be a public record.

(c) A volunteer shall be notified at the time the individual applies to volunteer that the local board of education may maintain a volunteer file on the individual, and that information in that file may be open to inspection in accordance with this section.

(d) This section shall not be construed to require a local school administrative unit to maintain records on volunteers, former volunteers, or individuals applying to be volunteers.

(e) As used in this section, the following terms mean:

(1) Volunteer. - An individual who provides services to a local board of education without expectation of compensation and with the understanding that the local board of education is under no obligation to continue accepting those services or to compensate the volunteer for them.

(2) Volunteer file. - Any information collected by the local board of education regarding volunteers, former volunteers, and individuals applying to be volunteers that relates to the individual's application, selection or nonselection, performance, disciplinary action, or termination, wherever that information is located or in whatever form it is maintained. (2003-353, s. 1.)

Article 13A.

State Advisory Council on Indian Education.

§ 115C-210. Council established.

There is hereby established an advisory council to the State Board of Education to be known as the "State Advisory Council on Indian Education". (1987 (Reg. Sess., 1988), c. 1084, s. 1.)

§ 115C-210.1. Membership - How appointed.

The Council shall consist of 15 members, as follows:

(1) Two legislative members (one senator appointed by the President Pro Tempore of the Senate and one representative appointed by the Speaker of the House);

(2) Two Indian members from higher education to be appointed by the Board of Governors of the University system;

(3) One Indian member from the North Carolina Commission on Indian Affairs to be appointed by that Commission;

(4) Eight Indian parents of students enrolled in public schools and two Indian educators from public elementary/secondary schools to be appointed by the State Board of Education from a list submitted by the North Carolina Commission on Indian Affairs;

(5) Indian members of the Council shall be broadly representative of North Carolina Indian tribes and organizations, specifically, the Eastern Band of Cherokee, Lumbee, Coharie, Waccamaw-Siouan, Haliwa Saponi, Meherrin, Person County Indians, Cumberland County Association for Indian People, the Guilford Native American Association, the Metrolina Native American Association, and any other Indian tribe gaining State recognition in the future. (1987 (Reg. Sess., 1988), c. 1084, s. 1; 1991, c. 739, s. 13; 1997-456, s. 27.)

§ 115C-210.2. Term of office.

The Legislative members, the higher education members, and the member from the North Carolina Commission on Indian Affairs shall serve for an unspecified term at the pleasure of their respective appointing authorities. The public school educators and the Indian parents shall each be divided into two classes, with one class being appointed initially for a term of one year and one class being appointed initially for a term of two years. Assignment of initial appointees to classes shall be by lot conducted by the State Board of Education just prior to the initial appointment. All subsequent terms shall be for a period of two years, and no member shall serve for more than two consecutive full terms. (1987 (Reg. Sess., 1988), c. 1084, s. 1.)

§ 115C-210.3. Organization, meetings, and compensation.

(a) At its initial meeting, the Council shall elect a chairperson from its membership.

(b) The Council shall meet in space to be provided by the Department of Public Instruction on such dates as are agreed on by the membership from meeting to meeting: provided, however, that the Council shall meet at least three, but no more than four times each year. The Council may meet at emergency meetings called by the chairperson. The Department of Public

Instruction shall provide necessary staff support and supplies to enable the Council to carry out its duties in an effective manner.

(c) Council members shall serve without pay, but shall receive travel allowances, lodging, subsistence and per diem as provided by G.S. 138-5. (1987 (Reg. Sess., 1988), c. 1084, s. 1.)

§ 115C-210.4. Duties of the Council.

It shall be the duty of the Advisory Council:

(1) To review annually relevant data on American Indian students using reports made available to the Council by the Department of Public Instruction. The review shall include, but not be limited to, data on academic performance, growth, suspension and expulsion events, dropouts, and graduation rates.

(2) To advocate for meaningful programs to reduce and eventually eliminate low achievement and concurrent high attrition rates among American Indian students.

(2a) To prepare an annual report that includes an action plan and make an annual presentation to the State Board of Education to advise the State Board on ways to meet the educational needs of American Indian students more effectively based on the State Board's strategies, policies, and information.

(3) To present and share the annual report with the Indian Tribes and Indian organizations referenced in Article 71A of the General Statutes and organizations holding membership on the North Carolina State Commission of Indian Affairs pursuant to G.S. 143B-407 at the statewide Indian Unity Conference and with the North Carolina State Commission of Indian Affairs, along with an action plan based on recommendations.

(4) To work closely with the Department of Public Instruction, Tribal Leaders, and Title VII Coordinators to improve coordination and communication between and among programs.

(4a) To improve consultations among the State Board of Education, the Department of Public Instruction, and American Indian tribal communities, students, parents, and educators.

(5) To advise the State Board of Education on any other aspect of American Indian education when requested by the State Board to do so. (1987 (Reg. Sess., 1988), c. 1084, s. 1; 1997-456, s. 27; 2013-295, s. 1.)

§§ 115C-211 through 115C-214. Reserved for future codification purposes.

Article 14.

Driver Education.

§ 115C-215. Administration of driver education program by the Department of Public Instruction.

(a) In accordance with criteria and standards approved by the State Board of Education, the State Superintendent of Public Instruction shall organize and administer a standardized program of driver education to be offered at the public high schools of this State for all physically and mentally qualified persons who (i) are older than 14 years and six months, (ii) are approved by the principal of the school, pursuant to rules adopted by the State Board of Education, (iii) are enrolled in a public or private high school within the State or are receiving instruction through a home school as provided by Part 3 of Article 39 of Chapter 115C of the General Statutes, and (iv) have not previously enrolled in the program. The State Board of Education shall use for this purpose all funds appropriated to it for this purpose and may use all other funds that become available for its use for this purpose.

(b) The driver education curriculum shall include the following:

(1) Instruction on the rights and privileges of the handicapped and the signs and symbols used to assist the handicapped relative to motor vehicles, including the "international symbol of accessibility" and other symbols and devices as provided in Article 2A of Chapter 20 of the General Statutes.

(2) At least six hours of instruction on the offense of driving while impaired and related subjects.

3) At least six hours of actual driving experience. To the extent practicable, this experience may include at least one hour of instruction on the techniques of defensive driving.

(4) At least one hour of motorcycle safety awareness training.

(c) The State Board of Education shall establish and implement a strategic plan for the driver education program. At a minimum, the strategic plan shall consist of goals and performance indicators, including the number of program participants as compared to the number of persons projected to be eligible to participate in the program, the implementation of a standard curriculum for the program, expenditures for the program, and the success rate of program participants in receiving a drivers license as reported by the Division of Motor Vehicles. The strategic plan shall also outline specific roles and duties of an advisory committee consisting of employees of the Division of Motor Vehicles and the Department of Public Instruction and other stakeholders in driver education.

(d) The State Board of Education shall adopt a salary range for the delivery of driver education courses by driver education instructors who are public school employees. The salary range shall be based on the driver education instructor's qualifications, certification, and licensure specific to driver education.

(e) The State Board of Education shall adopt rules to permit local boards of education to enter contracts with public or private entities to provide a program of driver education at public high schools. All driver education instructors shall meet the requirements established by the State Board of Education; provided, however, driver education instructors shall not be required to hold teacher certificates. (1953, c. 1196; 1955, c. 1372, art. 23, s. 4; 1959, c. 573, s. 16; 1981, c. 423, s. 1; 1991, c. 689, s. 32(b); 2011-145, s. 28.37(a); 2011-334, s. 1.)

§ 115C-216. Boards of education required to provide courses in operation of motor vehicles.

(a) Course of Training and Instruction Required in Public High Schools. - Local boards of education shall offer noncredit driver education courses in high schools using the standardized curriculum provided by the Department of Public Instruction.

(b) Inclusion of Expense in Budget. - The local boards of education shall include as an item of instructional service and as a part of the current expense fund of the budget of the high schools under their supervision, the expense necessary to offer the driver education course.

(c) to (f) Repealed by Session Laws 1991, c. 689, s. 32(c).

(g) Fee for Instruction. - The local boards of education may charge each student participating in a driver education course a fee of up to fifty-five dollars ($55.00) to offset the costs of providing the training and instruction. (1955, c. 817; 1965, c. 397; 1981, c. 423, s. 1; 1991, c. 689, s. 32(c); 2011-145, ss. 28.37(b), 31.1; 2013-360, s. 34.20(a).)

§§ 115C-217 through 115C-221. Reserved for future codification purposes.

Article 15.

North Carolina School of Science and Mathematics.

§§ 115C-222 through 115C-229: Repealed by Session Laws 1985, c. 757, s. 206(a).

Article 16.

Optional Programs.

Part 1. Educational Research.

§ 115C-230. Special projects.

Local boards of education are authorized to sponsor or conduct educational research and special projects pursuant to the provisions of G.S. 115C-47(8). (1981, c. 423, s. 1.)

Part 2. Adult Education.

§ 115C-231. Adult education programs; tuition; limitation of enrollment of pupils over 21.

(a) When in the judgment of the State Board of Education a program of adult education should be established as a part of the public school system and when appropriations have been made therefor, there shall be organized and administered under the general supervision of the Superintendent of Public Instruction, a course in adult education: Provided, that local boards of education, in their discretion, may institute and support such programs from local funds upon the approval of the State Board of Education.

(b) Tuition shall be free of charge to every person of the State 18 years of age, or over, who has not completed a standard high school course of study.

(c) Unless otherwise assigned by the local board of education, all persons of the district or attendance area who have not completed the prescribed course for graduation in the high school are entitled to attend the schools in the district or attendance area in which they reside: Provided, the superintendent, or the principal with the approval of the superintendent, of the local school administrative unit may, in his discretion, prohibit the enrollment of or remove from school any pupil who has attained the age of 21 years. (1955, c. 1372, art. 1, s. 1; art. 19, s. 3; art. 23, s. 2; 1963, c. 448, s. 24; 1971, c. 153; c. 704, s. 1; c. 1231, s. 1; 1981, c. 423, s. 1.)

Part 3. Summer Schools.

§ 115C-232. Local financing of summer schools.

Supplementary funds authorized in special tax elections for school purposes may be used to establish and maintain summer schools, as provided in G.S. 115C-501(a). (1981, c. 423, s. 1.)

§ 115C-233. Operation of summer schools.

Each local school administrative unit may establish and maintain summer schools. Such summer schools as may be established shall be administered by local boards of education and shall be conducted in accordance with standards developed by the State Board of Education. The standards so developed shall specify the requirements for approved curriculum, the qualifications of the personnel, the length of the session, and the conditions under which students may be granted credit for courses pursued during a summer school. In determining the eligibility of students for admission to summer schools, boards of education shall be governed by Article 9 of this Chapter, and G.S. 115C-366(b) and 115C-367 to 115C-370. Boards of education of local school administrative units may provide for summer schools from funds made available for that purpose by the State Board of Education, funds appropriated to the local school administrative unit by the tax-levying authority, and from any other revenues available for the purpose. (1975, c. 437, s. 11; 1981, c. 423, s. 1; 2006-69, s. 3(d).)

§§ 115C-234 through 115C-238. Reserved for future codification purposes.

Part 4. Performance-based Accountability Program.

§§ 115C-238.1 through 115C-238.4: Recodified as §§ 115C-105.20 through 115C-105.35.

§ 115C-238.5: Repealed by Session Laws 1995, c. 450, s. 14.

§§ 115C-238.6 through 115C-238.8: Recodified as §§ 115C-105.29 through 115C-105.32.

§ 115C-238.9. Reserved for future codification purposes.

§ 115C-238.10. Reserved for future codification purposes.

§ 115C-238.11. Reserved for future codification purposes.

Part 5. Outcome-Based Education Program.

§§ 115C-238.12 through 115C-238.19: Repealed by Session Laws 1995, c. 324, s. 17.2.

§ 115C-238.20. Reserved for future codification purposes.

§ 115C-238.21. Reserved for future codification purposes.

Part 6. Project Genesis Program.

§§ 115C-238.22 through 115C-238.25: Repealed by Session Laws 1997-18, s. 8.

§§ 115C-238.26 through 115C-238.29. Reserved for future codification purposes.

Part 6A. Charter Schools.

§ 115C-238.29A. Purpose of charter schools and establishment of North Carolina Charter Schools Advisory Board.

(a) Purpose of Charter Schools. - The purpose of this Part is to authorize a system of charter schools to provide opportunities for teachers, parents, pupils, and community members to establish and maintain schools that operate independently of existing schools, as a method to accomplish all of the following:

(1) Improve student learning;

(2) Increase learning opportunities for all students, with special emphasis on expanded learning experiences for students who are identified as at risk of academic failure or academically gifted;

(3) Encourage the use of different and innovative teaching methods;

(4) Create new professional opportunities for teachers, including the opportunities to be responsible for the learning program at the school site;

(5) Provide parents and students with expanded choices in the types of educational opportunities that are available within the public school system; and

(6) Hold the schools established under this Part accountable for meeting measurable student achievement results, and provide the schools with a method to change from rule-based to performance-based accountability systems.

(b) North Carolina Charter Schools Advisory Board. -

(1) [Advisory Board]. - There is created the North Carolina Charter Schools Advisory Board, hereinafter referred to in this Part as the Advisory Board. The Advisory Board shall be located administratively within the Department of Public Instruction and shall report to the State Board of Education.

(2) Membership. - The State Superintendent of Public Instruction, or the Superintendent's designee, shall be the secretary of the Advisory Board and a nonvoting member. The Advisory Board shall consist of the following 11 voting members:

a. Three members appointed by the Governor, including the chair of the Advisory Board.

b. Three members appointed by the General Assembly upon the recommendation of the President Pro Tempore of the Senate, in accordance with G.S. 120-121.

c. Three members appointed by the General Assembly upon the recommendation of the Speaker of the House of Representatives, in accordance with G.S. 120-121.

d. One member appointed by the State Board of Education.

e. The Lieutenant Governor or the Lieutenant Governor's designee.

(3) Covered board. - The Advisory Board shall be treated as a board for purposes of Chapter 138A of the General Statutes.

(4) Qualifications of members. - Members appointed to the Advisory Board shall collectively possess strong experience and expertise in public and nonprofit governance, management and finance, assessment, curriculum and instruction, public charter schools, and public education law. All appointed members of the Advisory Board shall have demonstrated an understanding of and a commitment to charter schools as a strategy for strengthening public education.

(5) Terms of office and vacancy appointments. - Appointed members shall serve four-year terms of office beginning on July 1. No appointed member shall serve more than eight consecutive years. Vacancy appointments shall be made by the appointing authority for the remainder of the term of office.

(6) Presiding officers and quorum. - The Advisory Board shall annually elect a vice-chair from among its membership. The chair shall preside over the Advisory Board's meetings. In the absence of the chair, the vice-chair shall preside over the Advisory Board's meetings. A majority of the Advisory Board constitutes a quorum.

(7) Meetings. - Meetings of the Advisory Board shall be held upon the call of the chair or the vice-chair with the approval of the chair.

(8) Expenses. - Members of the Advisory Board shall be reimbursed for travel and subsistence expenses at the rates allowed to State officers and employees by G.S. 138-6(a).

(9) Removal. - Any appointed member of the Advisory Board may be removed by a vote of at least two-thirds of the members of the Advisory Board at any duly held meeting for any cause that renders the member incapable or unfit to discharge the duties of the office.

(10) Powers and duties. - The Advisory Board shall have the following duties:

a. To make recommendations to the State Board of Education on the adoption of rules regarding all aspects of charter school operation, including time lines, standards, and criteria for acceptance and approval of applications, monitoring of charter schools, and grounds for revocation of charters.

b. To review applications and make recommendations to the State Board for final approval of charter applications.

c. To make recommendations to the State Board on actions regarding a charter school, including renewals of charters, nonrenewals of charters, and revocations of charters.

d. To undertake any other duties and responsibilities as assigned by the State Board. (1995 (Reg. Sess., 1996), c. 731, s. 2; 2013-355, s. 1(a).)

§ 115C-238.29B. Eligible applicants; contents of applications; submission of applications for approval.

(a) Any nonprofit corporation seeking to establish a charter school may apply to establish a charter school. If the applicant seeks to convert a public school to a charter school, the application shall include a statement signed by a majority of the teachers and instructional support personnel currently employed at the school indicating that they favor the conversion and evidence that a significant number of parents of children enrolled in the school favor conversion.

(b) The application shall contain at least the following information:

(1) A description of a program that implements one or more of the purposes in G.S. 115C-238.29A.

(2) A description of student achievement goals for the school's educational program and the method of demonstrating that students have attained the skills and knowledge specified for those student achievement goals.

(3) The governance structure of the school including the names of the initial members of the board of directors of the nonprofit, tax-exempt corporation and the process to be followed by the school to ensure parental involvement.

(3a) The local school administrative unit in which the school will be located.

(4) Admission policies and procedures.

(5) A proposed budget for the school and evidence that the financial plan for the school is economically sound.

(6) Requirements and procedures for program and financial audits.

(7) A description of how the school will comply with G.S. 115C-238.29F.

(8) Types and amounts of insurance coverage, including bonding insurance for the principal officers of the school, to be obtained by the charter school.

(9) The term of the charter.

(10) The qualifications required for individuals employed by the school.

(11) The procedures by which students can be excluded from the charter school and returned to a public school. Notwithstanding any law to the contrary, any local board may refuse to admit any student who is suspended or expelled from a charter school due to actions that would lead to suspension or expulsion from a public school under G.S. 115C-390.5 through G.S. 115C-390.11 until the period of suspension or expulsion has expired.

(12) The number of students to be served, which number shall be at least 65, and the minimum number of teachers to be employed at the school, which number shall be at least three. However, the charter school may serve fewer than 65 students or employ fewer than three teachers if the application contains a compelling reason, such as the school would serve a geographically remote and small student population.

(13) Information regarding the facilities to be used by the school and the manner in which administrative services of the school are to be provided.

(14) Repealed by Session Laws 1997-430, s. 1.

(c), (d) Repealed by Session Laws 2013-355, s. 1(b), effective July 25, 2013.

(e) The State Board shall establish reasonable fees of no less than five hundred dollars ($500.00) and no more than one thousand dollars ($1,000) for initial and renewal charter applications, in accordance with Article 2A of Chapter 150B of the General Statutes. No application fee shall be refunded in the event the application is rejected or the charter is revoked. (1995 (Reg. Sess., 1996), c. 731, s. 2; 1997-430, s. 1; 2011-282, s. 8; 2013-355, s. 1(b).)

§ 115C-238.29C: Repealed by Session Laws 2013-355, s. 1(c), effective July 25, 2013.

§ 115C-238.29D. Final approval of applications for charter schools.

(a) The State Board may grant final approval of an application if it finds (i) that the application meets the requirements set out in this Part and such other requirements as may be adopted by the State Board of Education, (ii) that the applicant has the ability to operate the school and would be likely to operate the school in an educationally and economically sound manner, and (iii) that granting the application would achieve one or more of the purposes set out in G.S. 115C-238.29A. The State Board shall act by January 15 of a calendar year on all applications and appeals it receives prior to a date established by the Office of Charter Schools for receipt of applications in the prior calendar year. In reviewing applications for the establishment of charter schools within a local school administrative unit, the State Board is encouraged to give preference to applications that demonstrate the capability to provide comprehensive learning experiences to students identified by the applicants as at risk of academic failure.

(b) Repealed by Session Laws 2011-164, s. 2(a), effective July 1, 2011.

(c) The State Board of Education may authorize a school before the applicant has secured its space, equipment, facilities, and personnel if the applicant indicates the authority is necessary for it to raise working capital. The State Board shall not allocate any funds to the school until the school has obtained space.

(d) The State Board of Education may grant the initial charter for a period not to exceed 10 years and may renew the charter upon the request of the chartering entity for subsequent periods not to exceed 10 years each. The State Board of Education shall review the operations of each charter school at least once every five years to ensure that the school is meeting the expected academic, financial, and governance standards.

(e) A material revision of the provisions of a charter application shall be made only upon the approval of the State Board of Education.

Except as provided in subsection (f) of this section, enrollment growth shall be considered a material revision of the charter application, and the State Board may approve such additional enrollment growth of greater than twenty percent (20%) only if the State Board finds all of the following:

(1)   The actual enrollment of the charter school is within ten percent (10%) of its maximum authorized enrollment.

(2)   The charter school has commitments for ninety percent (90%) of the requested maximum growth.

(3)   Repealed by Session Laws 2013-355, s. 1(d), effective July 25, 2013.

(4)   The charter school is not currently identified as low-performing.

(5)   The charter school meets generally accepted standards of fiscal management.

(6)   It is otherwise appropriate to approve the enrollment growth.

(f)   It shall not be considered a material revision of a charter application and shall not require prior approval of the State Board for a charter school to do any of the following:

(1)   Increase its enrollment during the charter school's second year of operation and annually thereafter by up to twenty percent (20%) of the school's previous year's enrollment.

(2)   Increase its enrollment during the charter school's second year of operation and annually thereafter in accordance with planned growth as authorized in its charter.

(3)   Expand to offer one grade higher than the charter school currently offers if the charter school has operated for at least three years and has not been identified as having inadequate performance as provided in G.S. 115C-238.29G(a1). (1995 (Reg. Sess., 1996), c. 731, s. 2; 1997-430, s. 3; 2000-67, s. 8.23; 2001-424, s. 28.26; 2003-354, s. 2; 2004-203, s. 45(a); 2011-164, ss. 1, 2(a), 3; 2013-355, s. 1(d); 2013-359, s. 2.)

§ 115C-238.29E. Charter school operation.

(a) A charter school that is approved by the State shall be a public school within the local school administrative unit in which it is located. All charter schools shall be accountable to the State Board for ensuring compliance with applicable laws and the provisions of their charters.

(b) A charter school shall be operated by a private nonprofit corporation that shall have received federal tax-exempt status no later than 24 months following final approval of the application.

(c) A charter school shall operate under the written charter signed by the State Board and the applicant. A charter school is not required to enter into any other contract. The charter shall incorporate the information provided in the application, as modified during the charter approval process, and any terms and conditions imposed on the charter school by the State Board of Education. No other terms may be imposed on the charter school as a condition for receipt of local funds.

(d) The board of directors of the charter school shall decide matters related to the operation of the school, including budgeting, curriculum, and operating procedures.

(e) A charter school's specific location shall not be prescribed or limited by a local board or other authority except a zoning authority. The school may lease space from a local board of education or as is otherwise lawful in the local school administrative unit in which the charter school is located. If a charter school leases space from a sectarian organization, the charter school classes and students shall be physically separated from any parochial students, and there shall be no religious artifacts, symbols, iconography, or materials on display in the charter school's entrance, classrooms, or hallways. Furthermore, if a charter school leases space from a sectarian organization, the charter school shall not use the name of that organization in the name of the charter school.

At the request of the charter school, the local board of education of the local school administrative unit in which the charter school will be located shall lease any available building or land to the charter school unless the board demonstrates that the lease is not economically or practically feasible or that the local board does not have adequate classroom space to meet its enrollment needs. Notwithstanding any other law, a local board of education may provide a school facility to a charter school free of charge; however, the charter school is responsible for the maintenance of and insurance for the school facility. If a charter school has requested to lease available buildings or land and is unable to reach an agreement with the local board of education, the charter school shall have the right to appeal to the board of county commissioners in which the building or land is located. The board of county commissioners shall have the final decision-making authority on the leasing of the available building or land.

(f) Except as provided in this Part and pursuant to the provisions of its charter, a charter school is exempt from statutes and rules applicable to a local board of education or local school administrative unit. (1995 (Reg. Sess., 1996), c. 731, s. 2; 1997-430, s. 4; 2013-355, s. 1(e).)

§ 115C-238.29F. General requirements.

(a) Health and Safety Standards. - A charter school shall meet the same health and safety requirements required of a local school administrative unit. The Department of Public Instruction shall ensure that charter schools provide parents and guardians with information about meningococcal meningitis and influenza and their vaccines at the beginning of every school year. This information shall include the causes, symptoms, and how meningococcal meningitis and influenza are spread and the places where parents and guardians may obtain additional information and vaccinations for their children.

The Department of Public Instruction shall also ensure that charter schools provide parents and guardians with information about cervical cancer, cervical dysplasia, human papillomavirus, and the vaccines available to prevent these diseases. This information shall be provided at the beginning of the school year to parents of children entering grades five through 12. This information shall include the causes and symptoms of these diseases, how they are transmitted, how they may be prevented by vaccination, including the benefits and possible side effects of vaccination, and the places where parents and guardians may obtain additional information and vaccinations for their children.

The Department of Public Instruction shall also ensure that charter schools provide students in grades seven through 12 with information annually on the preventable risks for preterm birth in subsequent pregnancies, including induced abortion, smoking, alcohol consumption, the use of illicit drugs, and inadequate prenatal care.

The Department of Public Instruction shall also ensure that charter schools provide students in grades nine through 12 with information annually on the manner in which a parent may lawfully abandon a newborn baby with a responsible person, in accordance with G.S. 7B-500.

The Department of Public Instruction shall also ensure that the guidelines for individual diabetes care plans adopted by the State Board of Education under G.S. 115C-12(31) are implemented in charter schools in which students with diabetes are enrolled and that charter schools otherwise comply with the provisions of G.S. 115C-375.3.

(a1)   Emergency Response Plan. - A charter school, in coordination with local law enforcement agencies, is encouraged to adopt an emergency response plan relating to incidents of school violence. These plans are not considered a public record as the term "public record" is defined under G.S. 132-1 and shall not be subject to inspection and examination under G.S. 132-6.

Charter schools are encouraged to provide schematic diagrams and keys to the main entrance of school facilities to local law enforcement agencies, in addition to implementing the provisions in G.S. 115C-105.49(b) and G.S. 115C-105.52.

(b)   School Nonsectarian. - A charter school shall be nonsectarian in its programs, admission policies, employment practices, and all other operations and shall not charge tuition or fees, except that a charter school may charge any fees that are charged by the local school administrative unit in which the charter school is located. A charter school shall not be affiliated with a nonpublic sectarian school or a religious institution.

(c)   Civil Liability and Insurance. -

(1)   The board of directors of a charter school may sue and be sued. The State Board of Education shall adopt rules to establish reasonable amounts and types of liability insurance that the board of directors shall be required by the charter to obtain. The board of directors shall obtain at least the amount of and types of insurance required by these rules to be included in the charter. Any sovereign immunity of the charter school, of the organization that operates the charter school, or its members, officers, or directors, or of the employees of the charter school or the organization that operates the charter school, is waived to the extent of indemnification by insurance.

(2)   No civil liability shall attach to the State Board of Education, or to any of their members or employees, individually or collectively, for any acts or omissions of the charter school.

(d) Instructional Program. -

(1) The school shall provide instruction each year for at least 185 days or 1,025 hours over nine calendar months.

(2) The school shall design its programs to at least meet the student performance standards adopted by the State Board of Education and the student performance standards contained in the charter.

(3) A charter school shall conduct the student assessments required by the State Board of Education.

(4) The school is subject to and shall comply with Article 9 of Chapter 115C of the General Statutes and The Individuals with Disabilities Education Improvements Act, 20 U.S.C. § 1400, et seq., (2004), as amended.

(5) The school is subject to and shall comply with Article 27 of Chapter 115C of the General Statutes, except that a charter school may also exclude a student from the charter school and return that student to another school in the local school administrative unit in accordance with the terms of its charter after due process.

(d1) Reading Proficiency and Student Promotion. -

(1) Students in the third grade shall be retained if the student fails to demonstrate reading proficiency by reading at or above the third grade level as demonstrated by the results of the State-approved standardized test of reading comprehension administered to third grade students. The charter school shall provide reading interventions to retained students to remediate reading deficiency, which may include 90 minutes of daily, uninterrupted, evidence-based reading instruction, accelerated reading classes, transition classes containing third and fourth grade students, and summer reading camps.

(2) Students may be exempt from mandatory retention in third grade for good cause but shall continue to receive instructional supports and services and reading interventions appropriate for their age and reading level. Good cause exemptions shall be limited to the following:

a. Limited English Proficient students with less than two years of instruction in an English as a Second Language program.

b.   Students with disabilities, as defined in G.S. 115C-106.3(1), whose individualized education program indicates the use of alternative assessments and reading interventions.

c.   Students who demonstrate reading proficiency appropriate for third grade students on an alternative assessment of reading comprehension. The charter school shall notify the State Board of Education of the alternative assessment used to demonstrate reading proficiency.

d.   Students who demonstrate, through a student reading portfolio, reading proficiency appropriate for third grade students.

e.   Students who have (i) received reading intervention and (ii) previously been retained more than once in kindergarten, first, second, or third grades.

(3)   The charter school shall provide notice to parents and guardians when a student is not reading at grade level. The notice shall state that if the student's reading deficiency is not remediated by the end of third grade, the student shall be retained unless he or she is exempt from mandatory retention for good cause. Notice shall also be provided to parents and guardians of any student who is to be retained under this subsection of the reason the student is not eligible for a good cause exemption, as well as a description of proposed reading interventions that will be provided to the student to remediate identified areas of reading deficiency.

(4)   The charter school shall annually publish on the charter school's Web site and report in writing to the State Board of Education by September 1 of each year the following information on the prior school year:

a.   The number and percentage of third grade students demonstrating and not demonstrating reading proficiency on the State-approved standardized test of reading comprehension administered to third grade students.

b.   The number and percentage of third grade students not demonstrating reading proficiency and who do not return to the charter school for the following school year.

c.   The number and percentage of third grade students who take and pass the alternative assessment of reading comprehension.

d. The number and percentage of third grade students retained for not demonstrating reading proficiency.

e. The number and percentage of third grade students exempt from mandatory third grade retention by category of exemption as listed in subdivision (2) of this subsection.

(e) Employees. -

(1) An employee of a charter school is not an employee of the local school administrative unit in which the charter school is located. The charter school's board of directors shall employ and contract with necessary teachers to perform the particular service for which they are employed in the school; at least fifty percent (50%) of these teachers shall hold teacher licenses. All teachers who are teaching in the core subject areas of mathematics, science, social studies, and language arts shall be college graduates.

The board also may employ necessary employees who are not required to hold teacher licenses to perform duties other than teaching and may contract for other services. The board may discharge teachers and nonlicensed employees.

(2) No local board of education shall require any employee of the local school administrative unit to be employed in a charter school.

(3) (Effective until June 30, 2018) If a teacher employed by a local school administrative unit makes a written request for a leave of absence to teach at a charter school, the local school administrative unit shall grant the leave for one year. For the initial year of a charter school's operation, the local school administrative unit may require that the request for a leave of absence be made up to 45 days before the teacher would otherwise have to report for duty. After the initial year of a charter school's operation, the local school administrative unit may require that the request for a leave of absence be made up to 90 days before the teacher would otherwise have to report for duty. A local board of education is not required to grant a request for a leave of absence or a request to extend or renew a leave of absence for a teacher who previously has received a leave of absence from that school board under this subdivision. A teacher who has career status under G.S. 115C-325 prior to receiving a leave of absence to teach at a charter school may return to a public school in the local school administrative unit with career status at the end of the leave of absence or upon the end of employment at the charter school if an appropriate position is available. If an appropriate position is unavailable, the teacher's name shall be

placed on a list of available teachers and that teacher shall have priority on all positions for which that teacher is qualified in accordance with G.S. 115C-325(e)(2).

(3) (Effective June 30, 2018) If a teacher employed by a local school administrative unit makes a written request for a leave of absence to teach at a charter school, the local school administrative unit shall grant the leave for one year. For the initial year of a charter school's operation, the local school administrative unit may require that the request for a leave of absence be made up to 45 days before the teacher would otherwise have to report for duty. After the initial year of a charter school's operation, the local school administrative unit may require that the request for a leave of absence be made up to 90 days before the teacher would otherwise have to report for duty. A local board of education is not required to grant a request for a leave of absence or a request to extend or renew a leave of absence for a teacher who previously has received a leave of absence from that school board under this subdivision. A teacher who has received a leave of absence to teach at a charter school may return to a public school in the local school administrative unit at the end of the leave of absence or upon the end of employment at the charter school if an appropriate position is available.

(4) The employees of the charter school shall be deemed employees of the local school administrative unit for purposes of providing certain State-funded employee benefits, including membership in the Teachers' and State Employees' Retirement System and the State Health Plan for Teachers and State Employees. The State Board of Education provides funds to charter schools, approves the original members of the boards of directors of the charter schools, has the authority to grant, supervise, and revoke charters, and demands full accountability from charter schools for school finances and student performance. Accordingly, it is the determination of the General Assembly that charter schools are public schools and that the employees of charter schools are public school employees. Employees of a charter school whose board of directors elects to become a participating employer under G.S. 135-5.3 are "teachers" for the purpose of membership in the North Carolina Teachers' and State Employees' Retirement System. In no event shall anything contained in this Part require the North Carolina Teachers' and State Employees' Retirement System to accept employees of a private employer as members or participants of the System.

(5) Education employee associations shall have equal access to charter school employees as provided in G.S. 115C-335.9.

(e1) Criminal History Checks. -

(1) If the local board of education of the local school administrative unit in which a charter school is located has adopted a policy requiring criminal history checks under G.S. 115C-332, then the board of directors of each charter school located in that local school administrative unit shall adopt a policy mirroring the local board of education policy that requires an applicant for employment to be checked for a criminal history, as defined in G.S. 115C-332. Each charter school board of directors shall apply its policy uniformly in requiring applicants for employment to be checked for a criminal history before the applicant is given an unconditional job offer. A charter school board of directors may employ an applicant conditionally while the board is checking the person's criminal history and making a decision based on the results of the check.

(2) There shall be no liability for negligence on the part of the State Board of Education or the board of directors of the charter school, or their employees, arising from any act taken or omission by any of them in carrying out the provisions of this subsection. The immunity established by this subsection shall not extend to gross negligence, wanton conduct, or intentional wrongdoing that would otherwise be actionable. The immunity established by this subsection shall be deemed to have been waived to the extent of indemnification by insurance, indemnification under Articles 31A and 31B of Chapter 143 of the General Statutes, and to the extent sovereign immunity is waived under the Tort Claims Act, as set forth in Article 31 of Chapter 143 of the General Statutes.

(f) Accountability. -

(1) The school is subject to the financial audits, the audit procedures, and the audit requirements adopted by the State Board of Education for charter schools. These audit requirements may include the requirements of the School Budget and Fiscal Control Act.

(2) The school shall comply with the reporting requirements established by the State Board of Education in the Uniform Education Reporting System.

(3) The school shall report at least annually to the State Board of Education the information required by the State Board.

(g) Admission Requirements. -

(1) Any child who is qualified under the laws of this State for admission to a public school is qualified for admission to a charter school.

(2) No local board of education shall require any student enrolled in the local school administrative unit to attend a charter school.

(3) Admission to a charter school shall not be determined according to the school attendance area in which a student resides, except that any local school administrative unit in which a public school converts to a charter school shall give admission preference to students who reside within the former attendance area of that school.

(4) Admission to a charter school shall not be determined according to the local school administrative unit in which a student resides.

(5) A charter school shall not discriminate against any student on the basis of ethnicity, national origin, gender, or disability. Except as otherwise provided by law or the mission of the school as set out in the charter, the school shall not limit admission to students on the basis of intellectual ability, measures of achievement or aptitude, athletic ability, disability, race, creed, gender, national origin, religion, or ancestry. Within one year after the charter school begins operation, the charter school shall make efforts for the population of the school to reasonably reflect the racial and ethnic composition of the general population residing within the local school administrative unit in which the school is located or the racial and ethnic composition of the special population that the school seeks to serve residing within the local school administrative unit in which the school is located. The school shall be subject to any court-ordered desegregation plan in effect for the local school administrative unit.

(5a) The charter school may give enrollment priority to any of the following:

a. Siblings of currently enrolled students who were admitted to the charter school in a previous year. For the purposes of this subsection, the term "siblings" includes any of the following who reside in the same household: half siblings, stepsiblings, and children residing in a family foster home.

b. Siblings of students who have completed the highest grade level offered by that school and who were enrolled in at least four grade levels offered by the charter school or, if less than four grades are offered, in the maximum number of grades offered by the charter school.

c. Limited to no more than fifteen percent (15%) of the school's total enrollment, unless granted a waiver by the State Board of Education, the following:

1. Children of the school's full-time employees.

2. For its first year of operation, children of the initial members of the charter school's board of directors.

d. A student who was enrolled in the charter school within the two previous school years but left the school (i) to participate in an academic study abroad program or a competitive admission residential program or (ii) because of the vocational opportunities of the student's parent.

(5b) Lottery procedures for siblings:

a. If siblings apply for admission to a charter school and a lottery is needed under G.S. 115C-238.29F(g)(6), the charter school may enter one surname into the lottery to represent all of the siblings applying at the same time. If that surname of the siblings is selected, then all of the siblings shall be admitted to the extent that space is available and does not exceed the grade level capacity.

b. If multiple birth siblings apply for admission to a charter school and a lottery is needed under G.S. 115C-238.29F(g)(6), the charter school shall enter one surname into the lottery to represent all of the multiple birth siblings applying at the same time. If that surname of the multiple birth siblings is selected, then all of the multiple birth siblings shall be admitted.

(6) During each period of enrollment, the charter school shall enroll an eligible student who submits a timely application, unless the number of applications exceeds the capacity of a program, class, grade level, or building. In this case, students shall be accepted by lot. Once enrolled, students are not required to reapply in subsequent enrollment periods.

(7) Notwithstanding any law to the contrary, a charter school may refuse admission to any student who has been expelled or suspended from a public school under G.S. 115C-390.5 through G.S. 115C-390.11 until the period of suspension or expulsion has expired.

(h) Transportation. - The charter school may provide transportation for students enrolled at the school. The charter school shall develop a transportation plan so that transportation is not a barrier to any student who resides in the local school administrative unit in which the school is located. The charter school is not required to provide transportation to any student who lives within one and one-half miles of the school. At the request of the charter school and if the local board of the local school administrative unit in which the charter school is located operates a school bus system, then that local board may contract with the charter school to provide transportation in accordance with the charter school's transportation plan to students who reside in the local school administrative unit and who reside at least one and one-half miles of the charter school. A local board may charge the charter school a reasonable charge that is sufficient to cover the cost of providing this transportation. Furthermore, a local board may refuse to provide transportation under this subsection if it demonstrates there is no available space on buses it intends to operate during the term of the contract or it would not be practically feasible to provide this transportation.

(i) Assets. - Upon dissolution of the charter school or upon the nonrenewal of the charter, all net assets of the charter school purchased with public funds shall be deemed the property of the local school administrative unit in which the charter school is located.

(j) Driving Eligibility Certificates. - In accordance with rules adopted by the State Board of Education, the designee of the school's board of directors shall do all of the following:

(1) Sign driving eligibility certificates that meet the conditions established in G.S. 20-11.

(2) Obtain the necessary written, irrevocable consent from parents, guardians, or emancipated juveniles, as appropriate, in order to disclose information to the Division of Motor Vehicles.

(3) Notify the Division of Motor Vehicles when a student who holds a driving eligibility certificate no longer meets its conditions.

(k) The Display of the United States and North Carolina Flags and the Recitation of the Pledge of Allegiance. - A charter school shall (i) display the United States and North Carolina flags in each classroom when available, (ii) require the recitation of the Pledge of Allegiance on a daily basis, and (iii) provide age-appropriate instruction on the meaning and historical origins of the flag and the Pledge of Allegiance. A charter school shall not compel any person to stand, salute the flag, or recite the Pledge of Allegiance. If flags are donated or are otherwise available, flags shall be displayed in each classroom.

(l)   North Carolina School Report Cards. - A charter school shall ensure that the report card issued for it by the State Board of Education receives wide distribution to the local press or is otherwise provided to the public. A charter school shall ensure that the overall school performance score and grade earned by the charter school for the current and previous four school years is prominently displayed on the school Web site. If a charter school is awarded a grade of D or F, the charter school shall provide notice of the grade in writing to the parent or guardian of all students enrolled in that school. (1995 (Reg. Sess., 1996), c. 731, s. 2; 1997-430, s. 5; 1997-443, s. 8.19; 1997-456, s. 55.4; 1998-212, s. 9.14A(a); 1999-243, s. 8; 2001-462, s. 1; 2004-118, s. 3; 2004-203, s. 45(b); 2006-69, s. 3(e); 2006-137, s. 2; 2007-59, s. 2; 2007-126, s. 2; 2007-323, s. 28.22A(o); 2007-345, s. 12; 2009-239, s. 1; 2009-563, s. 2; 2010-10, s. 2(a); 2011-93, s. 2(a); 2011-145, s. 7.29(b); 2011-164, s. 4; 2011-282, s. 9; 2012-142, ss. 7A.1(f), 7A.3(c), 7A.11(b); 2012-145, s. 2.5; 2012-179, s. 1(c); 2013-307, s. 1.1; 2013-355, s. 1(f); 2013-359, s. 1; 2013-360, ss. 8.43(a), 9.7(q).)

§ 115C-238.29G. Causes for nonrenewal or termination; disputes.

(a)   The State Board of Education may terminate, not renew, or seek applicants to assume the charter through a competitive bid process established by the State Board upon any of the following grounds:

(1)   Failure to meet the requirements for student performance contained in the charter;

(2)   Failure to meet generally accepted standards of fiscal management;

(3)   Violations of law;

(4)   Material violation of any of the conditions, standards, or procedures set forth in the charter;

(5)   Two-thirds of the faculty and instructional support personnel at the school request that the charter be terminated or not renewed; or

(6)   Other good cause identified.

(a1) The State Board shall adopt criteria for adequate performance by a charter school and shall identify charter schools with inadequate performance. The criteria shall include a requirement that a charter school which demonstrates no growth in student performance and has annual performance composites below sixty percent (60%) in any two years in a three-year period is inadequate.

(1) If a charter school is inadequate in the first five years of the charter, the charter school shall develop a strategic plan to meet specific goals for student performance that are consistent with State Board criteria and the mission approved in the charter school. The strategic plan shall be reviewed and approved by the State Board. The State Board is authorized to terminate or not renew a charter for failure to demonstrate improvement under the strategic plan.

(2) If a charter school is inadequate and has had a charter for more than five years, the State Board is authorized to terminate, not renew, or seek applicants to assume the charter through a competitive bid process established by the State Board. The State Board shall develop rules on the assumption of a charter by a new entity that include all aspects of the operations of the charter school, including the status of the employees. Public assets would transfer to the new entity and not revert to the local school administrative unit in which the charter school is located pursuant to G.S. 115C-238.29F(i).

(b) The State Board of Education shall develop and implement a process to address contractual and other grievances between a charter school and the local board of education during the time of its charter.

(c) The State Board and the charter school are encouraged to make a good-faith attempt to resolve the differences that may arise between them. They may agree to jointly select a mediator. The mediator shall act as a neutral facilitator of disclosures of factual information, statements of positions and contentions, and efforts to negotiate an agreement settling the differences. The mediator shall, at the request of either the State Board or a charter school, commence a mediation immediately or within a reasonable period of time. The mediation shall be held in accordance with rules and standards of conduct adopted under Chapter 7A of the General Statutes governing mediated settlement conferences but modified as appropriate and suitable to the resolution of the particular issues in disagreement.

Notwithstanding Article 33C of Chapter 143 of the General Statutes, the mediation proceedings shall be conducted in private. Evidence of statements made and conduct occurring in a mediation are not subject to discovery and are inadmissible in any court action. However, no evidence otherwise discoverable is inadmissible merely because it is presented or discussed in a mediation. The mediator shall not be compelled to testify or produce evidence concerning statements made and conduct occurring in a mediation in any civil proceeding for any purpose, except disciplinary hearings before the State Bar or any agency established to enforce standards of conduct for mediators. The mediator may determine that an impasse exists and discontinue the mediation at any time. The mediator shall not make any recommendations or public statement of findings or conclusions. The State Board and the charter school shall share equally the mediator's compensation and expenses. The mediator's compensation shall be determined according to rules adopted under Chapter 7A of the General Statutes. (1995 (Reg. Sess., 1996), c. 731, s. 2; 1997-430, s. 6; 2011-164, s. 5; 2013-355, s. 1(g).)

§ 115C-238.29H. State and local funds for a charter school.

(a) The State Board of Education shall allocate to each charter school:

(1) An amount equal to the average per pupil allocation for average daily membership from the local school administrative unit allotments in which the charter school is located for each child attending the charter school except for the allocation for children with disabilities and for the allocation for children with limited English proficiency;

(2) An additional amount for each child attending the charter school who is a child with disabilities; and

(3) An additional amount for children with limited English proficiency attending the charter school, based on a formula adopted by the State Board.

In accordance with G.S. 115C-238.29D(d), the State Board shall allow for annual adjustments to the amount allocated to a charter school based on its enrollment growth in school years subsequent to the initial year of operation.

In the event a child with disabilities leaves the charter school and enrolls in a public school during the first 60 school days in the school year, the charter school shall return a pro rata amount of funds allocated for that child to the State Board, and the State Board shall reallocate those funds to the local school administrative unit in which the public school is located. In the event a child with disabilities enrolls in a charter school during the first 60 school days in the school year, the State Board shall allocate to the charter school the pro rata amount of additional funds for children with disabilities.

(a1)   Funds allocated by the State Board of Education may be used to enter into operational and financing leases for real property or mobile classroom units for use as school facilities for charter schools and may be used for payments on loans made to charter schools for facilities, equipment, or operations. However, State funds shall not be used to obtain any other interest in real property or mobile classroom units. No indebtedness of any kind incurred or created by the charter school shall constitute an indebtedness of the State or its political subdivisions, and no indebtedness of the charter school shall involve or be secured by the faith, credit, or taxing power of the State or its political subdivisions. Every contract or lease into which a charter school enters shall include the previous sentence. The school also may own land and buildings it obtains through non-State sources.

(b)   If a student attends a charter school, the local school administrative unit in which the child resides shall transfer to the charter school an amount equal to the per pupil share of the local current expense fund of the local school administrative unit for the fiscal year. The per pupil share of the local current expense fund shall be transferred to the charter school within 30 days of the receipt of monies into the local current expense fund. The local school administrative unit and charter school may use the process for mediation of differences between the State Board and a charter school provided in G.S. 115C-238.29G(c) to resolve differences on calculation and transference of the per pupil share of the local current expense fund. The amount transferred under this subsection that consists of revenue derived from supplemental taxes shall be transferred only to a charter school located in the tax district for which these taxes are levied and in which the student resides.

(c)   The local school administrative unit shall also provide each charter school to which it transfers a per pupil share of its local current expense fund with all of the following information within the 30-day time period provided in subsection (b) of this section:

(1)   The total amount of monies the local school administrative unit has in each of the funds listed in G.S. 115C-426(c).

(2) The student membership numbers used to calculate the per pupil share of the local current expense fund.

(3) How the per pupil share of the local current expense fund was calculated.

(d) Prior to commencing an action under subsection (b) of this section, the complaining party shall give the other party 15 days' written notice of the alleged violation. The court shall award the prevailing party reasonable attorneys' fees and costs incurred in an action under subsection (b) of this section. The court shall order any delinquent funds, costs, fees, and interest to be paid in equal monthly installments and shall establish a time for payment in full that shall be no later than three years from the entry of any judgment. (1995 (Reg. Sess., 1996), c. 731, s. 2; 1997-430, s. 7; 1998-212, s. 9.20(f); 2003-423, s. 3.1; 2006-69, s. 3(f); 2013-355, s. 1(h).)

§ 115C-238.29I. Notice of the charter school process; review of charter schools.

(a) The State Board of Education shall distribute information announcing the availability of the charter school process described in this Part to each local school administrative unit and public postsecondary educational institution and, through press releases, to each major newspaper in the State.

(b) Repealed by Session Laws 1997-18, s. 15(i), effective July 1, 1999.

(c) The State Board of Education shall review and evaluate the educational effectiveness of the charter schools authorized under this Part and the effect of charter schools on the public schools in the local school administrative unit in which the charter schools are located. The Board shall report annually no later than January 1 to the Joint Legislative Education Oversight Committee on the following:

(1) The current and projected impact of charter schools on the delivery of services by the public schools.

(2) Student academic progress in the charter schools as measured, where available, against the academic year immediately preceding the first academic year of the charter schools' operation.

(3)   Best practices resulting from charter school operations.

(4)   Other information the State Board considers appropriate.

(d),   (e) Repealed by Session Laws 2013-355, s. 1(i), effective July 25, 2013. (1995 (Reg. Sess., 1996), c. 731, s. 2; 1997-18, s. 15(i); 1997-430, ss. 8, 9; 1999-27, s. 1; 2013-355, s. 1(i).)

§ 115C-238.29J: Repealed by Session Laws 2013-355, s. 1(j), effective July 25, 2013.

§ 115C-238.29K: Repealed by Session Laws 2013-355, s. 1(k), effective July 25, 2013.

Part 7. Extended Services Programs.

§ 115C-238.30. Purpose.

The General Assembly believes that all children can learn. It is the intent of the General Assembly that the mission of the public school community is to challenge with high expectations each child to learn, to achieve, and to fulfill his or her potential. With that mission as a guide, local school administrative units are encouraged to provide timely assistance to students who are at risk of school failure through the extended services programs described in this Part. (1993, c. 132.)

§ 115C-238.31. Extended services programs.

(a)   Local school administrative units are encouraged to implement extended services programs that will expand students' opportunities for educational success through high-quality, integrated access to instructional programming during nonschool hours. Extended services programs may be incorporated into school improvement plans developed in accordance with G.S. 115C-105.27.

Calendar alternatives include, but are not limited to, after-school hours, before-school hours, evening school, Saturday school, summer school, and year-round school. Instructional programming may include, but is not limited to, tutoring, direct instruction, enrichment activities, study skills, and reinforcement projects.

(b) Extended services programs shall be targeted primarily toward students who perform significantly below their age-level peers; however, these programs may be established for students who are achieving at or above grade level.

(c) Extended services programs should be accelerated and based on needs assessments of the students in the program. The programs shall build on, and be fully integrated with, existing classroom and school activities.

(d) Extended services programs may be based in schools, collaboratively between schools, or in other community-based locations. (1993, c. 132, s. 1; 1995 (Reg. Sess., 1996), c. 716, s. 24; 2011-145, s. 7.13(r); 2011-391, s. 14(b).)

§ 115C-238.32. Needs assessment; community-based collaboration.

(a) Before implementing an extended services program, the local school administrative unit shall conduct a needs assessment within the unit and in collaboration with local governmental and nongovernmental agencies to identify students, schools, and communities that need extended services. The needs assessment shall include an evaluation of existing school and community resources and programs and shall identify how instruction in the core curriculum could be improved to meet the needs of children at risk of school failure.

(b) Goals and expected outcomes for the program shall be based on the needs assessment. (1993, c. 132.)

§ 115C-238.33. Plan for effective use of fiscal resources; comprehensive plan to implement extended services programs.

(a) The State Board of Education shall develop model plans which show how to (i) deliver comprehensive extended services; (ii) effectively use all fiscal resources, including federal funds, and other resources under its control that support the goals of this Part; and (iii) maintain quality program evaluation. The model plans shall be communicated to local units and building-level committees.

(b)   Repealed by Session Laws, 1997-18, c. 15(j). (1993, c. 132, s. 1; 1997-18, s. 15(j).)

§§ 115C-238.34 through 115C-238.39. Reserved for future codification purposes.

Part 8. Intervention/Prevention Grant Program for North Carolina School Children.

§§ 115C-238.40 through 115C-238.47: Repealed by Session Laws 1995, c. 450, s. 16.

Part 9. Cooperative Innovative High School Programs.

§ 115C-238.50. Purpose.

(a)   The purpose of this Part is to authorize local boards of education to jointly establish with one or more boards of trustees cooperative innovative programs in high schools and colleges or universities that will expand students' opportunities for educational success through high quality instructional programming. These cooperative innovative high school programs shall target any of the following groups:

(1)   High school students who are at risk of dropping out of school before attaining a high school diploma.

(1a)   High school students with parents who did not continue education beyond high school.

(2)   High school students who would benefit from accelerated academic instruction.

(b) All the cooperative innovative high school programs established under this Part shall:

(1) Enable students to concurrently obtain a high school diploma and begin or complete an associate degree program, master a certificate or vocational program, or earn up to two years of college credit within five years.

(1a) Prepare students adequately for future learning in the workforce or in an institution of higher education.

(2), (3) Repealed by Session Laws 2011-145, s. 7.1A(j), effective January 1, 2012.

(4) Encourage the cooperative or shared use of resources, personnel, and facilities between public schools and colleges or universities, or both.

(5) Repealed by Session Laws 2011-145, s. 7.1A(j), effective January 1, 2012.

(6) Emphasize parental involvement and provide consistent counseling, advising, and parent conferencing so that parents and students can make responsible decisions regarding course taking and can track the students' academic progress and success.

(7) through (10) Repealed by Session Laws 2011-145, s. 7.1A(j), effective January 1, 2012.

(11) Develop methods for early identification of potential participating students in the middle grades and through high school and provide outreach to those students to promote academic preparation and awareness of the cooperative innovative high school programs.

(12) Repealed by Session Laws 2011-145, s. 7.1A(j), effective January 1, 2012.

(c) through (e) Repealed by Session Laws 2011-145, s. 7.1A(j), effective January 1, 2012.

(f) Students are eligible to attend these programs as early as ninth grade. (2003-277, s. 2; 2005-276, s. 7.33(a); 2010-31, s. 7.21(a); 2011-145, s. 7.1A(j).)

§ 115C-238.50A. Definitions.

The following definitions apply in this Part:

(1) Constituent institution. - A constituent institution as defined in G.S. 116-2(4).

(1a) Cooperative innovative high school. - A high school approved by the State Board of Education and the applicable governing Board that meets the following criteria:

a. It has no more than 100 students per grade level.

b. It partners with an institution of higher education to enable students to concurrently obtain a high school diploma and begin or complete an associate degree program, master a certificate or vocational program, or earn up to two years of college credit within five years.

c. It is located on the campus of the partner institution of higher education, unless the governing Board or the local board of trustees for a private North Carolina college specifically waives the requirement through adoption of a formal resolution.

(1b) Cooperative innovative high school allotment. - Funds appropriated by the General Assembly to the Department of Public Instruction to provide additional resources to approved cooperative innovative high schools.

(2) Education partner. - An education partner as provided in G.S. 115C-238.52.

(3) Governing Board. - The State Board of Community Colleges or the Board of Governors of The University of North Carolina.

(3a) Local board of education. - A local board as defined in G.S. 115C-5(5) or a regional school board of directors as defined in G.S. 115C-238.61(5).

(4) Local board of trustees. - The board of trustees of a community college, constituent institution of The University of North Carolina, or private college located in North Carolina.

(5) Partner institution of higher education. - A community college, constituent institution of The University of North Carolina, or private college located in North Carolina. (2005-276, s. 7.33(a); 2010-31, s. 7.21(c); 2011-145, s. 7.1A(j); 2011-241, s. 4; 2012-142, s. 7.11(a).)

§ 115C-238.51. Application process.

(a) A local board of education and at least one local board of trustees shall jointly apply to establish a cooperative innovative high school program under this Part.

(b) The application shall contain at least the following information:

(1) A description of a program that implements the purposes in G.S. 115C-238.50.

(2) A statement of how the cooperative innovative high school relates to the Economic Vision Plan adopted for the economic development region in which the cooperative innovative high school is to be located.

(3) The facilities to be used by the cooperative innovative high school and the manner in which administrative services of the school are to be provided.

(4) A description of student academic and vocational achievement goals and the method of demonstrating that students have attained the skills and knowledge specified for those goals.

(5) A description of how the cooperative innovative high school will be operated, including budgeting, curriculum, transportation, and operating procedures.

(6) The process to be followed by the cooperative innovative high school to ensure parental involvement.

(7) The process by which students will be selected for and admitted to the cooperative innovative high school.

(8) A description of the funds that will be used and a proposed budget for the first five years of the implementation of the cooperative innovative high

school. This description shall identify how the average daily membership (ADM) and full-time equivalent (FTE) students are counted. If additional funds are requested, a description of how those additional funds will be used shall be submitted. Additional funds may include the cooperative innovative high school allotment and tuition payments. For cooperative innovative high schools that have a community college as their partner institution of higher education, the proposed budget shall include the cost of including their students in calculations of budget full-time equivalent students for the North Carolina Community College System.

(9) The qualifications required for individuals employed in the cooperative innovative high school.

(10) The number of students to be served.

(11) A description of how the cooperative innovative high school's effectiveness in meeting the purposes in G.S. 115C-238.50 will be measured.

(c) The application shall be submitted to the State Board of Education and the applicable governing Board. If the partner institution of higher education is a private North Carolina college, the application shall be submitted solely to the State Board of Education.

(d), (e) Repealed by Session Laws 2012-142, s. 7.11(b), effective July 2, 2012. (2003-277, s. 2; 2005-276, s. 7.33(a); 2005-345, ss. 6(b), 6(c); 2011-145, s. 7.1A(j); 2012-142, s. 7.11(b).)

§ 115C-238.51A. Approval process.

(a) Joint Advisory Committee. - The State Board of Education and the applicable governing Board of the local board of trustees shall appoint a joint advisory committee to review the applications and to recommend approval for those applications that meet the requirements of this Part and achieve purposes set out in G.S. 115C-238.50. The recommendation shall indicate whether additional funds were requested in the application.

(b) No Additional Funds. - For applications which have not requested additional funds, the State Board of Education and the applicable governing Board may approve cooperative innovative high schools. In granting approval, consideration shall be given to the proposed budget and demonstration of sources of sustainable funding for the operation of the cooperative innovative high school. Approvals shall be made by June 30 of each year. No additional State funds, position allotments, earning of budget full-time equivalent students, or payments of tuition shall be provided to cooperative innovative high schools approved under this subsection.

(c) Additional Funds. - For applications which have requested additional funds, the State Board of Education and the applicable governing Board may approve cooperative innovative high schools contingent upon appropriation of the additional funds by the General Assembly. Contingent approval shall be made by April 1 of each year. The contingent approval shall expire if no appropriation is made by the General Assembly for the additional funds within one calendar year. No cooperative innovative high school shall open prior to the appropriation by the General Assembly of the full amount of the additional funds as requested in the application for that school under G.S. 115C-238.51 for the upcoming fiscal year or fiscal biennium, as appropriate. If no appropriation is made by the General Assembly, a revised application may be submitted under subsection (b) of this section. (2012-142, s. 7.11(c).)

§ 115C-238.52. Participation by other education partners.

(a) Any or all of the following education partners may participate in the development of a cooperative innovative high school under this Part that is targeted to high school students who would benefit from accelerated academic instruction:

(1), (2) Repealed by Session Laws 2005-276, s. 7.33(a), effective July 1, 2005.

(3) A private business or organization.

(4) The county board of commissioners in the county in which the cooperative innovative high school is located.

(b) Any or all of the education partners listed in subsection (a) of this section that participate shall:

(1) Jointly apply with the local board of education and the local board of trustees to establish a cooperative innovative high school under this Part.

(2) Be identified in the application.

(3) Sign the written agreement under G.S. 115C-238.53(b). (2003-277, s. 2; 2005-276, s. 7.33(a); 2012-142, s. 7.11(d).)

§ 115C-238.53. Operation of cooperative innovative high schools.

(a) A cooperative innovative high school approved by the State is accountable to the local board of education.

(b) A cooperative innovative high school approved under this Part shall operate under the terms of a written agreement signed by the local board of education, local board of trustees, State Board of Education, and applicable governing Board. The agreement shall incorporate the information provided in the application, as modified during the approval process, and any terms and conditions imposed on the school by the State Board of Education and the applicable governing Board. The agreement may be for a term of no longer than five school years.

(c) A cooperative innovative high school may be operated in a facility owned or leased by the local board of education, the local board of trustees, or the education partner, if any.

(d) A cooperative innovative high school approved under this Part shall provide instruction each school year for at least 185 days or 1,025 instructional hours during nine calendar months, shall comply with laws and policies relating to the education of students with disabilities, and shall comply with Article 27 of this Chapter. The requirements of G.S. 115C-84.2 shall not apply to the school calendar of a program approved under this Part.

(e) A cooperative innovative high school approved under this Part may use State, federal, and local funds allocated to the local school administrative unit, to the applicable governing Board, and to the partner institution of higher education to implement its program. If there is an education partner and if it is a public body, the cooperative innovative high school may use State, federal, and local funds allocated to that body.

(f) Except as provided in this Part and under the terms of the agreement, cooperative innovative high schools:

(1) Shall have the same exemptions from statutes and rules as charter schools operating under Part 6A of this Article, other than those pertaining to personnel.

(2) May be exempted by the State Board of Education or by the applicable governing Board from laws and rules applicable to a local board of education, a local school administrative unit, a community college, a constituent institution, or a local board of trustees. (2003-277, s. 2; 2005-276, s. 7.33(a); 2010-182, s. 1; 2012-142, ss. 7.11(e), 7A.11(c); 2012-145, s. 2.5.)

§ 115C-238.54. Funds for cooperative innovative high schools.

(a) The Department of Public Instruction shall assign a school code for each cooperative innovative high school that is approved under this Part. Notwithstanding G.S. 115C-105.25, once the cooperative innovative high school has been assigned a school code, the local board of education may use these funds for the school and may transfer these funds between funding allotment categories.

(a1) Repealed by Session Laws 2011-145, s. 7.1A(j), effective January 1, 2012.

(b) The local board of trustees may allocate State and federal funds for a cooperative innovative high school that is approved under this Part.

(c) An education partner under G.S. 115C-238.52 that is a public body may allocate State, federal, and local funds for a cooperative innovative high school that is approved under this Part.

(d) If not an education partner under G.S. 115C-238.52, a county board of commissioners in a county where a cooperative innovative high school is located may nevertheless appropriate funds to the school approved under this Part.

(e) The local board of education and the local board of trustees are strongly encouraged to seek funds from sources other than State, federal, and local appropriations. They are strongly encouraged to seek funds the Education Cabinet identifies or obtains under G.S. 116C-4.

(f) Students in cooperative innovative high schools shall not be charged tuition for courses taken through the partner institution of higher education.

(g) Students in cooperative innovative high schools that have a community college as their partner institution of higher education and were approved under G.S. 115C-238.51A(c) shall be included in calculations of budget full-time equivalent students for the North Carolina Community College System. Students in cooperative innovative high schools that have a community college as their partner institution of higher education and were approved under G.S. 115C-238.51A(b) shall not be included in calculations of budget full-time equivalent students for the North Carolina Community College System.

(h) The State Board of Education shall reimburse The University of North Carolina for tuition for courses taken by students at cooperative innovative high schools that have a constituent institution of The University of North Carolina as their partner institution of higher education and were approved under G.S. 115C-238.51A(c). Tuition payments shall not exceed the annual Board of Governors-approved undergraduate resident tuition rate calculated on a per credit hour basis and shall not include fees. In addition, the cooperative innovative high school students' credit hours shall be nonfundable under The University of North Carolina Semester Credit Hour Enrollment Change Funding Model. The State Board of Education shall not reimburse The University of North Carolina for tuition for courses taken by students at cooperative innovative high schools that have a constituent institution of The University of North Carolina as their partner institution of higher education and were approved under G.S. 115C-238.51A(b).

(i) The State Board of Education shall reimburse private North Carolina colleges for tuition for courses taken by students at cooperative innovative high schools that have a private North Carolina college as their partner institution of higher education and were approved under G.S. 115C-238.51A(c). Tuition payments shall not exceed the highest undergraduate resident rate approved by the Board of Governors for The University of North Carolina constituent institutions and shall not include fees. The State Board of Education shall not reimburse private North Carolina colleges for tuition for courses taken by students at cooperative innovative high schools that have a private North

Carolina college as their partner institution of higher education and were approved under G.S. 115C-238.51A(b). (2003-277, s. 2; 2005-276, s. 7.33(a); 2010-31, s. 7.21(b); 2011-145, s. 7.1A(j); 2012-142, s. 7.11(f).)

§ 115C-238.55. Evaluation of cooperative innovative high schools.

The State Board of Education and the governing Boards shall evaluate the success of students in cooperative innovative high schools approved under this Part. Success shall be measured by high school retention rates, high school completion rates, high school dropout rates, certification and associate degree completion, admission to four-year institutions, postgraduation employment in career or study-related fields, and employer satisfaction of employees who participated in and graduated from the schools. The Boards shall jointly report by January 15 of each year to the Joint Legislative Education Oversight Committee on the evaluation of these schools. (2003-277, s. 2; 2005-276, s. 7.33(a); 2009-305, s. 3; 2012-142, s. 7.11(g).)

§§ 115C-238.56 through 115C-238.59: Reserved for future codification purposes. (2003-277, s. 2.)

Part 10. Regional Schools.

§ 115C-238.60. Purpose.

(a)   The purpose of this Part is to authorize local boards of education to jointly establish a regional school to serve enrolled students in two or more local school administrative units that will expand student opportunities for educational success through high quality instructional programming. Regional schools may include partnerships with other education partners, including institutions of higher education and private businesses or organizations, and shall foster, encourage, and promote the development of knowledge and skills in career clusters of critical importance to the region.

(b) Except as otherwise provided in this Part, a regional school is exempt from statutes and rules applicable to a local board of education or local school administrative unit. (2011-241, s. 1.)

§ 115C-238.61. Definitions.

The following definitions apply in this Part:

(1) First generation student. - A student who has no parent who has completed a two- or four-year degree.

(2) Participating units. - A local school administrative unit whose local board of education has adopted a resolution to create a regional school that has been approved by the State Board of Education.

(3) Principal. - The principal of a regional school.

(4) Regional school. - A school created pursuant to G.S. 115C-238.62 which includes all of grades nine through twelve and may include grades seven and eight.

(5) Regional school board of directors or board of directors. - The governing board of a regional school appointed pursuant to G.S. 115C-238.63. (2011-241, s. 1.)

§ 115C-238.62. Creation of regional school.

(a) Resolution to Create a Regional School. - Any two or more local boards of education may create a regional school as provided in this Part. In order to create a regional school, each local board of education shall adopt a resolution stating its intent to create the regional school, which shall include the following:

(1) Name of the regional school.

(2) Names of all other local boards of education known to that local board of education adopting resolutions to create the regional school.

(3) Identification of one of the named local school administrative units to serve as the finance agent for the regional school.

(4) Identification of one of the named local school administrative units to provide, to the extent practicable, school food services to the regional school, if needed.

The local board of education shall develop a plan to provide transportation to the students domiciled in the district.

(b) Recognition of Regional School. - Each local board of education that adopts a resolution as provided in this section shall file a copy of the resolution with the State Board of Education. Upon receipt of resolutions from all local boards of education identified in each resolution for a named regional school, the State Board of Education shall approve the creation of the regional school.

(c) Expansion of Regional School. - A local board of education may adopt a resolution stating its intent to join an existing regional school, which shall include the name of the regional school and the names of all other local boards of education which have previously adopted resolutions to create the regional school. The local board of education shall file a copy of the resolution with the State Board of Education. Following receipt of the petition and after receiving comment from the regional school board of directors, the State Board of Education may approve the expansion of the regional school. (2011-241, s. 1.)

§ 115C-238.63. Regional school boards of directors; appointment; terms of office.

(a) Appointment. - A board of directors for a regional school shall consist of the following members. Appointed members of the board of directors shall be selected for their interest in and commitment to the importance of public education to regional economic development and to the purposes of the regional school.

(1) Local boards of education. - Each participating unit shall appoint one member to the board of directors from among the membership of the local board of education. Members appointed by local boards of education shall serve terms of four years.

(2) Local superintendents. - The local superintendent of the local school administrative unit identified as the finance agent for the regional school shall serve as an ex officio member of the board of directors. One additional superintendent shall be selected from among the superintendents of the participating units by those superintendents. The additional superintendent shall serve an initial term of two years. Subsequent appointees shall serve a term of four years.

(3) Business community. - The board of directors for the chamber of commerce of the county in which the regional school is located, in consultation with the North Carolina Economic Developers Association, shall appoint at least three members as representatives of the business community. At least fifty percent (50%) of the members of the board of directors for the regional school shall be representatives of the business community appointed in accordance with this subdivision. At least one of the appointees shall be a resident of the county in which the regional school is located. The appointees shall serve an initial term of two years. Subsequent appointees shall serve a term of four years.

(4) Parent Advisory Council. - The Parent Advisory Council established by G.S. 115C-238.69 shall appoint a member to the board of directors from among the Council membership. The member appointed by the Council shall serve a term of four years or until the child of the parent no longer attends the regional school.

(5) Higher education partners. - Any institution of higher education partner may appoint a representative of the institution of higher education to serve as an ex officio member of the board of directors.

(b) Vacancies. - Whenever an appointed member of the board of directors shall fail for any reason other than ill health or service in the interest of the State or nation to be present at three successive regular meetings of the board of directors, his or her place as a member of the board of directors shall be deemed vacant. Any member of the board of directors may be removed from office by the appointing authority for misfeasance, malfeasance, or nonfeasance in office. All vacancies shall be filled by the appointing authority for the remainder of the term of office. (2011-241, s. 1; 2013-360, s. 8.20.)

§ 115C-238.64. Board of directors; meetings; rules of procedure; officers.

(a) The board of directors shall meet at least four times a year and may hold special meetings at any time at the call of the chair or upon petition addressed to the chair by a majority of the members of the board of directors. All meetings of the board of directors shall be subject to the requirements of Article 33C of Chapter 143 of the General Statutes.

(b) The board of directors shall elect a chair and a vice-chair from among its members, who shall serve a two-year term.

(c) All members of the board of directors shall be voting members except for the chair, who may vote only on matters to break a tie.

(d) The board of directors shall determine its own rules of procedure and may delegate to such committees as it may create such of its powers as it deems appropriate.

(e) Members of the board of directors shall receive such per diem compensation and necessary travel and subsistence expenses while engaged in the discharge of their official duties as is provided by law for members of State boards and commissions. (2011-241, s. 1.)

§ 115C-238.65. Board of directors; corporate powers.

(a) The board of directors of the regional school shall be known and distinguished by the name of "The _____ Regional School Board of Directors" and shall continue as a body politic and corporate and by that name shall have perpetual succession and a common seal. It shall be able and capable in law to take, demand, receive, and possess all moneys, goods, and chattels that shall be given for the use of the regional school, and to apply to same according to the will of the donors; and by gift, purchase, or devise to receive, possess, enjoy, and retain forever any and all real and personal estate and funds, of whatsoever kind, nature, or quality the same may be, in special trust and confidence that the same, or the profits thereof, shall be applied to and for the use and purpose of establishing and endowing the regional school, and shall have power to receive donations from any source whatsoever, to be devoted exclusively to the purposes of the maintenance of the regional school, or according to the terms of the donation.

(b) The board of directors shall be able and capable in law to bargain, sell, grant, alien, or dispose of and convey and assure to the purchasers any and all such real and personal estate and funds as it may lawfully acquire when the condition of the grant to it or the will of the devisor does not forbid it; and shall be able and capable in law to sue and be sued in all courts whatsoever; and shall have power to open and receive subscriptions; and in general may do all such things as are usually done by bodies corporate and politic, or such as may be necessary for the promotion of learning and virtue. (2011-241, s. 1.)

§ 115C-238.66. Board of directors; powers and duties.

The board of directors shall have the following powers and duties:

(1) Academic program. -

a. The board of directors shall establish the standard course of study for the regional school. This course of study shall set forth the subjects to be taught in each grade and the texts and other educational materials on each subject to be used in each grade. The board of directors shall design its programs to meet at least the student performance standards adopted by the State Board of Education and the student performance standards contained in this Chapter.

b. The board of directors shall conduct student assessments required by the State Board of Education.

c. The board of directors shall provide the opportunity to earn or obtain credit toward degrees from a community college subject to Chapter 115D of the General Statutes or a constituent institution of The University of North Carolina.

d. The board of directors shall adopt a school calendar consisting of a minimum of 185 days or 1,025 hours of instruction covering at least nine calendar months.

(2) Standards of performance and conduct. - The board of directors shall establish policies and standards for academic performance, attendance, and conduct for students of the regional school. The policies of the board of directors shall comply with Article 27 of this Chapter.

(3) School attendance. - Every parent, guardian, or other person in this State having charge or control of a child who is enrolled in the regional school and who is less than 16 years of age shall cause such child to attend school continuously for a period equal to the time that the regional school shall be in session. No person shall encourage, entice, or counsel any child to be unlawfully absent from the regional school. Any person who aids or abets a student's unlawful absence from the regional school shall, upon conviction, be guilty of a Class 1 misdemeanor. The principal shall be responsible for implementing such additional policies concerning compulsory attendance as shall be adopted by the board of directors, including regulations concerning lawful and unlawful absences, permissible excuses for temporary absences, maintenance of attendance records, and attendance counseling.

(4) Reporting. - The board of directors shall comply with the reporting requirements established by the State Board of Education in the Uniform Education Reporting System.

(5) Assessment results. - The board of directors shall provide data to the participating unit in which a student is domiciled on the performance of that student on any testing required by the State Board of Education.

(6) Education of children with disabilities. - The board of directors shall require compliance with laws and policies relating to the education of children with disabilities.

(7) Health and safety. - The board of directors shall require that the regional school meet the same health and safety standards required of a local school administrative unit.

(7a) Emergency Response Plan. - A regional school, in coordination with local law enforcement agencies, is encouraged to adopt an emergency response plan relating to incidents of school violence. These plans are not considered a public record as the term "public record" is defined under G.S. 132-1 and shall not be subject to inspection and examination under G.S. 132-6. Regional schools are encouraged to provide schematic diagrams and keys to the main entrance of school facilities to local law enforcement agencies, in addition to implementing the provisions in G.S. 115C-105.49(b) and G.S. 115C-105.52.

(8) Driving eligibility certificates. - The board of directors shall apply the rules and policies established by the State Board of Education for issuance of driving eligibility certificates.

(9) Purchasing and contracts. - The board of directors shall comply with the purchasing and contract statutes and regulations applicable to local school administrative units.

(10) Exemption from the Administrative Procedures Act. - The board of directors shall be exempt from Chapter 150B of the General Statutes, except final decisions of the board of directors in a contested case shall be subject to judicial review in accordance with Article 4 of Chapter 150B of the General Statutes.

(11) North Carolina School Report Cards. - A regional school shall ensure that the report card issued for it by the State Board of Education receives wide distribution to the local press or is otherwise provided to the public. A regional school shall ensure that the overall school performance score and grade earned by the regional school for the current and previous four school years is prominently displayed on the school Web site. If a regional school is awarded a grade of D or F, the regional school shall provide notice of the grade in writing to the parent or guardian of all students enrolled in that school. (2011-241, ss. 1, 6(a); 2012-142, ss. 7A.3(d), 7A.11(d); 2012-145, s. 2.5; 2013-360, s. 8.43(b).)

§ 115C-238.67. Student admissions and assignment.

(a) Residency Requirement. - A student shall be domiciled in a participating unit to be eligible to attend the regional school. A student's eligibility to remain enrolled in the regional school shall terminate at the end of any school year during which a student ceases to satisfy the residency requirements.

(b) Participating Unit Allotments. - The number of student seats in the freshman class of the regional school shall be assigned proportionate to the total student population of the participating units, as determined by the participating unit's final average daily membership in the preceding school year. If fewer students residing in a participating unit elect to attend the regional school than available allotted seats, the remaining seats shall be divided proportionally among the other participating units.

(c) Admissions Criteria. - The board of directors shall establish criteria, standards, and procedures for admission of students. The admission criteria may give priority to first generation students and shall include the following:

(1) Demonstrated academic achievement.

(2) Demonstrated student interest in attendance.

(3) Documented parental support for student attendance.

(d) Lottery. - If the number of eligible students meeting the board of directors' admission criteria exceeds the seats available through the participating unit allotment, students shall be accepted by lot. (2011-241, s. 1.)

§ 115C-238.68. Employees.

The board of directors shall appoint all certified and noncertified staff.

(1) Principal. - The board of directors shall employ and contract with a principal for a term not to exceed three years. The principal shall meet the requirements for certification set out in G.S. 115C-284, unless waived by the State Board of Education upon submission of a request by the board of directors. The principal shall be responsible for school operations and shall exercise those duties and powers delegated by the board of directors.

(2) Teachers. - The board of directors shall employ and contract with necessary teachers to perform the particular service for which they are employed in the school. At least fifty percent (50%) of teachers employed by the board of directors shall hold teacher certificates, unless waived by the State Board of Education upon submission of a request by the board of directors.

(3) (Effective until July 1, 2014) Career status. - Employees of the board of directors shall not be eligible for career status. If a teacher employed by a local school administrative unit makes a written request for a leave of absence to teach at the regional school, the local school administrative unit shall grant the leave for one year. For the initial year of the regional school's operation, the local school administrative unit may require that the request for a leave of absence be made up to 45 days before the teacher would otherwise have to report for duty. After the initial year of the regional school's operation, the local

school administrative unit may require that the request for a leave of absence be made up to 90 days before the teacher would otherwise have to report for duty. A local board of education is not required to grant a request for a leave of absence or a request to extend or renew a leave of absence for a teacher who previously has received a leave of absence from that school board under this subdivision. A teacher who has career status under G.S. 115C-325 prior to receiving a leave of absence to teach at the regional school may return to a public school in the local school administrative unit with career status at the end of the leave of absence or upon the end of employment at the regional school if an appropriate position is available. If an appropriate position is unavailable, the teacher's name shall be placed on a list of available teachers in accordance with G.S. 115C-325(e)(2).

(3) (Effective July 1, 2014, until June 30, 2018) Leave of absence from local school administrative unit. - If a teacher employed by a local school administrative unit makes a written request for a leave of absence to teach at the regional school, the local school administrative unit shall grant the leave for one year. For the initial year of the regional school's operation, the local school administrative unit may require that the request for a leave of absence be made up to 45 days before the teacher would otherwise have to report for duty. After the initial year of the regional school's operation, the local school administrative unit may require that the request for a leave of absence be made up to 90 days before the teacher would otherwise have to report for duty. A local board of education is not required to grant a request for a leave of absence or a request to extend or renew a leave of absence for a teacher who previously has received a leave of absence from that school board under this subdivision. A teacher who has career status under G.S. 115C-325 prior to receiving a leave of absence to teach at the regional school may return to a public school in the local school administrative unit with career status at the end of the leave of absence or upon the end of employment at the regional school if an appropriate position is available. If an appropriate position is unavailable, the teacher's name shall be placed on a list of available teachers in accordance with G.S. 115C-325(e)(2).

(3) (Effective June 30, 2018) Leave of absence from local school administrative unit. - If a teacher employed by a local school administrative unit makes a written request for a leave of absence to teach at the regional school, the local school administrative unit shall grant the leave for one year. For the initial year of the regional school's operation, the local school administrative unit may require that the request for a leave of absence be made up to 45 days before the teacher would otherwise have to report for duty. After the initial year

of the regional school's operation, the local school administrative unit may require that the request for a leave of absence be made up to 90 days before the teacher would otherwise have to report for duty. A local board of education is not required to grant a request for a leave of absence or a request to extend or renew a leave of absence for a teacher who previously has received a leave of absence from that school board under this subdivision. A teacher who has received a leave of absence to teach at the regional school may return to a public school in the local school administrative unit at the end of the leave of absence or upon the end of employment at the regional school if an appropriate position is available.

(4)   Noncertified staff. - The board of directors also may employ necessary employees who are not required to hold teacher certificates to perform duties other than teaching and may contract for other services.

(5)   Employment dismissal. - An employee of the board of directors is not an employee of the local school administrative unit in which the regional school is located. The board of directors may discharge certified and noncertified employees according to the terms of the employment contract.

(6)   Employee benefits. - Employees of the board of directors shall participate in the Teachers' and State Employees' Retirement System and the State Health Plan on the same terms as employees employed by local boards of education.

(7)   Exemptions. - Employees of the board of directors shall be exempt from Chapter 126 of the General Statutes, except Articles 6 and 7. (2011-241, ss. 1, 6(b); 2013-360, s. 9.7(e), (r).)

§ 115C-238.69. Parent Advisory Council; purpose; appointments.

(a)   Purpose. - There shall be a Parent Advisory Council to serve as a resource and provide input to the board of directors as to the operation of a regional school. The board of directors shall consult the Parent Advisory Council when considering changes to the regional school's operations that may significantly impact students attending the regional school.

(b)   Appointment. - Each local board of education of the participating units shall appoint two members to the Parent Advisory Council for a term of four years or until the member's child no longer attends the regional school. Appointees shall be parents or guardians of students attending the regional school and shall, to the extent possible, reflect the demographic composition of the participating units. (2011-241, s. 1.)

§ 115C-238.70. State and local funds.

(a) The State Board of Education shall allocate to a regional school:

(1) An amount equal to the average per pupil allocation for average daily membership from the participating unit allotments for each child attending the regional school, except for the allocation for children with disabilities and for the allocation for children with limited English proficiency.

(2) An additional amount for each child attending the regional school who is a child with disabilities. In the event a child with disabilities leaves the regional school and enrolls in a public school during the first 60 school days in the school year, the regional school shall return a pro rata amount of funds allocated for that child to the State Board, and the State Board shall reallocate those funds to the local school administrative unit in which the public school is located. In the event a child with disabilities enrolls in the regional school during the first 60 school days in the school year, the State Board shall allocate to the regional school the pro rata amount of additional funds for children with disabilities.

(3) An additional amount for children with limited English proficiency attending the regional school, based on a formula adopted by the State Board.

(4) If the regional school has a final total average daily membership of 100 or more students, an amount to fund 12 months of employment for the school principal position.

(b) The State Board shall allow for annual adjustments to the amount allocated to the regional school based on its enrollment growth in school years subsequent to the initial year of operation.

(c) For each child who enrolls in the regional school, the participating unit in which the child resides shall transfer to the regional school an amount equal to the per pupil amount of all money appropriated to the local current expense fund for the participating unit for the fiscal year. The amount transferred under this subsection that consists of revenue derived from supplemental taxes shall be transferred only if the child enrolled in the regional school resides in that tax district. (2011-241, s. 1; 2013-363, s. 3.5.)

§ 115C-238.71. Finance and budget.

(a) The local school administrative unit identified as the finance agent by resolution pursuant to G.S. 115C-238.62 shall be the finance agent for the Board and shall have all the rights, duties, and obligations for receipt, accounting, and dispersing funds for the board of directors, including all the rights, duties, and obligations specified in Article 31 of this Chapter, which powers shall be exercised by the identified local school administrative unit for and on behalf of the board of directors. The board of directors shall provide reasonable compensation to the local school administrative unit for this service.

(b) No later than 10 days after the money is appropriated to the local current expense fund, each local board of education of a participating unit shall transfer to the board of directors the amount required under G.S. 115C-238.70(c) for each child enrolled in the school who resides in that participating unit. Once it has received funds from the local board of education, the board of directors shall be under no obligation to return the funds. (2011-241, s. 1.)

§ 115C-238.72. Participating units.

(a) Transportation. - Participating units shall develop a plan to provide transportation to the students domiciled in the district.

(b) Food Service. - The local school administrative unit identified by resolution shall provide, to the extent practicable, school food services to the regional school. For purposes of federal funding through the National School Lunch Program or other federally supported food service programs, the local school administrative unit identified by resolution shall be permitted to include eligible students enrolled in the regional school. Other participating units shall not include students enrolled in the regional school for purposes of federally supported food service programs. (2011-241, s. 1.)

§ 115C-238.73. Criminal history record checks.

(a)   As used in this section:

(1)   "Criminal history" means a county, state, or federal criminal history of conviction of a crime, whether a misdemeanor or a felony, that indicates an individual (i) poses a threat to the physical safety of students or personnel or (ii) has demonstrated that he or she does not have the integrity or honesty to fulfill his or her duties as school personnel. These crimes include the following North Carolina crimes contained in any of the following Articles of Chapter 14 of the General Statutes: Article 5A, Endangering Executive and Legislative, and Court Officers; Article 6, Homicide; Article 7A, Rape and Other Sex Offenses; Article 8, Assaults; Article 10, Kidnapping and Abduction; Article 13, Malicious Injury or Damage by Use of Explosive or Incendiary Device or Material; Article 14, Burglary and Other Housebreakings; Article 15, Arson and Other Burnings; Article 16, Larceny; Article 17, Robbery; Article 18, Embezzlement; Article 19, False Pretense and Cheats; Article 19A, Obtaining Property or Services by False or Fraudulent Use of Credit Device or Other Means; Article 20, Frauds; Article 21, Forgery; Article 26, Offenses Against Public Morality and Decency; Article 26A, Adult Establishments; Article 27, Prostitution; Article 28, Perjury; Article 29, Bribery; Article 31, Misconduct in Public Office; Article 35, Offenses Against the Public Peace; Article 36A, Riots and Civil Disorders; Article 39, Protection of Minors; and Article 60, Computer-Related Crime. These crimes also include possession or sale of drugs in violation of the North Carolina Controlled Substances Act, Article 5 of Chapter 90 of the General Statutes, and alcohol-related offenses such as sale to underage persons in violation of G.S. 18B-302 or driving while impaired in violation of G.S. 20-138.1 through G.S. 20-138.5. In addition to the North Carolina crimes listed in this subdivision, such crimes also include similar crimes under federal law or under the laws of other states.

(2)   "School personnel" means any of the following:

a.   Member of the board of directors.

b.   Employee of the regional school.

c.   Independent contractor or employee of an independent contractor of the regional school if the independent contractor carries out duties customarily performed by school personnel, whether paid with federal, State, local, or other funds, who has significant access to students or who has responsibility for the fiscal management of the regional school.

(b)   The board of directors shall adopt a policy on whether and under what circumstances school personnel shall be required to be checked for a criminal history. The board of directors shall apply its policy uniformly in requiring school personnel to be checked for a criminal history. The board of directors may grant conditional approval of an application while the board of directors is checking a person's criminal history and making a decision based on the results of the check.

The board of directors shall not require school personnel to pay for the criminal history record check authorized under this section.

(c)   The board of directors shall require the person to be checked by the Department of Justice (i) to be fingerprinted and to provide any additional information required by the Department of Justice to a person designated by the board of directors or to the local sheriff or the municipal police, whichever is more convenient for the person, and (ii) to sign a form consenting to the check of the criminal record and to the use of fingerprints and other identifying information required by the repositories. The board of directors shall consider refusal to consent when making employment decisions and decisions with regard to independent contractors. The fingerprints of the individual shall be forwarded to the State Bureau of Investigation for a search of the State criminal history record file, and the State Bureau of Investigation shall forward a set of fingerprints to the Federal Bureau of Investigation for a national criminal history record check. The Department of Justice shall provide to the board of directors the criminal history from the State and National Repositories of Criminal Histories of any school personnel for which the board of directors requires a criminal history record check.

The board of directors shall not require school personnel to pay for the fingerprints authorized under this section.

(d)   The board of directors shall review the criminal history it receives on an individual. The board of directors shall determine whether the results of the review indicate that the individual (i) poses a threat to the physical safety of students or personnel or (ii) has demonstrated that he or she does not have the integrity or honesty to fulfill his or her duties as school personnel and shall use the information when making employment decisions and decisions with regard to independent contractors. The board of directors shall make written findings with regard to how it used the information when making employment decisions and decisions with regard to independent contractors. The board of directors may delegate any of the duties in this subsection to the principal.

(e) The board of directors, or the principal if designated by the board of directors, shall provide to the State Board of Education the criminal history it receives on a person who is certificated, certified, or licensed by the State Board of Education. The State Board of Education shall review the criminal history and determine whether the person's certificate or license should be revoked in accordance with State laws and rules regarding revocation.

(f) All the information received by the board of directors through the checking of the criminal history or by the State Board of Education in accordance with this section is privileged information and is not a public record but is for the exclusive use of the board of directors or the State Board of Education. The board of directors or the State Board of Education may destroy the information after it is used for the purposes authorized by this section after one calendar year.

(g) There shall be no liability for negligence on the part of the board of directors, or its employees, or the State Board of Education, or its employees, arising from any act taken or omission by any of them in carrying out the provisions of this section. The immunity established by this subsection shall not extend to gross negligence, wanton conduct, or intentional wrongdoing that would otherwise be actionable. The immunity established by this subsection shall be deemed to have been waived to the extent of indemnification by insurance, indemnification under Articles 31A and 31B of Chapter 143 of the General Statutes, and to the extent sovereign immunity is waived under the Tort Claims Act, as set forth in Article 31 of Chapter 143 of the General Statutes.

(h) Any applicant for employment who willfully furnishes, supplies, or otherwise gives false information on an employment application that is the basis for a criminal history record check under this section shall be guilty of a Class A1 misdemeanor. (2011-241, s. 1.)

Article 17.

Supporting Services.

Part 1. Transportation.

§ 115C-239. Authority of local boards of education.

Each local board of education is hereby authorized to acquire, own, lease, contract and operate school buses for the transportation of pupils enrolled in the public schools of such local school administrative unit, and of persons employed in the operation of such schools in accordance with rules and regulations adopted by the State Board of Education under the authority of G.S. 115C-12(17) and within the limitations set forth in G.S. 115C-239 to 115C-246, 115C-248 to 115C-254 and 115C-256 to 115C-259. Boards of education which own and operate school buses for the transportation of pupils shall have authority to establish separate systems of transportation for pupils attending elementary schools and for pupils attending middle schools, junior high schools, or senior high schools. Each such board may operate such buses to and from such of the schools within the local school administrative unit, and in such number, as the board shall from time to time find practicable and appropriate for the safe, orderly and efficient transportation of such pupils and employees to such schools. (1955, c. 1372, art. 21, s. 1; 1973, c. 586, s. 1; 1981, c. 423, s. 1; 1983, c. 630, s. 2; 2001-97, s. 3.)

§ 115C-240. Authority and duties of State Board of Education.

(a)   The State Board of Education shall promulgate rules and regulations for the operation of a public school transportation system.

(b)   The State Board of Education shall be under no duty to supply transportation to any pupil or employee enrolled or employed in any school. Neither the State nor the State Board of Education shall in any manner be liable for the failure or refusal of any local board of education to furnish transportation, by school bus or otherwise, to any pupil or employee of any school, or for any neglect or action of any county or city board of education, or any employee of any such board, in the operation or maintenance of any school bus.

(c)   The State Board of Education shall from time to time adopt such rules and regulations with reference to the construction, equipment, color, and maintenance of school buses, the number of pupils who may be permitted to ride at the same time upon any bus, and the age and qualifications of drivers of school buses as it shall deem to be desirable for the purpose of promoting safety in the operation of school buses. Every school bus that is capable of operating on diesel fuel shall be capable of operating on diesel fuel with a minimum biodiesel concentration of B-20, as defined in G.S. 143-58.4. No school bus shall be operated for the transportation of pupils unless such bus is constructed and maintained as prescribed in such regulations and is equipped with adequate heating facilities, a standard signaling device for giving due notice that the bus is about to make a turn, an alternating flashing stoplight on the front of the bus, an alternating flashing stoplight on the rear of the bus, and such other warning devices, fire protective equipment and first aid supplies as may be prescribed for installation upon such buses by the regulation of the State Board of Education.

(d)   The State Board of Education shall assist local boards of education by establishing guidelines and a framework through which local boards may establish, review and amend school bus routes prepared pursuant to G.S. 115C-246. The State Board shall also require local boards to implement the Transportation Information Management System or an equivalent system approved by the State Board of Education, no later than September 1, 1992. The State Board of Education shall also assist local boards of education with reference to the acquisition and maintenance of school buses or any other question which may arise in connection with the organization and operation of school bus transportation systems of local boards.

(e)   The State Board of Education shall allocate to the respective local boards of education funds appropriated from time to time by the General Assembly for the purpose of providing transportation to the pupils enrolled in the public schools within this State. Such funds shall be allocated by the State Board of Education in accordance with the number of pupils to be transported, the length of bus routes, road conditions and all other circumstances affecting the cost of the transportation of pupils by school bus to the end that the funds so appropriated may be allocated on a fair and equitable basis, according to the needs of the respective local school administrative units and so as to provide the most efficient use of such funds. Such allocation shall be made by the State Board of Education at the beginning of each fiscal year, except that the State Board may reserve for future allocation from time to time within such fiscal year as the need therefor shall be found to exist, a reasonable amount not to exceed ten percent (10%) of the total funds available for transportation in such fiscal year from such appropriation. If there is evidence of inequitable or inefficient use of funds, the State Board of Education shall be empowered to review school bus routes established by local boards pursuant to G.S. 115C-246 as well as other factors affecting the cost of the transportation of pupils by school bus.

(f) The respective local boards shall use such funds for the purposes of replacing, maintaining, insuring, and operating public school buses and service vehicles in accordance with the provisions of G.S. 115C-239 to 115C-246, 115C-248 to 115C-254 and 115C-256 to 115C-259 and for no other purpose, but in the making of expenditures for such purposes shall be subject to rules and regulations promulgated by the State Board of Education. (1955, c. 1372, art. 21, p. 2; 1981, c. 423, s. 1; 1983, c. 630, ss. 3-6; 1989 (Reg. Sess., 1990), c. 1066, s. 96(a); 1991 (Reg. Sess., 1992), c. 900, s. 77(a); 2007-423, s. 1.)

§ 115C-241. Assignment of school buses to schools.

The superintendent of the schools of each local school administrative unit which shall elect to operate a school bus transportation system, shall, prior to the commencement of each regular school year and subject to the approval of the local board of education, allocate and assign to the respective public schools within the jurisdiction of such local school administrative unit the school buses which the local board shall own and direct to be operated during such school year. From time to time during such school year, subject to the directions of the local board of education, the superintendent may revise such allocation and assignment of school buses in accordance with the changing transportation needs and conditions at the respective schools of such local school administrative unit, and may, pursuant to such revision, assign an additional bus or buses to a school or withdraw a bus or buses from a school in such local school administrative unit. (1955, c. 1372, art. 21, s. 3; 1981, c. 423, s. 1.)

§ 115C-242. Use and operation of school buses.

Public school buses may be used for the following purposes only, and it shall be the duty of the superintendent of the school of each local school administrative unit to supervise the use of all school buses operated by such local school administrative unit so as to assure and require compliance with this section:

(1) A school bus may be used for the transportation of pupils enrolled in and employees in the operation of the school to which such bus is assigned by the superintendent of the local school administrative unit. Except as otherwise herein provided, such transportation shall be limited to transportation to and

from such school for the regularly organized school day, and from and to the points designated by the principal of the school to which such bus is assigned, for the receiving and discharging of passengers. No pupil or employee shall be so transported upon any bus other than the bus to which such pupil or employee has been assigned pursuant to the provisions of this Article: Provided, that children enrolled in a Headstart program or any More at Four program may be transported on public school buses, and any additional costs associated with such contractual arrangements shall be incurred by the benefitting Head Start or More at Four program: Provided further, that children with disabilities may be transported to and from the nearest appropriate private school having a special education program approved by the State Board of Education if the children to be transported are or have been placed in that program by a local school administrative unit as a result of the State or the unit's duty to provide such children with a free appropriate public education.

(2) In the case of illness or injury requiring immediate medical attention of any pupil or employee while such pupil or employee is present at the school in which such pupil is enrolled or such employee is employed, the principal of such school may, in his discretion, permit such pupil or employee to be transported by a school bus to a doctor or hospital for medical treatment, and may, in his discretion, permit such other person as he may select to accompany such pupil.

(3) The board of education of any local school administrative unit may operate the school buses of such unit one day prior to the opening of the regular school term for the transportation of pupils and employees to and from the school to which such pupils are assigned or in which they are enrolled and such employees are employed, for the purposes of the registration of students, the organization of classes, the distribution of textbooks, and such other purposes as will, in the opinion of the superintendent of the schools of such unit, promote the efficient organization and operation of such public schools.

(4) A local board of education which elects to operate a school bus transportation system, shall not be required to provide transportation for any school employee, nor shall such board be required to provide transportation for any pupil living within one and one half miles of the school in which such pupil is enrolled.

(5) Local boards of education, under rules adopted by the State Board of Education, may permit the use and operation of school buses for the transportation of pupils and instructional personnel as the board deems necessary to serve the instructional programs of the schools. Included in the

use permitted by this section is the transportation of children with disabilites, and children enrolled in programs that require transportation from the school grounds during the school day, such as special vocational or occupational programs. On any such trip, a city or county-owned school bus shall not be taken out of the State.

If State funds are inadequate to pay for the transportation approved by the local board of education, local funds may be used for these purposes. Local boards of education shall determine that funds are available to such boards for the transportation of children to and from the school to which they are assigned for the entire school year before authorizing the use and operation of school buses for other services deemed necessary to serve the instructional program of the schools.

Children with disabilities may be transported to and from the nearest appropriate private school having a special education program approved by the State Board of Education if the children to be transported have been placed in that program by a local school administrative unit as a result of the State or the unit's duty to provide those children with a free appropriate public education.

(6)   School buses owned by a local board of education may be used for emergency management purposes in any state of disaster or local state of emergency declared under Chapter 166A of the General Statutes. Under rules and regulations adopted by a local board of education, its school buses may be used with its permission for the purpose of testing emergency management plans; however, neither the State Board of Education nor the local board of education shall be liable for the operating cost, any compensation claims or any tort claims resulting from the test.

(7)   Uses authorized by G.S. 115C-243. (1955, c. 1372, art. 21, s. 4; 1957, c. 1103; 1969, c. 47; 1973, c. 869; 1977, c. 830, ss. 2, 3; 1977, 2nd Sess., c. 1280, s. 2; 1979, c. 885; 1981, c. 423, s. 1; 1983, c. 630, s. 7; c. 768, s. 8; 1987, c. 827, s. 49; 2006-66, s. 7.18(i); 2006-69, s. 3(g).)

§ 115C-243. Use of school buses by senior citizen groups.

(a)   Any local board of education may enter into agreements with the governing body of any county, city, or town, or with any State agency, or any agency established or identified pursuant to Public Law 89-73, Older Americans

Act of 1965, to provide for the use of school buses to provide transportation for the elderly.

(b) Each agreement entered into under this section must provide the following:

(1) That the board of education shall be reimbursed in full for the proportionate share of any and all costs, both fixed and variable, of such buses attributable to the uses of the bus pursuant to the agreement.

(2) That the board of education shall be held harmless from any and all liability by virtue of uses of the buses pursuant to the agreement.

(3) That adequate liability insurance is maintained under G.S. 115C-42 to insure the board of education, and that adequate insurance is maintained to protect the property of the board of education. The minimum limit of liability insurance shall not be less than the maximum amount of damages which may be awarded under the Tort Claims Act, G.S. 143-291. The costs of said insurance shall be paid by the agency contracting for the use of the bus, either directly or through the fee established by the agreement.

(c) Before any board of education shall enter into any agreement under this section, it must by resolution establish a policy for use of school buses by the elderly. The policy must give first priority to school uses under G.S. 115C-242 and 115C-42. The resolution must provide for a schedule of charges under this section. Such resolution, if adopted, shall be amended or readopted at least once per year to provide for adjustments to the schedule of charges or to provide for maintaining the same schedule of charges. If the price bid for the service by a private bus carrier is less than the schedule of charges adopted by the board of education, then the board of education may not enter into the agreement.

(d) No board of education shall be under any duty to sign any agreement under this section.

(e) No bus operated under the provisions of this section shall travel outside of the area consisting of the county or counties where the local board of education is located and the county or counties contiguous to that county or counties, but not outside of the State of North Carolina.

(f) Before any agreement under this section may be signed, the State Board of Education shall adopt a uniform schedule of charges for the use of buses under this section. Such schedule shall include a charge by the hour and by the mile which shall cover all costs both fixed and variable, including depreciation, gasoline, fuel, labor, maintenance, and insurance. The schedule may be amended by the State Board of Education. The schedule of charges adopted by the local board of education under subsection (c) may vary from the State schedule only to cover changes in wages. (1977, 2nd Sess., c. 1280, s. 1; 1981, c. 423, s. 1; 1983, c. 717, s. 92; 1985 (Reg. Sess., 1986), c. 955, ss. 17, 18; 2006-203, s. 32.)

§ 115C-244. Assignment of pupils to school buses.

(a) The superintendent or superintendent's designee shall assign the pupils and employees who may be transported to and from school upon the bus or buses assigned to each school and shall implement and enforce the plan developed under G.S. 115C-246. No pupil or employee shall be permitted to ride upon any school bus to which such pupil or employee has not been so assigned by the superintendent or superintendent's designee, except by the express direction of the superintendent or superintendent's designee.

(b) In the event that the superintendent or superintendent's designee assigns a school bus to be used in the transportation of pupils to two or more schools, the superintendent or superintendent's designee shall assign the pupils to be transported to and from each school by that bus, and the principals of the respective schools shall implement and enforce this assignment of pupils.

(c) Any pupil enrolled in any school, or the parent or guardian of any such pupil, or the person standing in loco parentis to such pupil, may apply to the principal of such school for transportation of such pupil to and from such school by school bus for the regularly organized school day. The principal shall deliver the application to the superintendent or superintendent's designee, who shall assign a pupil to a school bus if the pupil is entitled to school bus transportation under this Article and the rules of the State Board of Education. Such assignment shall be made by the superintendent or superintendent's designee so as to provide for the orderly, safe and efficient transportation of pupils to such school and so as to promote the orderly and efficient administration of the school and the health, safety and general welfare of the pupils to be so transported. Assignments of pupils and employees to school buses may be changed by the superintendent or superintendent's designee as he may from time to time find proper for the safe and efficient transportation of such pupils and employees.

(d) The parent or guardian of any pupil enrolled in any school, or the person standing in loco parentis to any such pupil, who shall apply under subsection (c) of this section for the transportation of such pupil to and from such school by school bus, may, if such application is denied, or if such pupil is assigned to a school bus not satisfactory to such parent, guardian, or person standing in loco parentis to such pupil, pursuant to rules and regulations established by the local board of education, apply to such board for such transportation upon a school bus designated in such application, and shall be entitled to a prompt and fair hearing by such board in accordance with the rules and regulations established by it. The majority of such board shall be a quorum for the purpose of holding such hearing and passing upon such application, and the decision of the majority of the members present at such hearing shall be the decision of the board. If, at such hearing, the board shall find that pupil is entitled to be transported to and from such school upon the school bus designated in such application, or if the board shall find that the transportation of such pupil upon such bus to and from such school will be for the best interests of such pupil, will not interfere with the proper administration of such school, or with the safe and efficient transportation by school bus of other pupils enrolled in such school and will not endanger the health or safety of the children there enrolled, the board shall direct that such child be assigned to and transported to such school upon such bus.

(e) A decision of a local board under subsection (d) is final and, except as provided in this subsection, is subject to judicial review in accordance with Article 4 of Chapter 150B of the General Statutes. A person seeking judicial review shall file a petition in the superior court of the county where the local board made its decision.

(f) No employee shall be assigned to or permitted to ride upon a school bus when to do so will result in the overcrowding of such bus or will prevent the assignment to such bus of a pupil entitled to ride thereon, or will otherwise, in the opinion of the superintendent or superintendent's designee, be detrimental to the comfort or safety of the pupils assigned to such bus, or to the safe, efficient and proper operation of such bus. (1955, c. 1372, art. 21, s. 5; 1981, c. 423, s. 1; 1987, c. 827, ss. 47, 48; 1998-220, s. 3.)

§ 115C-245. School bus drivers; monitors; safety assistants.

(a) Each local board, which elects to operate a school bus transportation system, shall employ the necessary drivers for such school buses. The drivers shall have all qualifications prescribed by the regulations of the State Board of Education herein provided for and must be at least 18 years old and have at least six months driving experience as a licensed operator of a motor vehicle before employment as a regular or substitute driver, but the selection and employment of each driver shall be made by the local board of education, and the driver shall be the employee of such local school administrative unit. Each local board of education shall assign the bus drivers employed by it to the respective schools within the jurisdiction of such board, and the superintendent or superintendent's designee shall assign the drivers to the school buses to be driven by them. No school bus shall at any time be driven or operated by any person other than the bus driver assigned to such bus except by the express direction of the superintendent or superintendent's designee or in accordance with rules and regulations of the appropriate local board of education.

(b) The driver of a school bus subject to the direction of the superintendent or superintendent's designee shall have complete authority over and responsibility for the operation of the bus and the maintaining of good order and conduct upon such bus, and shall report promptly to the principal any misconduct upon such bus or disregard or violation of the driver's instructions by any person riding upon such bus. The principal may take such action with reference to any such misconduct upon a school bus, or any violation of the instructions of the driver, as he might take if such misconduct or violation had occurred upon the grounds of the school.

(c) The driver of any school bus shall permit no person to ride upon such bus except pupils or school employees assigned thereto or persons permitted by the express direction of the superintendent or superintendent's designee to ride thereon.

(d) The superintendent or superintendent's designee may, in his discretion, appoint a monitor for any bus assigned to any school. It shall be the duty of such monitor, subject to the direction of the driver of the bus, to preserve order upon the bus and do such other things as may be appropriate for the safety of the pupils and employees assigned to such bus while boarding such bus, alighting therefrom or being transported thereon, and to require such pupils and employees to conform to the rules and regulations established by the local board of education for the safety of pupils and employees upon school buses.

Such monitors shall be unpaid volunteers who shall serve at the pleasure of the superintendent or superintendent's designee.

(e)   A local board of education may, in its discretion within funds available, employ transportation safety assistants upon recommendation of the principal through the superintendent. The safety assistants thus employed shall assist the bus drivers with the safety, movement, management, and care of children boarding the bus, leaving the bus, or being transported in it. The safety assistant should be either an adult or a certified student driver who is available as a substitute bus driver. (1955, c. 1372, art. 21, s. 6; 1979, c. 719, ss. 1-4; 1979, 2nd Sess., c. 1156; 1981, c. 423, s. 1; 1987, c. 276; 1989, c. 558, s. 2; 1998-220, s. 4.)

§ 115C-246. School bus routes.

(a)   The superintendent of the local school administrative unit shall, prior to the commencement of each regular school year, prepare a plan for a definite route, including stops for receiving and discharging pupils, for each school bus so as to assure the most efficient use of such bus and the safety and convenience of the pupils assigned thereto. The superintendent may, in his discretion, obtain the advice of the State Board of Education with reference to the plan. The buses shall be operated upon the route so established and not otherwise, except as provided in this Article. From time to time the principal may suggest changes in any such bus route as he shall deem proper for the said purposes, and the same shall be effective when approved by the superintendent of the local school administrative unit.

(b)   Unless road or other conditions make it inadvisable, public school buses shall be routed on state-maintained highways, municipal streets, or other streets with publicly dedicated right-of-way. The local board of education shall not be responsible for damage to the roadway. Each public school bus shall be routed so that the bus passes within one mile of the residence of each pupil assigned to that bus. A pupil who lives one and one-half miles or more from the school to which the pupil is assigned shall be eligible for school bus transportation.

(c)   All bus routes when established pursuant to this section shall be filed in the office of the board of education of the local school administrative unit, and all changes made therein shall be filed in the office of such board within 10 days after such change shall become effective.

(d) Repealed by Session Laws 1985 (Regular Session, 1986), c. 975, s. 24.

(e) No provision of this Article shall be construed to place upon the State, or upon any county or city, any duty to supply any funds for the transportation of pupils, or any duty to supply funds for the transportation of pupils who live within the corporate limits of the city or town in which is located the public school in which such pupil is enrolled or to which such pupil is assigned, even though transportation to or from such school is furnished to pupils who live outside the limits of such city or town. (1955, c. 1372, art. 21, s. 7; 1959, c. 573, s. 15; 1963, c. 990, ss. 2, 3; 1965, c. 1095, ss. 2, 3; 1981, c. 423, s. 1; 1985 (Reg. Sess., 1986), c. 975, s. 24; 1987, c. 827, s. 49; 1989 (Reg. Sess., 1990), c. 1066, s. 96(b); 2005-151, s. 1.)

§ 115C-247. Purchase of activity buses by local boards.

The several local boards of education in the State are hereby authorized and empowered to take title to school buses purchased with local or community funds for the purpose of transporting pupils to and from athletic events and for other local school activity purposes, and commonly referred to as activity buses.

Each local board of education that operates activity buses shall adopt a policy relative to the proper use of the vehicles. The policy shall permit the use of these buses for travel to athletic events during the regular season and playoffs and for travel to other school-sponsored activities.

The provisions of G.S. 115C-42 shall be fully applicable to the ownership and operation of such activity school buses. Activity buses may also be used as provided in G.S. 115C-243. (1955, c. 1256; 1957, c. 685; 1959, c. 573, s. 2; 1961, c. 1102, s. 4; 1977, 2nd Sess., c. 1280, s. 3; 1981, c. 423, s. 1; 2006-208, s. 1.)

§ 115C-248. Inspection of school buses and activity buses; report of defects by drivers; discontinuing use until defects remedied.

(a) The superintendent of each local school administrative unit, shall cause each school bus owned or operated by such local school administrative unit to be inspected at least once each 30 days during the school year for mechanical defects, or other defects which may affect the safe operation of such bus. A report of such inspection, together with the recommendations of the person making the inspection, shall be filed promptly in the office of the superintendent of such local school administrative unit, and a copy thereof shall be forwarded to the principal of the school to which such bus is assigned.

(b)   It shall be the duty of the driver of each school bus to report promptly to the principal of the school, to which such bus is assigned, any mechanical defect or other defect which may affect the safe operation of the bus when such defect comes to the attention of the driver, and the principal shall thereupon report such defect to the superintendent of the local school administrative unit. It shall be the duty of the superintendent of the local school administrative unit to cause any and all such defects to be corrected promptly.

(c)   If any school bus is found by the principal of the school, to which it is assigned, or by the superintendent of the local school administrative unit, to be so defective that the bus may not be operated with reasonable safety, it shall be the duty of such principal or superintendent to cause the use of such bus to be discontinued until such defect is remedied, in which event the principal of the school, to which such bus is assigned, may permit the use of a different bus assigned to such school in the transportation of the pupils and employees assigned to the bus found to be defective.

(d)   The superintendent of each local school administrative unit, shall cause each activity bus which is used for the transportation of students by such local school administrative unit or any public school system therein to be inspected for mechanical defects, or other defects which may affect the safe operation of such activity bus, at the same time and in the same way and manner as the regular public school buses for the normal transportation of public school pupils are inspected. A report of such inspection, together with the recommendations of the person making the inspection, shall be filed with the principal of the school which uses and operates such activity bus and a copy shall be forwarded to the superintendent of the local school administrative unit involved. It shall be the duty of the driver of each activity bus to make the same reports to the principal of the school using and operating such activity bus as is required by this section. If any public school activity bus is found to be so defective that the activity bus may not be operated with reasonable safety, it shall be the duty of such principal to cause the use of such activity bus to be discontinued until such defect is remedied to the satisfaction of the person making the inspection and a report to this effect has been filed in the manner herein prescribed. Nothing in this subsection shall authorize the use of State funds for the purchase, operation or repair of any activity bus. (1955, c. 1372, art. 21, s. 8; 1961, c. 474; 1975, c. 150, s. 2; 1981, c. 423, s. 1.)

§ 115C-249. Purchase and maintenance of school buses, materials and supplies.

(a) To the extent that the funds shall be made available to it for such purpose, a local board of education is authorized to purchase from time to time such additional school buses and service vehicles or replacements for school buses and service vehicles, as may be deemed by such board to be necessary for the safe and efficient transportation of pupils enrolled in the schools within such local school administrative unit. Any school bus so purchased shall be constructed and equipped as prescribed by the provisions of this Article and by the regulations of the State Board of Education issued pursuant thereto. Any school bus so purchased that is capable of operating on diesel fuel shall be capable of operating on diesel fuel with a minimum biodiesel concentration of B-20, as defined in G.S. 143-58.4. At least two percent (2%) of the total volume of fuel purchased annually by local school districts statewide for use in school bus diesel engine motor vehicles shall be biodiesel fuel of a minimum blend of B-20, to the extent that biodiesel blend is available and compatible with the technology of the vehicles or equipment used.

(b) The tax-levying authorities of any county are hereby authorized to make provision from time to time in the capital outlay budget of the county for the purchase of such school buses or service vehicles.

(c) Any funds appropriated from time to time by the General Assembly for the purchase of school buses or service vehicles shall be allocated by the State Board of Education to the respective local boards of education in accordance with the requirements of such boards as determined by the State Board of Education, and thereupon shall be paid over to the respective local boards of education in accordance with such allocation.

(c1) In determining which school buses in the statewide fleet are to be replaced with State funds in a given year, the State Board of Education shall give highest priority to safety concerns.

A bus is eligible for replacement with State funds based on its age and mileage when it is either 20 years old by model year or has been operated for 250,000 miles, except as follows:

(1)   A bus that has been operated for less than 150,000 miles is not eligible for replacement regardless of its model year.

(2)   A bus that is less than 15 years old by model year is not eligible for replacement until the bus has been operated for 300,000 miles.

(c2)   The State Board of Education may authorize the replacement of up to 30 buses each year due to safety concerns regarding the bus or mechanical or structural problems that would place an undue burden on a local school administrative unit.

(c3)   A local school administrative unit shall receive an incentive payment of two thousand dollars ($2,000) at the beginning of each school year for each bus that it continues to operate although the bus is eligible for replacement, until the bus is 23 years old by model year. The local school administrative unit may use these bonus funds for the additional maintenance costs of operating buses with higher mileage or for any other school purpose.

(d)   The title to any additional or replacement school bus or service vehicle purchased pursuant to the provisions of this section, shall be taken in the name of the board of education of such local school administrative unit, and such bus shall in all respects be maintained and operated pursuant to the provisions of this Article in the same manner as any other public school bus.

(e)   It shall be the duty of the county board of education to provide adequate buildings and equipment for the storage and maintenance of all school buses and service vehicles owned or operated by the board of education of any local school administrative unit in such county. It shall be the duty of the tax-levying authorities of such county to provide in its capital outlay budget for the construction or acquisition of such buildings and equipment as may be required for this purpose.

(f)   In the event of the damage or destruction of any school bus or service vehicle by fire, collision, or otherwise, the board of education of the local school administrative unit which shall own or operate such bus or service vehicle may apply to the State Board of Education for funds with which to replace it. If the State Board of Education finds that such bus or service vehicle has been destroyed or damaged to the extent that it cannot be made suitable for further use, and if the State Board of Education finds that the replacement of such bus or service vehicle is necessary in order to enable such local school administrative unit to operate properly its school bus transportation system, the State Board of Education shall allot to the board of education of such local school administrative unit from the funds now held by the State Board of Education for the replacement of school buses or service vehicles, or from funds hereafter appropriated by the General Assembly for that purpose, a sum sufficient to purchase a new school bus or service vehicle to be used as a replacement for such damaged or destroyed bus or service vehicle and upon such allocation such sum shall be paid over to or for the account of the board of education of such local school administrative unit for such purpose.

(g) Repealed by Session Laws 2003-147, s. 3, effective for a local school administrative unit when the unit is certified as being E-Procurement compliant, or April 1, 2004, whichever occurs first.

(h) Appropriations by the General Assembly for the purchase of public school buses shall not revert to the General Fund. Any unexpended portion of those appropriations shall at the end of each fiscal year be transferred to a reserve account and be held, together with any other funds appropriated for the purpose, for the purchase of public school buses. (1955, c. 1372, art. 21, s. 9; 1961, c. 833, s. 16; 1975, c. 879, s. 46; 1981, c. 423, s. 1; 1987, c. 827, s. 49; 1991 (Reg. Sess., 1992), c. 1039, s. 24; 2003-147, s. 3; 2004-203, s. 72(b); 2007-423, s. 2; 2013-360, s. 8.11(a).)

§ 115C-249.1. Purchase of tires for school buses; repair or refurbishment of tires for school buses.

(a) Definitions. - The following terms apply in this section:

(1) Critical tire information. - Tire brand name, tire line name, tire identification numbers, load and pressure markings, tire size designation, service descriptions such as load and speed ratings, and other information and specifications placed on the original tire sidewall by the original tire manufacturer.

(2) School bus. - A vehicle as defined in G.S. 20-4.01(27)d3. and G.S. 20-4.01(27)d4. that is owned, rented, or leased by a local board of education.

(b) Forensic Tire Standards. - In order to preserve critical tire information, a local board of education shall procure and install for school buses only tires that possess the original, unaltered, and uncovered tire sidewall. Furthermore, a local board of education shall not execute a contract for the repair or refurbishment of tires for school buses that provides for the removal, covering, or other alteration in any manner of the critical tire information contained on the original tire sidewall.

(c) Tire Purchase and Contract Standards Applicability. - All contracts for the purchase, repair, or refurbishment of tires for school buses, or contracts for the purchase of products or services related to the repair or refurbishment of tires for school buses, executed on or after the date this section becomes effective shall comply with the provisions of this section.

(d) Exemption. - Notwithstanding the provisions of this section, a local board of education that owns or has a legally binding contract in place for the future purchase of tires having altered or covered sidewalls prior to the date that this section becomes effective shall perform its existing contractual obligations related thereto and may continue to use those tires on school buses for the useful life of the retreaded tire. (2011-145, s. 28.36(b).)

§ 115C-250. Authority to expend funds for transportation of children with disabilities.

(a) The State Board of Education and local boards of education may expend public funds for transportation of children with disabilities who are unable because of their disability to ride the regular school buses and who have been placed in programs by a local school board as a part of its duty to provide these children with a free appropriate education under Article 9 of this Chapter. At the option of the local board of education with the concurrence of the State Board of Education, funds appropriated to the State Board of Education for contract transportation of children with disabilities may be used to purchase buses and minibuses as well as for the purposes authorized in the budget. The State Board of Education shall adopt rules concerning the construction and equipment of these buses and minibuses.

The Departments of Health and Human Services, Juvenile Justice and Delinquency Prevention, and Correction may also expend public funds for transportation of children with disabilities who are unable because of their disability to ride the regular school buses and who have been placed in programs by one of these agencies as a part of that agency's duty to provide these children with a free appropriate public education under Article 9 of this Chapter.

If a local area mental health center places a child with a disability in an educational program, the local area mental health center shall pay for the transportation of the child who is unable due to the disability to ride the regular school buses to the program.

(b)   Funds appropriated for the transportation of children with disabilities may be used to pay transportation safety assistants employed in accordance with G.S. 115C-245(e) for buses to which children with disabilities are assigned. (1955, c. 1372, art. 21, s. 6; 1973, c. 1351, s. 1; 1975, c. 678, ss. 9, 10; 1977, c. 830, s. 1; 1979, c. 719, ss. 1-4; 1979, 2nd Sess., c. 1156; 1981, c. 423, s. 1; c. 912, s. 1; 1981 (Reg. Sess., 1982), c. 1282, s. 31; 1985, c. 479, s. 26(b); 1987, c. 769; 1997-443, s. 11A.118(a); 1998-202, s. 4(n); 2000-137, s. 4(q); 2006-69, s. 3(h).)

§ 115C-251. Transportation supervisors.

The State Board of Education shall from time to time adopt such rules and regulations with regard to the qualifications of persons employed by local boards of education as chief mechanic or supervisor of transportation as it shall deem necessary or desirable for the purpose of assuring the proper maintenance and safety of school buses. A local board of education shall not employ any person as chief mechanic or supervisor of transportation if that person does not meet the qualifications established by the State Board. (1977, c. 314; 1981, c. 423, s. 1.)

§ 115C-252. Aid in lieu of transportation.

(a)   When, by reason of road conditions or otherwise, any local board of education, which shall elect to operate a school bus transportation system, shall find it impracticable to furnish to a pupil transportation by school bus to the school in which such pupil is enrolled, or to which such pupil is assigned, the board may assign such pupil to such other school within such local school administrative unit as the board shall deem advisable, unless the parent or guardian of such pupil or the person standing in loco parentis to such pupil, shall notify the principal of the school, in which such pupil is enrolled or to which such pupil is assigned, of the desire of such pupil to continue to attend such school without the benefit of transportation by school bus.

(b)   In the event that any local board of education, which shall operate a system of school bus transportation, shall find it impracticable to furnish to a pupil such transportation to the school in which such pupil is enrolled or to which such pupil is assigned, and if, as a result thereof, such pupil shall be required to obtain board and lodging at a place other than the residence of such pupil in order to attend a school, such board may, in its discretion, provide for the payment to the parent or guardian of such pupil of a sum not to exceed fifty dollars ($50.00) per month for each school month that such pupil shall so obtain board and lodging at a place other than the residence of the pupil for the purpose of attending a school. (1955, c. 1372, art. 21, s. 10; 1973, c. 932; 1981, c. 423, s. 1.)

§ 115C-253. Contracts for transportation.

Any local board of education may, in lieu of the operation by it of public school buses, enter into a contract with any person, firm or corporation for the transportation by such person, firm or corporation of pupils enrolled in the public schools of such local school administrative unit for the same purposes for which such local school administrative unit is authorized by this Article to operate public school buses. Any vehicle used by such person, firm or corporation for the transportation of such pupils shall be constructed and equipped as provided in rules and regulations promulgated by the State Board of Education, and the driver of such vehicle shall possess all of the qualifications prescribed by rules and regulations promulgated by the State Board of Education. Where a contract for transportation of pupils is entered into between a local board of education and any person, firm or corporation which contemplates the use of an automobile or vehicle other than a bus for the transportation of 16 pupils or less, the automobile or vehicle shall not be required to be constructed and equipped as provided for in G.S. 115C-240(c), but shall be constructed and equipped pursuant to rules and regulations promulgated by the State Board of Education. In the event that any local board of education shall enter into such a contract, the board may use for such purposes any funds which it might use for the operation of school buses owned by the board, and the tax-levying authorities of the county or of the city may provide in the county or city budget such additional funds as may be necessary to carry out such contracts. (1955, c. 1372, art. 21, s. 11; 1975, c. 382; 1981, c. 423, s. 1; 1987, c. 827, ss. 49, 50; 2007-423, s. 3.)

§ 115C-254. Use of school buses by State defense militia or North Carolina National Guard.

When requested to do so by the Governor, the board of education of any local school administrative unit is authorized and directed to furnish a sufficient number of school buses to the North Carolina State Defense Militia or the North Carolina National Guard for the purpose of transporting members of the State defense militia or members of the North Carolina National Guard to and from authorized places of encampment, or to and from places to which members of the State defense militia or members of the North Carolina National Guard are ordered to proceed for the purpose of suppressing riots or insurrections, repelling invasions or dealing with any other emergency. Public school buses so furnished by any local school administrative unit to the State defense militia or the North Carolina National Guard shall be operated by members or employees of the State defense militia or North Carolina National Guard, and all expense of such operation, including any repair or replacement of any bus occasioned by such operation, shall be paid by the State from the appropriations available for the use of the State defense militia or the North Carolina National Guard. (1955, c. 1372, art. 21, s. 12; 1981, c. 423, s. 1; 1999-456, s. 33(e); 2009-281, s. 1; 2011-183, s. 77.)

§ 115C-255. Liability insurance and waiver of immunity as to certain acts of bus drivers.

The securing of liability insurance and the waiver of immunity as to certain torts of school bus drivers, school transportation service vehicle drivers and school activity bus drivers, is subject to the provisions of G.S. 115C-42, except when such vehicles are operated with funds from the State Public School Fund. (1981, c. 423, s. 1.)

§ 115C-256. School bus drivers under Workers' Compensation Act.

Awards to school bus drivers under the Workers' Compensation Act shall be made pursuant to the provisions of G.S. 115C-337(b). (1981, c. 423, s. 1.)

§ 115C-257. Attorney General to pay claims.

The Attorney General is hereby authorized to pay reasonable medical expenses, not to exceed three thousand dollars ($3,000), incurred within one year from the date of accident to or for each pupil who sustains bodily injury or death caused by accident, while boarding, riding on, or alighting from a school bus operated by any local school administrative unit. (1955, c. 1372, art. 22, s. 1; 1981, c. 423, s. 1; c. 576, s. 1; 1998-212, s. 9.17(a).)

§ 115C-258. Provisions regarding payment.

The claims authorized herein may be paid, regardless of whether the injury received by the pupil was due to negligence on the part of the school bus driver, the injured pupil, or any other person. To the extent of payments made under this Article, the Attorney General shall be subrogated to the right of the pupil against any third party legally responsible for the injury. Further, any amounts paid shall constitute a credit against any obligation arising under the provisions of the Tort Claims Act. (1955, c. 1372, art. 22, s. 2; 1981, c. 423, s. 1; c. 576, s. 1.)

§ 115C-259. Claims must be filed within one year.

The right to payment as authorized herein shall be forever barred unless a claim be filed with the Attorney General within one year after the accident. (1955, c. 1372, art. 22, s. 3; 1981, c. 423, s. 1; c. 576, s. 1.)

§§ 115C-260 through 115C-261: Repealed by Session Laws 1981, c. 576, s. 2.

§ 115C-262. Liability insurance and tort liability.

Liability insurance and tort liability of local boards of education for actions arising out of activities conducted pursuant to this Part, are subject to the provisions of G.S. 115C-42. (1981, c. 423, s. 1.)

Part 2. Food Service.

§ 115C-263. Required provision of services.

As a part of the function of the public school system, local boards of education shall provide to the extent practicable school food services in the schools under their jurisdiction. All school food services made available under this authority shall be provided in accordance with standards and regulations recommended by the Superintendent of Public Instruction and approved by the State Board of Education. (1955, c. 1372, art. 5, s. 34; 1965, c. 912; 1967, c. 990; 1975, c. 384; 1981, c. 423, s. 1.)

§ 115C-264. Operation.

(a) In the operation of their public school nutrition programs, the public schools shall participate in the National School Lunch Program established by the federal government. The program shall be under the jurisdiction of the Division of School Support, Child Nutrition Services of the Department of Public Instruction and in accordance with federal guidelines as established by the Food and Nutrition Service of the United States Department of Agriculture.

(b) For nutritional purposes, the public schools shall not (i) use cooking oils in their school food programs that contain trans-fatty acids or (ii) sell processed foods containing trans-fatty acids that were formed during the commercial processing of the foods.

(c) All school food services shall be operated on a nonprofit basis, and any earnings therefrom over and above the cost of operation as defined herein shall be used to reduce the cost of food, to serve better food, or to provide free or reduced-price lunches to indigent children and for no other purpose. The term "cost of operation" means the actual cost incurred in the purchase and preparation of food, the salaries of all personnel directly engaged in providing food services, and the cost of nonfood supplies as outlined under standards adopted by the State Board of Education. "Personnel" means child nutrition supervisors or directors, bookkeepers directly engaged in food service record keeping and those persons directly involved in preparing and serving food. Child nutrition personnel shall be paid from the funds of food services only for services rendered in behalf of the child nutrition program. Any cost incurred in the provisions and maintenance of school food services over and beyond the cost of operation shall be included in the budget request filed annually by local boards of education with boards of county commissioners. Public schools are not required to comply with G.S. 115C-522(a) in the purchase of supplies and food for such school food services. (1955, c. 1372, art. 5, s. 34; 1965, c. 912; 1967, c. 990; 1975, c. 384; 1981, c. 423, s. 1; 1991 (Reg. Sess., 1992), c. 900, s. 78; 2003-147, s. 5; 2004-124, s. 7.29(a); 2004-203, ss. 72(a), (b); 2005-253, s. 1.)

§ 115C-264.1. Preference to high-calcium foods and beverages in purchasing contracts.

(a) In addition to any requirements established by the United States Department of Agriculture under the National School Lunch Program, the School Breakfast Program, or other federally supported food service programs, local boards of education shall give preference in purchasing contracts to high-calcium foods and beverages. For purposes of this section, "high-calcium foods and beverages" means foods and beverages that contain a higher level of calcium and that are equal to or lower in price than other products of the same type or quality.

(b) Notwithstanding the provisions of subsection (a) of this section, if a local school board determines that a high-calcium food or beverage would interfere with the proper treatment and care of an individual receiving services from the public school food program, the local school board shall not be required to purchase a high-calcium food or beverage for that individual. A local school board that has entered into a contract with a supplier to purchase food or beverages before the effective date of this section is not required to purchase high-calcium foods or beverages for the duration of that contract if purchasing those products would change the terms of the contract. (2003-257, s. 1.)

§ 115C-264.2. Vending machine sales.

(a) Each school may, with the approval of the local board of education, sell to students beverages in vending machines during the school day so long as:

(1) Soft drinks are not sold (i) during the breakfast and lunch periods, (ii) at elementary schools, or (iii) contrary to the requirements of the National School Lunch Program;

(2) Sugared carbonated soft drinks, including mid-calorie carbonated soft drinks, are not offered for sale in middle schools;

(3) Not more than fifty percent (50%) of the offerings for sale to students in high schools are sugared carbonated soft drinks;

(4) Diet carbonated soft drinks are not considered in the same category as sugared carbonated soft drinks; and

(5) Bottled water products are available in every school that has beverage vending.

(b) Nothing in subsection (a) of this section prohibits a school from adopting stricter policies with respect to beverage vending.

(c) Snack vending in all schools shall, by school year 2006-2007, meet the Proficient Level of the NC Eat Smart Nutrition Standards, such that in elementary schools, no snack vending is available to students, and in middle and high schools, seventy-five percent (75%) of snack vending products have not more than 200 calories per portion or snack vending package. (2005-253, s. 2.)

§ 115C-264.3. Child Nutrition Program standards.

The State Board of Education, in direct consultation with a cross section of local directors of child nutrition services, shall establish statewide nutrition standards for school meals, a la carte foods and beverages, and items served in the After School Snack Program administered by the Department of Public Instruction and child nutrition programs of local school administrative units. The nutrition standards will promote gradual changes to increase fruits and vegetables, increase whole grain products, and decrease foods high in total fat, trans fat, saturated fat, and sugar. The nutrition standards adopted by the State Board of Education shall be implemented initially in elementary schools. All elementary schools shall achieve a basic level by the end of the 2009-2010 school year, followed by middle schools and then high schools. (2005-457, s. 1; 2007-323, s. 7.36A(a); 2008-107, s. 7.25(a).)

Part 3. Library/Media Personnel.

§ 115C-265. Rules and regulations for distribution of library/media personnel funds; employment of personnel.

(a) The State Board of Education is authorized to promulgate rules and regulations for the distribution of library/media personnel funds, on the basis of average daily membership (ADM), to each local school administrative unit of the State.

(b) Each local school administrative unit in the State shall employ library/media personnel in accordance with State library/media guidelines approved by the State Board of Education insofar as funds are approved for that purpose by the North Carolina General Assembly. (1977, c. 1088, ss. 2, 3; 1981, c. 423, s. 1.)

§§ 115C-266 through 115C-270. Reserved for future codification purposes.

SUBCHAPTER V. PERSONNEL.

Article 18.

Superintendents.

§ 115C-271. Selection by local board of education, term of office.

(a) It is the policy of the State that each local board of education has the sole discretion to elect a superintendent of schools. However, the State Board shall adopt rules that establish the qualifications for election. At a minimum, each superintendent shall have been a principal in a North Carolina public school or shall have other leadership, management, and administrative experience. In addition, the State Board shall adopt rules that include minimum credentials, educational prerequisites, and relevant experience requirements that would qualify a person to serve as a superintendent without having direct experience or certification as an educator. It is the duty of each local board to elect a superintendent who is qualified. If a local board elects a superintendent who is not qualified or who cannot qualify under this section, then the election and contract are null and void, and the board shall elect a person who is qualified.

(b) Each local board of education shall elect a superintendent under a written contract of employment for a term of no more than four years, ending on June 30 of the final months of the contract. Contracts of employment for a period of less than one year shall be governed and limited by G.S. 115C-275. Each local board shall file a copy of the contract with the State Board of Education before the individual is eligible for this office.

(c) At any time after the first 12 months of the contract, a local board may, with the written consent of the current superintendent, extend or renew the term of the superintendent's contract for a term of no more than four years from the date of the extension. If new board members have been elected or appointed and are to be sworn in, a board shall not act to extend or renew the current superintendent's contract until after the new members have been sworn in.

(d) A local board may terminate the superintendent's contract before the contract term of employment has expired so long as all the following conditions are met:

(1) No State funds are used for this purpose.

(2) Local funds appropriated for teachers, textbooks, or classroom materials, supplies, and equipment are not transferred or used for this purpose.

(3) The local board makes public the funds that are to be transferred or used for this purpose.

(4) The local board notifies the State Board of the funds that are to be transferred or used for this purpose.

(5) No funds acquired through donation or fund-raising are used for this purpose, except for funds raised specifically for this purpose or for funds donated by private for-profit corporations.

Immediately upon receipt of the notification from a local board under this subsection, the State Board shall review the accounts of that local school administrative unit. If the State Board finds that the local board failed to meet all the conditions set out in this subsection, the State Board shall issue a warning to the local board as provided in G.S. 115C-451 and, in addition to any other actions the State Board may take under G.S. 115C-451, shall order the local board to take action to comply with this subsection. (1981, c. 423, s. 1; 1983, c. 478; 1983 (Reg. Sess., 1984), c. 1103, s. 3; 1987, c. 389; 1989, c. 339; 1991, c. 238, s. 1; 1997-443, s. 8.7; 2001-174, s. 1.)

§ 115C-272. Residence, oath of office, and salary of superintendent.

(a) Every superintendent shall reside in the county in which he is employed. The superintendent shall not teach, nor be regularly employed in any other capacity that may limit or interfere with his duties as superintendent. Each superintendent, before entering upon the duties of his office, shall take an oath for the faithful performance thereof. The salary of the superintendent shall be in accordance with a State standard salary schedule, fixed and determined by the State Board of Education as provided by law; and such salary schedule for superintendents shall be determined on the same basis for both county and city superintendents and shall take into consideration the amount of work inherent to the office of both county and city superintendents; and such schedule shall be published in the same way and manner as the schedules for teacher and principal salaries are now published.

(b) Superintendents shall be paid promptly when their salaries are due provided the legal requirements for their employment and service have been met. All superintendents employed by any local school administrative unit who are paid from local funds shall be paid promptly as provided by law and as State allotted superintendents are paid. Superintendents paid from State funds shall be paid as follows:

(1) Each local board of education shall establish a set date on which monthly salary payments to superintendents shall be made. This set pay date may differ from the end of the calendar month of service. Superintendents shall only be paid for the days employed as of the set pay date. Payment for a full month when days employed are less than a full month is prohibited as this constitutes prepayment. The daily rate of pay shall equal the number of weekdays in the pay period. Included within their term of employment shall be annual vacation leave at the same rate provided for State employees. Included within the 12 months' employment each local board of education shall designate the same or an equivalent number of legal holidays as those designated by the State Human Resources Commission for State employees.

(2) Notwithstanding any provisions of this section to the contrary no person shall be entitled to pay for any vacation day not earned by that person. Vacation days shall not be used for extending the term of employment of individuals and shall not be cumulative from one fiscal year to another fiscal year: Provided, that superintendents may accumulate annual vacation leave days as follows: annual leave may be accumulated without any applicable maximum until June 30 of each year. On June 30 of each year, any superintendent with more than 30 days of accumulated leave shall have the excess accumulation converted to sick leave so that only 30 days are carried forward to July 1 of the same year. All vacation leave taken by the superintendent will be upon the authorization of his immediate supervisor and under policies established by the local board of education. An employee shall be paid in a lump sum for accumulated annual leave not to exceed a maximum of 240 hours or 30 days when separated from service due to resignation, dismissal, reduction in force, death, or service retirement. Upon separation from service due to service retirement, any annual vacation leave over 30 days will convert to sick leave and may be used for creditable service at retirement in accordance with G.S. 135-4(e). If the last day of terminal leave falls on the last workday in the month, payment shall be made for the remaining nonworkdays in that month. Employees retiring on disability retirement may exhaust annual leave rather than be paid in a lump sum. The provisions of this subdivision shall be accomplished without additional State and local funds being appropriated for this purpose. The State Board of Education shall adopt rules and regulations for the administration of this subdivision.

(3) Each local board of education shall sustain any loss by reason of an overpayment to any superintendent paid from State funds.

(4) All of the foregoing provisions of this section shall be subject to the requirement that at least fifty dollars ($50.00), or other minimum amount

required by federal social security laws, of the compensation of each school employee covered by the Teachers' and State Employees' Retirement System or otherwise eligible for social security coverage shall be paid in each of the four quarters of the calendar year.

(c) The State Board of Education, in fixing the State standard salary schedule of superintendents as authorized by law, shall provide that superintendents who entered the armed or auxiliary forces of the United States after September 16, 1940, and who left their positions for such service, shall be allowed experience increments for the period of such service as though the same had not been interrupted thereby, in the event such persons return to the position of teachers, principals or superintendents in the public schools of the State after having been honorably discharged from the armed or auxiliary forces of the United States. (1955, c. 1372, art. 6, s. 1; art. 17, s. 9; art. 18, s. 6; 1961, c. 1085; 1971, c. 1052; 1973, c. 647, s. 1; 1975, cc. 383, 608; c. 834, ss. 1, 2; 1979, c. 600, ss. 1-5; 1981, c. 423, s. 1; c. 946, s. 1; 1983, c. 872, s. 1; 1985, c. 757, s. 145(c); 1985 (Reg. Sess., 1986), c. 975, s. 15; 1987, c. 414, s. 4; 1989 (Reg. Sess., 1990), c. 1066, s. 93; 1993, c. 321, s. 73(a); 1995, c. 450, s. 17; 1997-443, s. 8.38(f); 1999-237, s. 28.26(c); 2013-382, s. 9.1(c).)

§ 115C-273. Salary schedule for superintendents.

Every local board of education may adopt, as to assistant or associate superintendents not paid out of State funds, a salary schedule similar to the State salary schedule, but it likewise shall recognize a difference in salaries based on different duties, training, experience, professional fitness, and continued service in the same school system; but if any local board of education shall fail to adopt such a schedule, the State salary schedule shall be in force. (1955, c. 1372, art. 5, s. 32; 1965, c. 584, s. 3; 1981, c. 423, s. 1.)

§ 115C-274. Removal.

(a) Local boards of education are authorized to remove a superintendent who is guilty of immoral or disreputable conduct or who shall fail or refuse to perform the duties required of him by law. In case the State Board of Education has sufficient evidence at any time that any superintendent of schools is not capable of discharging, or is not discharging, the duties of his office as required by law or is guilty of immoral or disreputable conduct, the State Board of Education shall report this matter to the board of education employing said superintendent of schools. It shall then be the duty of that board of education to hear the evidence in the case and, if after careful investigation it shall find the charges true, it shall declare the office vacant at once and proceed to elect a successor: Provided, that such superintendent shall have the right to try his title to office in the courts of the State.

(b) If the superintendent shall fail in the duties enumerated in G.S. 115C-276(g), 115C-276(h), 115C-276(i), or any other duties as may be assigned him, he shall be subject, after notice, to an investigation by the State Board of Education or by his board of education for failure to perform his duties. For persistent failure to perform these duties, the State Board of Education may revoke the superintendent's certificate and the superintendent may be dismissed by his board of education.

(c) The identification by the State Board of Education of more than half the schools in a local school administrative unit as low-performing under G.S. 115C-105.37 is evidence that the superintendent is unable to fulfill the duties of the office, and the State Board may appoint an interim superintendent to carry out the duties of the superintendent under G.S. 115C-105.39, may revoke the superintendent's certificate under this section, may dismiss the superintendent under G.S. 115C-105.39, or may take any combination of these actions. (1955, c. 1372, art. 5, s. 25; art. 6, s. 4; 1981, c. 423, s. 1; 1995 (Reg. Sess., 1996), c. 716, s. 6.)

§ 115C-275. Vacancies in office of superintendent.

In case of vacancy by death, resignation, or otherwise, in the office of a superintendent, such vacancy shall be filled by the local board of education in which such vacancy occurred. If the vacancy is filled on a temporary basis, subject to the same approvals and to the same educational qualifications as provided for superintendents, the individual appointed to fill the vacancy on a temporary basis shall be paid the salary provided for superintendents. During the time any superintendent is on an approved leave of absence, without pay, an acting superintendent may be appointed in the same manner to serve during the interim period, which appointment shall be subject to the same approvals and to the same educational qualifications as provided for superintendents. In case such position is not filled immediately on a permanent or temporary basis, or in case of absence of a superintendent on account of illness or other approved reason, the board of education, by resolution duly adopted and recorded in the minutes of such board, may assign to an employee of such school board, with the approval of the Superintendent of Public Instruction, any duty or duties of such superintendent which necessity requires be performed during such time. If the superintendent's duty of signing warrants and checks is assigned, the board shall give proper notice immediately to the State Controller and to the appropriate local disbursing official. (1955, c. 1372, art. 6, s. 2; 1959, c. 573, s. 3; 1977, c. 298; 1981, c. 423, s. 1; 1987 (Reg. Sess., 1988), c. 1025, s. 11; 1991, c. 542, s. 1.)

§ 115C-276. Duties of superintendent.

(a) In General. - All acts of local boards of education, not in conflict with State law, shall be binding on the superintendent, and it shall be his duty to carry out all rules and regulations of the board.

All the powers, duties and responsibilities imposed by law upon the superintendents of county administrative units shall, with respect to city administrative units, be imposed upon, and exercised by, the superintendents of city administrative units, in the same manner and to the same extent, insofar as applicable thereto, as such powers and duties are exercised and performed by superintendents of county administrative units with reference to said county administrative units.

(b) To Serve as Secretary to Board. - Superintendents shall be ex officio secretary to their respective boards of education. As secretary to the board of education, the superintendent shall record all proceedings of the board, issue all notices and orders that may be made by the board, and otherwise be executive officer of the board of education. He shall see that the minutes of the meetings of the board of education are promptly and accurately recorded in the minute book which shall be kept in the office of the board of education and be open at all times to public inspection.

(c) To Monitor Condition of School Plants. - It shall be the duty of every superintendent to visit the schools of his unit, to keep his board of education informed at all times as to the condition of the school plants in his administrative unit, and to make immediate provisions to remedy any unsafe or unsanitary conditions existing in any school building.

(d) To Attend Professional Meetings. - It shall be the duty of every superintendent to attend professional meetings conducted by the State Superintendent of Public Instruction and such other professional meetings as are necessary to keep him informed on educational matters.

(e) To Report Certain Information to the Superintendent of Public Instruction. - It shall be the duty of every superintendent to furnish as promptly as possible to the State Superintendent when requested by him, information and statistics on any phase of the school work in his administrative unit.

(f) To Administer Oaths When Required. - The superintendent shall have authority to administer oaths to teachers and all other school officials when an oath is required of the same.

(g) To Familiarize Himself with and to Implement State Policies and Rules. - It shall be the duty of the superintendent to keep himself thoroughly informed as to all policies promulgated and rules adopted by the State Superintendent of Public Instruction and the State Board of Education, for the organization and government of the public schools. The superintendent shall notify and inform his board of education, supervisors, principals, teachers, janitors, bus drivers, and all other persons connected with the public schools, of such policies and rules. In the performance of these duties, the superintendent shall confer, work, and plan with all school personnel to achieve the best methods of instruction, school organization and school government.

(h) To Hold Necessary Teachers' Meetings. - The superintendent shall hold each year such teachers' meetings and study groups as in his judgment will improve the efficiency of the instruction in the schools of his unit.

(i) To Distribute Certain Supplies and Information. - The superintendent shall distribute to all school personnel all blanks, registers, report cards, record books, bulletins, and all other supplies and information furnished by the State Superintendent and the State Board of Education and give instruction for their proper use.

(j) To Assist the Local Board in Electing School Personnel. - It shall be the duty of the superintendent to recommend and the board of education to elect all principals, teachers, and other school personnel in the administrative unit.

(k) To Submit Organization Reports and Other Information to the State Board. - Each year the superintendent of each local school administrative unit shall submit to the State Board of Education statistical reports, certified by the chairman of the board of education, showing the organization of the schools in his or her unit and any additional information the State Board may require. At the end of the second month of school each year, local boards of education, through the superintendent, shall report school organization, employees' duties, and class sizes to the State Board. As of February 1 each year, local boards of education, through the superintendent, shall report all exceptions to individual class size maximums in kindergarten through third grade that occur at that time.

(l)   (Effective until July 1, 2014) To Maintain Personnel Files and to Participate in Firing and Demoting of Staff. - The superintendent shall maintain in his office a personnel file for each teacher that contains complaints, commendations, or suggestions for correction or improvement about the teacher and shall participate in the firing and demoting of staff, as provided in G.S. 115C-325.

(l)   (Effective July 1, 2014) To Maintain Personnel Files and to Participate in Firing and Demoting of Staff. - The superintendent shall maintain in his or her office a personnel file for each teacher that contains complaints, commendations, or suggestions for correction or improvement about the teacher and shall participate in the firing and demoting of staff, as provided in Part 3 of Article 22 of this Chapter.

(m)   To Furnish Boundaries of Special Taxing Districts. - It shall be the duty of county superintendents, and of city superintendents where their administrative units are not coterminous with city or township limits, to furnish tax listers at tax listing time the boundaries of each taxing district and city administrative unit in which a special tax will be levied to the end that all property in such district or unit may be properly listed.

(n)   To Issue Salary Vouchers. - The authority for a superintendent to issue vouchers for the salary of all school employees, whether paid from State or local funds, shall be a monthly payroll, prepared on forms furnished by the State Board of Education and containing all information required by the State Board of Education. This monthly payroll shall be signed by the principal of the school. If any voucher so drawn is chargeable against district funds, the amount so charged and the district to which said amount is charged shall be specified on the voucher. The superintendent shall not approve the vouchers for the pay of principals or teachers until the monthly and annual reports required by the local board of education are made.

(o) To Participate in the School Budget and Finances. - The superintendent shall participate in the school budget and finances, as provided in Article 31 of this Chapter.

(p) To Require Teachers and Principals to Make Reports. - The superintendents may require teachers to make reports to the principals and principals to make reports to the superintendent. Any superintendent who knowingly and willfully makes or procures another to make any false report or records, requisitions, or payrolls, respecting daily attendance of pupils in the public schools, payroll data sheets, or other reports required to be made to any board or officer in the performance of his duties, shall be guilty of a Class 1 misdemeanor and the certificate of such person to teach in the public schools of North Carolina shall be revoked by the Superintendent of Public Instruction.

(q) To Assign School Principals. - Subject to local board policy, the superintendent shall have the authority to assign principals to school buildings. When making an assignment, the superintendent shall consider (i) whether a principal has demonstrated the leadership ability to increase student achievement at a school where conditions indicated a significant risk of low student performance; and (ii) how to maintain stability at a school where, during the time the principal has been at a school, there has been significant improvement on end-of-course or end-of-grade tests and other accountability measures developed by the State Board of Education.

(r) To Maintain Student Discipline. - The superintendent shall maintain student discipline in accordance with Article 27 of this Chapter and shall keep data on each student to whom corporal punishment was administered, who was suspended for more than 10 days, who was reassigned for disciplinary reasons, or who was expelled. This data shall include the race, gender, age, grade level, ethnicity, and disability status of each student, the duration of suspension for each student, whether alternative education services were provided for each student, and whether a student had multiple suspensions in that academic year.

(s) To Provide for Annual Evaluations and Mandatory Improvement Plans. - The superintendent shall provide for the annual evaluation of all licensed employees assigned to low-performing schools that did not receive an assistance team. The superintendent shall determine whether all principals and assistant principals who evaluate licensed employees are trained in the proper administration of the employee evaluations and the development of appropriate mandatory improvement plans. The superintendent also shall arrange for principals and assistant principals who evaluate licensed employees to receive the appropriate training.

(t) Repealed by Session Laws 2012-142, s. 7.13(c), effective July 1, 2012. (1955, c. 1372, art. 5, s. 24; art. 6, ss. 3-6, 10, 15; art. 17, s. 6; art. 18, s. 7; 1959, c. 1294; 1963, c. 688, s. 3; 1965, c. 584, ss. 5, 6, 16; 1969, c. 539; 1973, c. 770, ss. 1, 2; 1975, c. 965, s. 3; 1977, c. 1088, s. 4; 1981, c. 423, s. 1; 1985 (Reg. Sess., 1986), c. 975, ss. 17, 18, 24; 1987 (Reg. Sess., 1988), c. 1025, s. 12; c. 1086, s. 89(c); 1993, c. 169, s. 2; c. 210, s. 4; c. 539, s. 882; 1994, Ex. Sess., c. 24, s. 14(c); 1995, c. 386, s. 2; 1995 (Reg. Sess., 1996), c. 716, s. 25; 1998-5, s. 6; 1998-182, s. 38; 1998-220, s. 10; 2011-282, s. 10; 2011-348, s. 4; 2012-142, s. 7.13(c); 2013-360, s. 9.7(f); 2013-363, s. 3.3(c).)

§ 115C-277. Office, equipment, and clerical assistance to be provided by board.

It shall be the duty of the various boards of education to provide the superintendent of schools with an appropriate office. Likewise, it shall be the duty of the various boards of education to furnish adequately the superintendent's office and provide all necessary office supplies. Authority is hereby given to boards of education to employ sufficient clerical assistants and purchase sufficient office machines and equipment to the end that the business of the superintendent of schools shall always be conducted in a prompt and efficient manner. (1955, c. 1372, art. 5, s. 23; 1981, c. 423, s. 1.)

§ 115C-278. Assistant superintendent and associate superintendent.

Local boards of education shall have authority to employ an assistant superintendent, in addition to those that may be furnished by the State when, in the discretion of the board of education, the schools of the administrative unit can thereby be more efficiently and more economically operated and when funds for the same are provided in the current expense fund budget. The duties of such assistant superintendent shall be assigned by the superintendent with the approval of the board of education.

Local boards of education may, upon the recommendation of the superintendent, elect assistant or associate superintendents for a term of from one to four years. The term may not, however, exceed the expiration date of the superintendent's contract, unless the remaining time of the superintendent's contract is less than one year. If there is less than one year remaining on the superintendent's contract, the assistant or associate superintendent shall be given a contract through the next school year.

The term of employment shall be stated in a written contract which shall be entered into between the board of education and the assistant or associate superintendent, a copy of which shall be filed with the Superintendent of Public Instruction as a matter of information. The assistant or associate superintendent may not be dismissed during the term to which he is elected except for misconduct of such a nature as to indicate he is unfit to continue in his position, incompetence, neglect of duty, or failure or refusal to carry out validly assigned duties. (1955, c. 1372, art. 5, s. 27; 1971, c. 1188, s. 1; 1973, c. 733; 1981, c. 423, s. 1.)

§§ 115C-279 through 115C-283. Reserved for future codification purposes.

Article 19.

Principals and Supervisors.

§ 115C-284. Method of selection and requirements.

(a) Principals and supervisors shall be elected by the local boards of education upon the recommendation of the superintendent, in accordance with the provisions of G.S. 115C-276(j).

(b) In the city administrative units, principals shall be elected by the board of education of such administrative unit upon the recommendation of the superintendent of city schools.

(b1) To qualify for certification as a school administrator, an individual must meet all of the following requirements:

(1) Submit a complete application to the State Board.

(2) Pay the applicable fee.

(3) Have a bachelor's degree from an accredited college or accredited university.

(4) Have one of the following:

a. A graduate degree from a public school administration program that meets the public school administration program approval standards established by the State Board of Education.

b. A master's degree from an accredited college or accredited university and, by December 31, 1999, have completed a public school administration program that meets the public school administration program approval standards set by the State Board of Education.

c. Education and training determined by the State Board of Education as equivalent.

(5) Pass the exam adopted by the State Board.

(c) The State Board of Education shall have entire control of certifying all applicants for supervisory and professional positions in all public elementary and high schools of North Carolina; and it shall prescribe the rules and regulations for the renewal and extension of all certificates, and shall determine and fix the salary for each grade and type of certificate which it authorizes. The State Board of Education shall require each applicant for an initial certificate or graduate certificate to demonstrate the applicant's academic and professional preparation by achieving a prescribed minimum score at least equivalent to that required by the Board on November 30, 1972, on a standard examination appropriate and adequate for that purpose. If the Board shall specify the National Teachers Examination for this purpose, the required minimum score shall not be lower than that which the Board required on November 30, 1972. The Board shall not issue provisional certificates for principals.

The Board shall issue a one-year provisional assistant principal's certificate to an employee of a local board only if: (i) the local board determines there is a shortage of persons who hold or are qualified to hold a principal's certificate and the employee enrolls in an approved program leading to a masters degree in school administration before the provisional certificate expires; or (ii) the employee is enrolled in an approved masters in school administration program and is participating in the required internship under the masters program. The Board shall extend the provisional certificate for a total of no more than two additional years while the employee is completing the program.

(c1) It is the policy of the State of North Carolina to maintain the highest quality principal and assistant principal education programs in order to enhance the competence of professional personnel certified in North Carolina. To ensure that principal and assistant principal preparation programs are upgraded to reflect a more rigorous course of study, the State Board of Education shall submit to the General Assembly not later than March 1, 1992, a plan to promote this policy. In developing this plan, the State Board shall consider (i) requiring these programs to include additional preparation for site-based decision making and for the additional autonomy being granted to local school units, (ii) enhancing program entrance requirements to include assessment of an applicant's ability to complete the program and to perform as a principal, and (iii) enhancing the overall content of the programs.

The State Board of Education, as lead agency in coordination and cooperation with the University Board of Governors and such other public and private agencies as are necessary, shall refine the several certification requirements, standards for approval of institutions of principal and assistant principal education, standards for institution-based innovative and experimental programs, and standards for improved efficiencies in the administration of the approved programs.

(c2) The State Board of Education shall adopt new standards by July 1, 2008, for school administrator preparation programs. The new standards shall:

(1) Be aligned with the revised standards for the evaluation of school executives and specifically address the use of the results of the Teacher Working Conditions Survey;

(2) Require evidence of a high level of institutional commitment, including dedicated resources, for administrator preparation program improvements and redesign;

(3) Require the use of cross-functional work teams to determine a common curriculum framework that (i) is designed to align with defined standards, (ii) includes rigorous core courses, and (iii) will produce administrators who meet the defined standards. The cross-functional work teams shall include school-

based personnel, faculty from schools of education and other disciplines from institutions of higher education, and representatives of State agencies;

(4) Require the use of cross-functional work teams to design and periodically update specific standards regarding placement, required activities, and evaluations of clinical experiences. These standards shall include appropriate training for the school leaders who agree to accept and supervise interns;

(5) Require written agreements between the institution of higher education and a local school administrative unit to govern their shared responsibility for (i) recruitment and preparation of school administrators, especially with regard to clinical experiences including the internship, and (ii) a new administrator's success once employed;

(6) Require authentic partnerships between adjunct faculty and full-time faculty to fully address the need for both practical, field-based experience and academic, theory-based experience. These partnerships may require a change in the institution of higher education's definition of scholarly activity and its reward system;

(7) Require all candidates to complete a year-long internship; and

(8) Require the development of portfolios for emerging leaders that provide evidence they are applying their training to actual school needs and challenges.

Institutions of higher education shall redesign their school administrator preparation programs to meet the new standards and report to the State Board of Education on the redesign by July 1, 2009.

(c3) (Effective July 1, 2017) The State Board of Education shall require that all students in school administrator preparation programs demonstrate competencies in (i) using digital and other instructional technologies and (ii) supporting teachers and other school personnel to use digital and other instructional technologies to ensure provision of high-quality, integrated digital teaching and learning to all students. The State Board of Education shall include continuing education in high-quality, integrated digital teaching and learning as a requirement of licensure renewal.

(d) Repealed by Session Laws 1989, c. 385, s. 1.

(d1) It is the policy of the State of North Carolina that, subsequent to the adoption of a system of classroom teacher differentiation and prerequisites to candidacy for principal, a classroom teacher must have attained at least the second level of differentiation, have at least four years of classroom teaching experience, and possess, at least, a Masters Degree in Education Administration. This subsection shall not apply to educational personnel certified as of July 1, 1984.

(e) It shall be unlawful for any board of education to employ or keep in service any principal or supervisor who neither holds nor is qualified to hold a certificate in compliance with the provision of the law or in accordance with the regulations of the State Board of Education.

(f) The allotment of classified principals shall be one principal for each duly constituted school with seven or more state-allotted teachers.

(g) Local boards of education shall have authority to employ supervisors in addition to those that may be furnished by the State when, in the discretion of the board of education, the schools of the local school administrative unit can thereby be more efficiently and more economically operated and when funds for the same are provided in the current expense fund budget. The duties of such supervisors shall be assigned by the superintendent with the approval of the board of education.

(h) All principals and supervisors employed in the public schools of the State or in schools receiving public funds, shall be required either to hold or be qualified to hold a certificate in compliance with the provision of the law or in accordance with the regulations of the State Board of Education. (1955, c. 1372 art. 5, ss. 4, 27; art. 6, s. 6; art. 18, ss. 1-4; 1963, c. 688, s. 3; 1965, c. 584, ss. 6, 20.1; 1969, c. 539; 1971, c. 1188, s. 1; 1973, cc. 236, 733; c. 770, ss. 1, 2; 1975, c. 437, s. 7; c. 686, s. 1; c. 731, ss. 1, 2; c. 965, s. 3; 1977, c. 1088, s. 4; 1981, c. 423, s. 1; 1983 (Reg. Sess., 1984), c. 1103, s. 4; 1985 (Reg. Sess., 1986), c. 975, s. 16; 1989, c. 385, s. 1; 1991, c. 689, s. 200(a); 1991 (Reg. Sess., 1992), c. 1030, s. 28; 1993, c. 392, s. 2; 1999-30, s. 1; 1999-394, s. 1; 2006-264, s. 56(b); 2007-517, s. 1; 2008-187, s. 43; 2013-11, s. 2.)

§ 115C-285. Salary.

(a) Principals and supervisors shall be paid promptly when their salaries are due provided the legal requirements for their employment and service have been met. All principals and supervisors employed by any local school administrative unit who are to be paid from local funds shall be paid promptly as provided by law and as state-allotted principals and supervisors are paid.

Principals and supervisors paid from State funds shall be paid as follows:

(1)   Classified principals and State-allotted supervisors shall be employed for a term of 12 calendar months. Each local board of education shall establish a set date on which monthly salary payments to classified principals and State-allotted supervisors shall be made. This set pay date may differ from the end of the calendar month of service. Classified principals and State-allotted supervisors shall only be paid for the days employed as of the set pay date. Payment for a full month when days employed are less than a full month is prohibited as this constitutes prepayment. They shall earn annual vacation leave at the same rate provided for State employees. On a day that employees are required to report for a workday but pupils are not required to attend school due to inclement weather, an employee may elect not to report due to hazardous travel conditions and to take one of his annual vacation days or to make up the day at the time agreed upon by the employee and his immediate supervisor. They shall be provided by the board the same or an equivalent number of legal holidays as those designated by the State Human Resources Commission for State employees.

(2)   Supervisors and classified principals paid on an hourly or other basis whether paid from State or from local funds may accumulate annual vacation leave days as follows: annual leave may be accumulated without any applicable maximum until June 30 of each year. On June 30 of each year, any supervisor or principals with more than 30 days of accumulated leave shall have the excess accumulation converted to sick leave so that only 30 days are carried forward to July 1 of the same year. All vacation leave taken by the employee will be upon the authorization of his immediate supervisor and under policies established by the local board of education. An employee shall be paid in a lump sum for accumulated annual leave not to exceed a maximum of 240 hours or 30 days when separated from service due to resignation, dismissal, reduction in force, death, or service retirement. Upon separation from service due to service retirement, any annual vacation leave over 30 days will convert to sick leave and may be used for creditable service at retirement in accordance with G.S. 135-4(e). If the last day of terminal leave falls on the last workday in the month, payment shall be made for the remaining nonworkdays in that month. Employees retiring on disability retirement may exhaust annual leave rather than be paid in a lump sum. The provisions of this subdivision shall be accomplished without additional State and local funds being appropriated for

this purpose. The State Board of Education shall adopt rules and regulations for the administration of this subdivision.

(3) Notwithstanding any provisions of this section to the contrary no person shall be entitled to pay for any vacation day not earned by that person. Vacation days shall not be used for extending the term of employment of individuals and shall not be cumulative from one fiscal year to another fiscal year, except as provided in subdivision (5) of this section.

(4) Each local board of education shall sustain any loss by reason of an overpayment to any principal or supervisor paid from State funds.

(5) All of the foregoing provisions of this section shall be subject to the requirement that at least fifty dollars ($50.00), or other minimum amount required by federal social security laws, of the compensation of each school employee covered by the Teachers' and State Employees' Retirement System or otherwise eligible for social security coverage shall be paid in each of the four quarters of the calendar year.

(6) The State Board of Education, in fixing the State standard salary schedule of principals as authorized by law, shall provide that principals who entered the armed or auxiliary forces of the United States after September 16, 1940, and who left their positions for such service, shall be allowed experience increments for the period of such service as though the same had not been interrupted thereby, in the event such persons return to the position of teachers, principals or superintendents in the public schools of the State after having been honorably discharged from the armed or auxiliary forces of the United States.

(7) (Effective until July 1, 2014) All persons employed as principals in the schools and institutions listed in subsection (p) of G.S. 115C-325 shall be compensated at the same rate as are teachers in the public schools in accordance with the salary schedule adopted by the State Board of Education.

(7) (Effective July 1, 2014) All persons employed as principals in the schools and institutions listed in G.S. 115C-325.10 shall be compensated at the same rate as are teachers in the public schools in accordance with the salary schedule adopted by the State Board of Education.

(8) A teacher who becomes an assistant principal without a break in service shall be paid, on a monthly basis, at least as much as he or she would earn as a teacher employed by that local school administrative unit.

(b) Every local board of education may adopt, as to principals and supervisors not paid out of State funds, a salary schedule, but it likewise shall recognize a difference in salaries based on different duties, training, experience, professional fitness, and continued service in the same school system; but if any local board of education shall fail to adopt such a schedule, the State salary schedule shall be in force.

(c) The board of education may withhold the salary of any supervisor or principal who delays or refuses to render such reports as are required by law, but when the reports are delivered in accordance with law, the salary shall be paid forthwith. (1955, c. 1372, art. 5, s. 32; art. 6, s. 13; art. 17, s. 9; art. 18, s. 6; 1961, c. 1085; 1965, c. 584, s. 3; 1971, c. 1052; 1973, c. 315, s. 2; c. 647, s. 1; 1975, c. 383; c. 437, s. 9; c. 608; c. 834, ss. 1, 2; 1979, c. 600, ss. 1-5; 1981, c. 423, s. 1; c. 639, s. 4; c. 946, s. 2; 1983, c. 872, s. 2; 1985, c. 757, s. 145(d); 1985 (Reg. Sess., 1986), c. 975, s. 15; 1987, c. 414, s. 5; 1989, c. 386, s. 1; 1993, c. 321, s. 73(b); 1995, c. 450, s. 18; 1997-443, s. 8.38(g); 1999-237, s. 28.26(d); 2009-451, s. 7.22(a); 2013-360, s. 9.7(g); 2013-382, s. 9.1(c).)

§115C-286. Rules for conduct of principals and supervisors.

The conduct of principals and supervisors, the kind of reports they shall make, and their duties in the care of school property are subject to the rules of the local board, as provided in G.S. 115C-47(18). (1981, c. 423, s. 1.)

§ 115C-286.1. Evaluations of principals.

Local school administrative units shall evaluate all principals and assistant principals at least once each year. Either the superintendent or the superintendent's designee shall conduct the evaluations.

The State Board of Education shall ensure that the standards and criteria for the evaluations include the accountability measures of teacher retention, teacher support, and school climate. The State Board shall revise its evaluation instruments to include these measures. A local board shall use the performance standards and criteria adopted by the State Board unless the board develops an alternative evaluation that is properly validated and that includes standards and criteria similar to those adopted by the State Board. (2005-276, s. 7.29.)

§ 115C-287: Repealed by Session Laws 1993, c. 210, s. 5.

§ 115C-287.1. (Applicable to employees employed before July 1, 2014) Method of employment of principals, assistant principals, supervisors, and directors.

(a)   (1) Beginning July 1, 1995, all persons employed as school administrators shall be   employed pursuant to this section.

(2)   Notwithstanding G.S. 115C-287.1(a)(1), the following school administrators shall be employed pursuant to G.S. 115C-325:

a.   School administrators who, as of July 1, 1995, are serving in a principal or supervisor position with career status in that position; and

b.   School administrators who, as of July 1, 1995, are serving in a principal or supervisor position and who are eligible to achieve career status on or before June 30, 1997.

A school administrator shall cease to be employed pursuant to G.S. 115C-325 if the school administrator: (i) voluntarily relinquishes career status or the opportunity to achieve career status through promotion, resignation, or otherwise; or (ii) is dismissed or demoted or whose contract is not renewed pursuant to G.S. 115C-325.

(3)   For purposes of this section, school administrator means a:

a.   Principal;

b.   Assistant principal;

c.   Supervisor; or

d.   Director,

whose major function includes the direct or indirect supervision of teaching or of any other part of the instructional program.

(4)   Nothing in this section shall be construed to confer career status on any assistant principal or director, or to make an assistant principal eligible for career status as an assistant principal or a director eligible for career status as a director.

(b)   Local boards of education shall employ school administrators who are ineligible for career status as provided in G.S. 115C-325(c)(3), upon the recommendation of the superintendent. The initial contract between a school administrator and a local board of education shall be for two to four years, ending on June 30 of the final 12 months of the contract. In the case of a subsequent contract between a principal or assistant principal and a local board of education, the contract shall be for a term of four years. In the case of an initial contract between a school administrator and a local board of education, the first year of the contract may be for a period of less than 12 months provided the contract becomes effective on or before September 1. A local board of education may, with the written consent of the school administrator, extend, renew, or offer a new school administrator's contract at any time after the first 12 months of the contract so long as the term of the new, renewed, or extended contract does not exceed four years. Rolling annual contract renewals are not allowed. Nothing in this section shall be construed to prohibit the filling of an administrative position on an interim or temporary basis.

(c)   The term of employment shall be stated in a written contract that shall be entered into between the local board of education and the school administrator. The school administrator shall not be dismissed or demoted during the term of the contract except for the grounds and by the procedure by which a career teacher may be dismissed or demoted as set forth in G.S. 115C-325.

(d)   If a superintendent intends to recommend to the local board of education that the school administrator be offered a new, renewed, or extended contract, the superintendent shall submit the recommendation to the local board for action. The local board may approve the superintendent's recommendation or decide not to offer the school administrator a new, renewed, or extended school administrator's contract.

If a superintendent decides not to recommend that the local board of education offer a new, renewed, or extended school administrator's contract to the school administrator, the superintendent shall give the school administrator written notice of his or her decision and the reasons for his or her decision no later than May 1 of the final year of the contract. The superintendent's reasons may not be arbitrary, capricious, discriminatory, personal, or political. No action by the local board or further notice to the school administrator shall be necessary unless the school administrator files with the superintendent a written request, within 10 days of receipt of the superintendent's decision, for a hearing before the local board. Failure to file a timely request for a hearing shall result in a waiver of the right to appeal the superintendent's decision. If a school administrator files a timely request for a hearing, the local board shall conduct a hearing pursuant to the provisions of G.S. 115C-45(c) and make a final decision on whether to offer the school administrator a new, renewed, or extended school administrator's contract.

If the local board decides not to offer the school administrator a new, renewed, or extended school administrator's contract, the local board shall notify the school administrator of its decision by June 1 of the final year of the contract. A decision not to offer the school administrator a new, renewed, or extended contract may be for any cause that is not arbitrary, capricious, discriminatory, personal, or political. The local board's decision not to offer the school administrator a new, renewed, or extended school administrator's contract is subject to judicial review in accordance with Article 4 of Chapter 150B of the General Statutes.

(e)   Repealed by Session Laws 1995, c. 369, s. 1.

(f)   If the superintendent or the local board of education fails to notify a school administrator by June 1 of the final year of the contract that the school administrator will not be offered a new school administrator's contract, the school administrator shall be entitled to 30 days of additional employment or severance pay beyond the date the school administrator receives written notice that a new contract will not be offered.

(g)   If, prior to appointment as a school administrator, the school administrator held career status as a teacher in the local school administrative unit in which he or she is employed as a school administrator, a school administrator shall retain career status as a teacher if the school administrator is not offered a new, renewed, or extended contract by the local board of education, unless the school administrator voluntarily relinquished that right or is dismissed or demoted pursuant to G.S. 115C-325.

(h)   An individual who holds a provisional assistant principal's certificate and who is employed as an assistant principal under G.S. 115C-284(c) shall be considered a school administrator for purposes of this section. Notwithstanding subsection (b) of this section, a local board may enter into one-year contracts with a school administrator who holds a provisional assistant principal's certificate. If the school administrator held career status as a teacher in the local school administrative unit prior to being employed as an assistant principal and the State Board for any reason does not extend the school administrator's provisional assistant principal's certificate, the school administrator shall retain career status as a teacher unless the school administrator voluntarily relinquished that right or is dismissed or demoted under G.S. 115C-325. Nothing in this subsection or G.S. 115C-284(c) shall be construed to require a local board to extend or renew the contract of a school administrator who holds a provisional assistant principal's certificate. (1993, c. 210, s. 6; 1993 (Reg. Sess., 1994), c. 677, s. 16(a); 1995, c. 369, s. 1; 1998-220, s. 16; 1999-30, s. 3; 2003-291, s. 1.)

Vision Books Order Form

Fax Orders:	1-980-299-5965
Phone Orders:	1-704-898-0770
E-mail Orders:	www.visionbooks.org
Mail Orders:	Vision Books, LLC P.O. Box 42406 Charlotte, NC 28215

Shipp To:
Name_____
Address_____
City_____State_____Zip_____
Phone_____Fax_____
Email_____@_____

Bill To: We can bill a third party on your behalf.
Name_____
Address_____
City_____State_____Zip_____
Phone____(_____)_____Fax_____
Email_____@_____

Pamphlet Number ($15.00 Each)	Qty	Total Cost
_____	_____	_____
_____	_____	_____
_____	_____	_____
_____	_____	_____
_____	_____	_____
_____	_____	_____
_____	_____	_____
_____	_____	_____
<u>Full Volume Set 1-92</u>	<u>92 Pamphlets</u>	<u>1,380.00</u>

Free Shipping Shipping & Handling on Full Volume Orders
Add $1.00 Shipping & Handling per pamphlet $_____

Total Cost $_____

Thank you for your support. Management!

DID YOU ENJOY THIS BOOK?

Vision Books, LLC would like to hear from you! If you or someone you know has been fasely imprisoned, we would like to hear your story. If the 'North Carolina Criminal Law and Procedure' has had an effect in your life or if you have suggestions, we would like to hear from you. Send your letters to:

Vision Books, LLC
Attn: Staff Writers
P.O. Box 42406
Charlotte, NC 28215
Email: staff@visionbooks.org

Order Additional Copies:

Fax Orders: 1-980-299-5965

Phone Orders: 1-704-898-0770

E-mail Orders: www.visionbooks.org

Mail Orders: Vision Books, LLC
                       P.O. Box 42406
                       Charlotte, NC 28215

www.ingramcontent.com/pod-product-compliance
Lightning Source LLC
Chambersburg PA
CBHW051630170526
45167CB00001B/127